"Grant plops himself in the town of Natchez, Mississippi, during its annual Tableaux. He chronicles the antebellum-themed pageant's organizers' struggles to keep it relevant—and their deeper conflicts about what it represents—with empathy, skepticism, and exquisitely dry wit. One local's quip to Grant sums it up perfectly: 'This whole town is like a Southern *Twin Peaks*.'"
—Jonathan Miles, *Garden & Gun*

"Travel writer Grant sensitively probes the complex and troubled history of the oldest city on the Mississippi River through the eyes of a cast of eccentric and unexpected characters."
—Juliana Rose Pignataro, *Newsweek* ("25 Must-Read Fall Books to Escape the Chaos of 2020")

"With the easygoing manner—social and literary—displayed in *Dispatches from Pluto*, Richard Grant has slipped into the gossipy waters of Natchez and allowed the vexed and deeper history of race to bubble to the surface—where, it turns out, it's been lurking all along."
—Geoff Dyer, National Book Critics Circle Award–winning author of *Otherwise Known as the Human Condition*

"Richard Grant's skilled writing shows how Mississippi as a place reveals itself in its unique and memorable stories. It is through his careful weaving together of tales told by the book's cast of lively characters that the reader engages with a narrative that reaches beyond the borders of the small river town of Natchez. In the end, *The Deepest South of All* is not just a book about Mississippi or the South. This is a book about America and how we as a nation tend to grasp our myths so tightly that we begin to obscure what is real, what looms right before our very eyes."
—W. Ralph Eubanks, author of *Ever Is a Long Time* and *The House at the End of the Road*

"Richard Grant traveled down to old Natchez to discover a whole new Southern Gothic—marked by prayer gossip, deeply weird historical pageantry, slave-quarters B&B hosts, mean-girl garden clubs, militant revisionists, and gay-black-mayor-adoring racists—all positioning themselves, helplessly, along an ancient divide."
—Jack Hitt, author of *Bunch of Amateurs*

"I grew up in a town in the Mississippi Delta barely three hours away, but Natchez might as well have been a separate universe—albeit a small and insular one. Grant does a singular and surprisingly nuanced job of capturing that universe and its inhabitants, with their wild (and often carefully cultivated) eccentricities, their obsession with genealogy and houses, their deeply ingrained habit of rewriting the past. He captures the paradoxes— ladies of the old guard still 'receive' tourists in hoop skirts during the annual Pilgrimage but the enormously popular mayor is a gay African American. There are crazy feuds, wild bits of lore, and great 'characters' to be sure, but the book is much more than a rollicking tale of colorful Southerners. Grant deftly weaves in the city's painful and violent history so that the end result is a page-turner that's nothing short of a masterpiece. Think *Midnight in the Garden of Good and Evil* with a conscience."

—Julia Reed, author of *South Toward Home*

"Like an intrepid explorer, Richard Grant has discovered another American eccentricity and delivers in *The Deepest South of All* a riotous tale of Natchez, Mississippi, a hothouse populated by remnants of a faded aristocracy as well as resentful descendants of slaves in a river town governed by a gay black mayor but really ruled by two bickering garden clubs paying homage to the Confederacy."

—Curtis Wilkie, author of *The Fall of the House of Zeus*

"Yes, bourbon and hoopskirts. But also an eighteenth-century West African prince and an anti-Klan paramilitary group. Natchez is a place we call 'unlikely,' by which we mean its strangeness runs deeper, its violence burns brighter, even its openings for reconciliation seem wider. Yet Grant wisely suggests that these eye-popping tales reveal a story about race that is neither curious nor unique, but wholly American. In this testament to how stories define us all, Grant, frank and empathetic, makes us root for Natchez the way we should root for our own towns."

—Katy Simpson Smith, author of *The Everlasting*

THE
DEEPEST
SOUTH
of ALL

TRUE STORIES FROM
NATCHEZ, MISSISSIPPI

RICHARD GRANT

Simon & Schuster Paperbacks

New York   London   Toronto   Sydney   New Delhi

Simon & Schuster Paperbacks
An Imprint of Simon & Schuster, Inc.
1230 Avenue of the Americas
New York, NY 10020

Copyright © 2020 by Richard Grant

First Simon & Schuster trade paperback edition August 2021

SIMON & SCHUSTER and colophon are registered trademarks of
Simon & Schuster, Inc.

For information about special discounts for bulk purchases, please
contact Simon & Schuster Special Sales at 1-866-506-1949 or
business@simonandschuster.com

The Simon & Schuster Speakers Bureau can bring authors to your
live event. For more information or to book an event contact the Simon &
Schuster Speakers Bureau at 1-866-248-3049 or visit our website at
www.simonspeakers.com.

Interior design by Erika R. Genova

Manufactured in the United States of America

10   9   8   7   6   5   4   3   2   1

Library of Congress Control Number: 2020941300

ISBN 978-1-5011-7782-8
ISBN 978-1-5011-7784-2 (pbk)
ISBN 978-1-5011-7783-5 (ebook)

I have felt many times there a sense of place as powerful as if it were visible and walking and could touch me.

—Eudora Welty, *Some Notes on River Country*

THE
DEEPEST
SOUTH
of ALL

PROLOGUE

O ne summer night in Natchez, the old Mississippi river town that once boasted more millionaires than anywhere else in America, I walked past antebellum mansions and moss-hung trees to a Victorian house on a side street. The front-door knocker was the metal head of a cat with the tail of a steel mouse between its teeth. When I knocked the mouse against the doorplate, Elodie Pritchartt's dog Versace, a half-pug, half-beagle mix, began barking hysterically. Elodie dealt with Versace and then opened the door. A blogger who writes about the loveliness and lunacy in her hometown, she was dressed all in red, with her graying hair cut short, a glass of bourbon resting in her hand, and a big, friendly smile that contained a glint of mischief. A cocktail party was in full swing behind her.

She introduced me to the guests. An older gay man called Norbert had a kind of studied pomposity and a partner who didn't say much. A beautiful young archaeologist named Kerry Dicks was telling a story about a friend of her father's, "a very nice man who thought that characters from children's books were coming out of the wallpaper and talking to people." Holding court and smoking a cigar on the back deck was a woman named TJ, wearing a man's suit and tie with her dark hair slicked back. Her partner, Laurie, was sweetly feminine in a floral print blouse, and she beamed with pride as TJ told story after story about flat refusing to take any guff.

Elodie poured me a huge measure of bourbon and handed me a printed note card that she had found while going through some old boxes. It dated from the civil rights era and reflected the panic of white people in Natchez at the prospect of black people voting: "HELP! HELP! HELP! TOTAL WHITE VOTER REGISTRATION is necessary for our very survival." Elodie, an anti-racist liberal, was passing out these cards as ironic party favors.

She told a story about a woman she knew who was obsessed with helicopters and had fallen in love with a serial killer. He was in prison for killing prostitutes and had been arrested with a severed breast in his pocket. It was a desperately strange story and my head was starting to swim. Then a man named Denver started talking about the former mental hospital that he lives in for part of the year, and the various people that have taken up residence there without his permission. One of them is a professional magician. "I don't know where he came from, but he says it's against the magicians' union rules for him to do any housework, or clean up after himself, so long as he's wearing his magician clothes," Denver said. "So he wears his black magician clothes all the time. He can do magic, but no physical labor. He says he's like Picasso."

"He's a charlatan!" snapped Norbert.

Denver continued, "Then there's the No-Necks. There's a mother and her daughter, and a little redneck boy—"

"Sluts! Slatterns!" Norbert yelled. "You go to bed in the master bedroom and it's full of pubic hairs."

"That's a problem," Denver admitted. "We don't know who's been sleeping in my bed. But anyway, the little redneck boy—"

"He should be arrested. Incarcerate the trash!"

"Calm yourself, Norbert. He's not even ten years old."

"He's a vicious little shit."

Other tenants included an Andrew Jackson impersonator and two bishops who perform funerals for $500 and walk around in full regalia. "They're frauds," said Norbert. "One of them got ordained in Canada and ordained the other one. The porcine bishop drank an entire quart of single-malt Scotch because he says that's all he can drink."

Kerry Dicks asked how many rooms were in the building. "He has six bedrooms and fourteen chandeliers," said Norbert acidly. It sounded like a crazy short story that Flannery O'Connor might have written, but Denver and Norbert and some of the other guests insisted that it was all true. "There's still graffiti from the mental patients in the attic and enough air-conditioning units up there to chill a piece of meat," said Denver. "Why they would need to get the attic down to forty degrees I have no idea. Most of the graffiti is religious, and the windows are plexiglass so the patients couldn't smash them and escape."

I struggled to make sense of the incoming information. Why had Denver, a highly educated and sophisticated man, decided to make his second home in a decommissioned lunatic asylum in Mississippi? Why had he allowed a lazy magician, the No-Neck rednecks, and two fraudulent bishops to live in this home without permission? Why did he continue to do so? Why would a mental hospital need so many air conditioners in the attic?

But there was no opportunity to get answers to these questions because Elodie was now telling a story about her boyfriend Tommy's grandfather, who was the only white doctor in the Natchez area who would tend to black patients during the Depression. "One night he was helping a black woman in childbirth and it was going badly wrong," said Elodie. "She was going to die. He knew it, and she knew it. She had a little boy already, and she said, 'Please take care of my son.' And that's what Tommy's grandfather did. They named the little boy Rooster and they raised him on the back porch. There was a big old trunk out there and he slept in one of the drawers. Isn't that just the most wonderful, beautiful story?"

"He slept in a drawer? On the back porch?" said Denver sarcastically.

"It was the Depression!" said Elodie. "Tommy's dad—the doctor's own son—slept in a drawer too because they'd rented out the house to boarders."

I said, "Rooster? Why not George or Henry? Why did they name the boy after a chicken?"

Meanwhile, Versace the dog was experiencing terrible flatulence. "Oh my Lord, that stink would drive a buzzard off a gut pile," said one of the men. Kerry picked up one of the HELP! HELP! HELP! cards and used it as a fan. When Norbert and his partner got up to say their goodbyes, she took stock of the situation: "Okay, the queens are leaving, the dog is farting, and I'm fanning myself with white-supremacist literature."

Elodie poured more drinks and told a story about her late father, a conservative who found himself unable to vote for McCain and Palin in 2008: "Daddy thought Obama was a better candidate, but he couldn't bring himself to vote for a black man, so he abstained and went to bed early on election night. I stayed up and watched the whole thing. I went into his bedroom the next morning and told him the result. Daddy let out a big sigh of relief and said, 'Thank God that nigger won.'"

Elodie and the other guests convulsed into laughter. Then Denver started talking about the Magician's three-year stint in federal penitentiary for hacking bank websites, and his little clamshell computer that had lines of code constantly running across it. "The Magician could get internet when we had no internet," said Denver. "He got paid good money every year to go to DEF CON—the underground hackers' conference—and he would go by bus or train, so he wouldn't have to show his driver's license. He insisted he was just going there to perform magic tricks."

Then there was Denver's eccentric heiress friend, Miss Christine, and the Kabuki ladies, and the Acrobat, and it wasn't clear if they lived at the old mental hospital or showed up there for the Christmas parties. I sat there shaking my head, wishing it would stop, but the weird stories kept on coming. Denver's cousin Edward has over two hundred Studebakers on his property and a sign that reads THIS IS NOT A JUNKYARD. IT'S A MORGUE.

Then Denver got his phone out and started scrolling through photographs, and there they were, even stranger looking and more improbable than I had imagined them: the charlatan bishops, the Magician in his black clothes, the No-Necks, the Kabuki ladies, who were white women in rice-flour makeup, and some kind of neo-Confederate militia that showed up at his parties in military uniforms and drank up all the booze.

"It's just the South," he said, as Versace let out another atrocious fart and the women fanned themselves with HELP! HELP! HELP! cards. "It's just the South. There's no point trying to explain it."

I first heard about Natchez from a chef and cookbook writer named Regina Charboneau. I met her on the opening night of the Hot Tamale literary-culinary festival, which took place in a repurposed cotton gin surrounded by bare fields in the Mississippi Delta. The hulking old tin structure was hung with chandeliers and furnished with banqueting tables. Wineglasses and silverware glinted on white tablecloths. There were artisanal charcuterie stations, hundreds of well-dressed people milling around, a small army of bartenders pouring free wine and liquor.

Regina and I were both signing copies of our latest books at the author tables. I had written a true account of moving to rural Mississippi as an Englishman chewed up by New York City. Regina had published a handsome cookbook about the local cuisines along the length of the Mississippi River. She was warmhearted, witty and cosmopolitan, with a natural air of authority. She wore vintage cat-eye glasses and her dark hair in a bob. For many years she had owned a fashionable restaurant and a blues club in San Francisco, and her friends included Lily Tomlin and the Rolling Stones.

Now she had sold everything in San Francisco and moved back to her hometown of Natchez, Mississippi, where her family has lived for seven generations. I confessed that I knew nothing about Natchez, although I recognized its name, which rhymes with *matches*, from an old Howlin' Wolf song. "Natchez is wonderful," she said. "We're known for our history and our antebellum homes, and we're very different from the rest of Mississippi. People often describe Natchez as a little New Orleans, but it's really off in its own universe."

Her husband Doug, a native Minnesotan—they met in Alaska while Regina was cooking at a bush camp—poured me a shot of the white rum he was distilling in Natchez. It tasted raw and alive and faintly of tequila. They showed me photographs of their house, an antebellum Greek Revival home named Twin Oaks with white columns and Gothic-looking trees. "You must come and stay with us," said Regina. "I'll cook, and there's always a party, and you can do a book signing at King's Tavern." This was her latest restaurant, housed in one of the oldest standing buildings in Mississippi, circa 1789.

This was an impossible invitation to refuse, and soon afterwards I drove to Natchez for the first time. The town is tucked away in a remote corner of southwest Mississippi, on a bluff overlooking the Mississippi River. The nearest airport is ninety miles away in Baton Rouge, Louisiana, and there's no passenger train or interstate-highway connection. To get to Natchez, you've got to be going there, as Mississippians often say, because it's not on the way to anywhere else.

Country roads took me through a gently undulating landscape of woods and pastures, with occasional shacks and farmhouses and small fundamentalist churches. Scrolling through the radio, there was a babble of preachers, white and African American. I passed a derelict gas station with a forlorn sign:

PUMPING TO PLEASE
SOUL FOOD

Soon afterwards I entered the scruffy, unremarkable outskirts of Natchez. It was the usual Southern strip of fast-food joints and tractor-supply shops, easy loans, dollar stores, gas stations, and churches. There was a Mexican restaurant, a basic-looking supermarket, a swooping overpass leading to the Walmart.

The road to King's Tavern took me through an African American neighborhood that looked poor and tired. I pulled over to read a historical marker and a chill went through me. I was standing on the site of the second-largest slave market in the Deep South, a place known as the Forks of the Road. I could see a small memorial on a side street, and I walked over to take a look.

There were a few illustrated panels and a set of manacles mounted in a concrete block. The panels were thoughtful, informative, and deeply unsettling, with reproduced historical drawings of slaves, slave traders, and newspaper advertisements for the human commodity: "Negroes! Negroes! Just received, an addition of TWENTY-FIVE likely young field hands—Also, a fine Carriage Driver and Dining Room servants, for sale by R.H. ELAM, Forks of the Road."

Tens of thousands of people were sold here. They were transported by riverboats up and down the Mississippi. They were marched overland all the way from Virginia and Maryland to the booming new cotton frontier in the Lower Mississippi Valley, of which Natchez was the capital and the epicenter. The men were bound together in wrist chains and neck manacles and forced to march the thousand miles in lockstep. The women were usually roped together and the children put in wagons with the injured and heavily pregnant. These caravans of misery were known as coffles and flanked by men on horseback with whips and guns.

The slaves were told to sing as they marched, to keep up morale, but the coffle song lyrics that survive are mostly sad and mournful, because so many of the people singing had been sold away from their families.

> *The way is long before me, love*
> *And all my love's behind me;*
> *You'll seek me down by the old gum tree*
> *But none of you will find me*

As the coffle neared Natchez, the slave traders would stop and camp for a while. The human merchandise, which had not been unshackled for bodily functions or any other reason for months, was finally bathed, rested, fattened up, and made ready for sale. The women were typically put into calico dresses with pink ribbons at the neck. The men were dressed up in top hats, white shirts, vests, and corduroy velvet trousers. Pot liquor, the greasy residue of vegetables boiled with pork fat, was rubbed into their skin to make it shine. Thus prepared and ordered to "step lively" to encourage their own sale, they were herded into the pens at the Forks of the Road slave market.

Prospective buyers examined teeth, hefted breasts, poked and prodded, leered, mocked, and humiliated in the usual way, but there was no auction block here. Purchasing a human being at the Forks was like buying a car today. You agreed on a price with the dealer, made a down payment, and signed a contract agreeing to make further payments until you owned the property outright. Only the very rich bought slaves without financing.

Considering the volume of suffering and degradation generated here, and the global economic consequences of slavery's expansion into the Lower Mississippi Valley, the richest cotton land on earth, it seemed like such a modest little memorial: a few signboards, a set of manacles, a small patch of mown grass with flowerbeds. Most of the site was occupied by small businesses—a tire shop, a car wash—and low-income housing where all the tenants appeared to be African American, living on the same patch of ground where their ancestors were bought and sold.

———

I drove on past vacant lots, boarded-up buildings, nice old houses in need of paint and repair, a handsome Gothic Revival church. Then I crossed Martin Luther King Street, which appeared to be the demarcation line between black Natchez and white Natchez, and two different income brackets. Now the old houses were well maintained and freshly painted with attractive front gardens. The downtown historic district, originally laid out by the Spanish in the 1790s, was charming and lovely and from the high bluff there was a spectacular view of the Mississippi River.

Driving around, I saw some of the antebellum mansions for which Natchez is best known. The town and the surrounding area contain the greatest concentration of antebellum homes in the American South, including some of the most opulent and extravagant. Looking at these Federal, Greek Revival, and Italianate mansions, their beauty seemed inseparable from the horrors of the regime that created them. The soaring white columns, the manacles, the dingy apartment buildings at the Forks of the

Road, the tendrils of Spanish moss hanging from the gnarled old trees, the humid fragrant air itself: everything seemed charged with the lingering presence of slavery, in a way that I'd never experienced anywhere else.

I parked outside King's Tavern, a two-story building of brick and timber, still recognizable through its restorations as an eighteenth-century tavern. Pushing open a stout wooden door, I came into a low-ceilinged room with heavy beams, exposed-brick walls, and a bar made out of whiskey-barrel staves. Regina Charboneau hugged me like an old friend.

She led me up a steep, narrow staircase to the room where I would sign and sell books. I set out my wares and greeted my customers. They were far more sophisticated than I was expecting in a small, isolated Mississippi town. I talked with an extremely well-read woman who had lived all over the world before coming back to Natchez, where she grew up. The way of life here, she had decided, suited her best.

Asked to describe it, she said, "We're house-crazy. We adore old homes, antiques, throwing parties, making it fabulous. Gay men love it here. Natchez is very liberal and tolerant in some ways, and very conservative and racist in other ways, although I will say that our racists aren't generally hateful or mean. Nor do they think they're racists. There's still a lot of denial in the white community about the fact that this whole town was built on slavery. Most black people don't like thinking about slavery either, although they're acutely aware of it."

She talked about the insularity of the town, and the singularity of its culture. "We look more to New Orleans than the rest of Mississippi. The Catholic influence is strong in both the black and white communities. We're obsessed with our history, but it's often a self-serving mythological version of that history.

Genealogy is big. And there's a whole spectrum of behavior that we refer to politely as 'eccentricity.'"

I wondered aloud if Natchez might be an interesting place to write about. She made me swear to keep her out of it and warned me against bird-watching: "A lot of outsiders come down here like bird-watchers, studying the inhabitants, observing their quirks and colorful plumage. Well, guess what: the birds are looking right back at you. And sooner or later, one of them is going to talk ugly about you."

Gay couples wandered through and were greeted warmly and casually. Regina brought me a platter of slow-cooked, peppery brisket with horseradish on wood-fired flatbread, and a glass of good Spanish wine to wash it down. My antennae were swiveling. Natchez didn't remind me of anywhere else. I liked it here, yet I felt a creeping sense of unease. King's Tavern is allegedly haunted by the ghosts of murdered women and children, but that wasn't it. Slave coffles were still marching through my brain. Greasy rags were polishing dark skin. The past had split open like a badly stitched wound and was leaking into the present.

"Do you have a suit and tie?" Regina asked, as I packed up my unsold books. "There's a party tonight at Stanton Hall. I think you'll find it interesting."

"You should have warned me." I said, standing there in dark jeans and boots. "I do have a sports coat."

"That'll be fine," she said. "You have a British accent." We drove to Doug and Regina's house as darkness fell on the town. I caught glimpses of a church spire, graceful old houses that could have been in New Orleans, a 1950s malt shop that still had its white and colored takeout windows, although they were no longer observed. Then we pulled in through trees and old brick walls and parked behind an 1852 Greek Revival home. This was Twin Oaks, and my room was in a long, low wooden building across the walled garden, now functioning as a stylish and comfortable bed-and-breakfast for tourists.

I put on my sports coat and walked up to the big house. An owl hooted, fountains trickled in the darkness. I climbed some steep stone steps and opened the door into the kitchen. There were three big refrigerators, a six-burner restaurant stove, ice-cream makers, bread machines. Regina poured some wine and led me through to the next room, which had comfortable modern sofas and a television. She pointed to a painting of a skinny white man with spiky hair and a guitar. "I like to say we're the only antebellum home in Natchez with a self-portrait of Ronnie Wood," she said, referring to the Rolling Stones guitarist, who had given her the painting. "He has his issues, of course, but he's really a sweet man."

She led me through another door, and I stepped back in time. Apart from the electric lightbulbs in the chandelier, Regina's magnificent dining room contained very little evidence that the twentieth century had occurred. An antique table was set with gorgeous antique china and glassware. The walls were green and hung with enormous prints of the birds that John James Audubon had shot and then painted during his time in Natchez in the 1820s. An odd contraption hung from the ceiling, a carved wooden board of some kind.

"That's a punkah," Regina explained. "It's a type of fan that came to Natchez from British India via the Caribbean. You see a lot of them in Natchez homes."

"In Natchez, you only use the word *home* if it's antebellum," said Doug. "If your house was built after the Civil War, it's trashy to call it a home."

In British India, a junior servant called a punkah wallah pulled the rope to keep the punkah fanning the air. Here, the task was performed by house slaves, then by former slaves and their descendants, until the advent of electric fans and air-conditioning turned punkahs into antique curiosities, kept around for nostalgia's sake, like so many things in Natchez.

"When I was growing up here, slavery was hardly ever mentioned," said Regina. "Or people would say that the slaves were happy and well looked after, and the Civil War was about states' rights and honor. You still hear that, of course, but we are finally making some progress. The best thing we can do about our awful history is to acknowledge it openly and honestly."

She invited me to look around the rest of the house while she dressed for the party. I had two surprises in quick succession. Almost literally, I bumped into Janet, a middle-aged black woman who worked for Regina as a cook and housekeeper and had helped raise her children. A few moments later, I was startled by a large oil painting of a young man wearing a Confederate officer's uniform with a saber at his waist. This was not some antique family heirloom, but recently painted. Regina seemed liberal and forward-thinking, so what was this hagiographic Confederate portrait doing on the wall of her front parlor?

"That's Miss Regina's son Jean-Luc," said Janet. "He was King of Pilgrimage a few years ago."

I asked her what that meant, and she told me to ask Miss Regina. When Regina emerged, wearing a long black dress, I questioned her about the painting. "Oh," she said, and gave a little laugh. "His brother Martin says he might as well have a swastika on his back, but Luc wanted to be King, which totally surprised us, and the tradition has always been that the men in the court wear these uniforms. I didn't even realize they were

Confederate uniforms until quite recently, I'm embarrassed to admit. They were just the uniforms the guys always wore in the pageant."

Now I was even more puzzled. "What's the pageant?"

Regina said, "It's the Tableaux that the garden clubs put on every year. The children dance the Little Maypole, Big Maypole, the Soirée, and so on, and the Royal Court comes out with the King and Queen, but the whole thing is really about the social standing of the mothers. It's always so hard to explain."

Leaving for the party, I felt badly underdressed and completely baffled by all the unfamiliar terminology. As we drove through the quiet dark streets, Regina said the party was for the Pilgrimage Garden Club, of which she was president. "I'm amazed that you have time for gardening," I said, thinking about her cookbooks, her restaurant, her catering business, and the bed-and-breakfast.

"Oh." She gave another little laugh. "The garden clubs don't do any gardening, although we do appreciate flowers."

Doug said, "The garden clubs are about raising money, social prestige, tourism, and the historic preservation of antebellum buildings. They're run by women, and they have a lot of power. Natchez is probably the closest thing to a matriarchy that you're going to find in America."

We parked outside a mansion of staggering enormity and opulence. Stanton Hall occupies an entire city block in the middle of Natchez, and it's one of the grandest homes in the South to survive the Civil War. Its monumental size and massive Corinthian columns are softened and feminized by lacy ironwork on the balconies, and gorgeous trees and flower gardens in its grounds. It's one of the jewels in the crown of the Pilgrimage Garden Club, which operates it as a house museum for tourists, and a social venue for balls and parties such as this one.

We climbed up the white stone steps and entered the main hallway, which is more than seventy feet long. All the furniture, draperies, and paintings were antebellum antiques, which gave the impression that the clock had stopped on the eve of the Civil War. This impression was deepened by the fact that all the guests were white, and all the serving staff were African Americans in black-and-white uniforms.

"You can't win with that one," said Doug. "If you hire white people, you're discriminating against black people by denying them employment. If you hire black people, you're perpetuating the racial dynamics of slavery in an antebellum setting. So we do what we want, and most of the time we hire black people. They're friends of our friends, they need the work, and they do a good job. If you've got a problem with that, I can't help you."

It occurred to me that hiring black and white staff might be an option, but I didn't press the point. Regina and Doug went off to circulate, and I wandered through the vast mansion to the back gallery, where the bar was set up. I asked the bartender for a glass of red wine. He gave me a look that I couldn't interpret—was it something to do with my accent, or my attire? Then he said, "How about white wine?"

Standing behind me was a large bearish man with bright blue eyes and a slightly sad, soulful look. "It's the rugs," he explained. "The antique rugs in the dining room are a pale creamy color. They never serve red wine at Stanton Hall so the garden club ladies don't have to murder anyone for spilling it."

I ordered a Scotch on the rocks. I had the persistent feeling that I'd walked into a movie set, that none of this was real. I was transfixed by the older women. They were in their eighties and nineties, glittering with diamonds, hair swept up into chignons and bouffants. They carried themselves with regal grace and dignity and in moments of repose they looked like waxworks.

I watched carefully as they seated themselves on antique chairs along one wall of the dining room. These were the grandes dames of the Pilgrimage Garden Club, true power brokers in Natchez high society, and younger women lined up to pay court to them. Since the grandes dames were seated, the younger women were forced to crouch down awkwardly, or kneel in an attitude of complete supplication, to avoid talking down to their social superiors. The older women sometimes clasped a hand to help them balance.

One poor woman, crouching in front of a high-ranking octogenarian, accidentally knocked a glass of Coca-Cola onto the pale antique rug. The old dowager stiffened. Then she cut the offender dead with a slight adjustment of her eye muscles, the beginnings of a fake smile halted too soon, and an almost imperceptible turn of her jaw to the side, as the woman wailed her apologies and tried desperately to blot up the stain with a table napkin. It seemed entirely possible that she might be removed from the party and garroted under the live oaks.

I made the acquaintance of Bettye Jenkins, who was ninety and looking fabulous in a black pantsuit with gold shoes and her white hair in a perfect chignon. I told her it was my first time in Natchez, and I had been hearing about Pilgrimage. Could she explain it?

"Why, yes, that's when we put on our hoopskirts and receive," she said in a refined Southern drawl.

"Receive?"

"Yes, we receive visitors in our homes as guests."

"You'll have to excuse my ignorance, but what are hoopskirts?"

"Surely you've seen *Gone with the Wind*. Those are hoop-skirts, like our great-grandmothers wore before the War."

Miss Bettye, as people referred to her, showing respect for her seniority, struck me as the epitome of a grand and gracious Southern lady from a bygone era, and I was amazed to hear that she ran a tugboat company on the Mississippi River with her daughter Carla. "Miss Bettye still goes to work every day except when she's at the beauty parlor," said Regina when I found her on the back gallery. "There's another woman in her nineties who runs a radio station. We've always had a lot of strong, capable, powerful women in this town."

Mansplaining—the tendency of men to interrupt women, hijack the conversation, and explain how things really are—was strikingly absent from this social scene. Women dominated the conversations and interrupted the men, who responded by fading obligingly into the background. Even charismatic big-shouldered oilmen held their tongues. I asked a wealthy genteel business-man how power and social prestige works in Natchez, and he said, "Why on earth are you asking me? We just do what the matrons tell us to do, and for God's sake don't quote me using the word *matron*."

Regina worked the party, currying favor, placating egos, sooth-ing conflicts, dissolving tensions, gleaning information, hinting at opportunities, applying pressure, asking after loved ones and children. There were important things to do, huge sums of money to raise. For starters, Stanton Hall needed a new roof and other repairs, and that was going to cost the garden club $750,000.

Portraits of the Stanton family stared down from the walls. Frederick Stanton, who built this mansion with enslaved labor, was an Irishman from Belfast who transformed himself into a Southern planter, slave owner, and cotton merchant. Very few of the Natchez nabobs, as the antebellum millionaires were known, were products of the American South. They were outsiders, mostly from Pennsylvania, who quickly mastered the skills of acquiring land and growing cotton with slaves, a system of production that one historian describes as "capitalism with its clothes off."

I tried to broach the subject of slavery with one of the dowagers. "There were no slaves in Natchez," she insisted haughtily. "We had field hands on our plantations, of course, but they were out of town or across the river. Here in Natchez, we had servants and we loved them. They were part of our families."

When I relayed this to Regina, she rolled her eyes, sighed, and said, "I'm sure that's what she's been told her whole life, and some people probably did love their servants and mammies, but those people were owned, they were enslaved, they could be bought and sold, and so could their children. You can't just leave that part out!"

The most surprising thing about Natchez slaveholders is that many of them were Unionists. Even though the local economy was utterly dependent on slavery, Natchez voted not to secede from the Union, predicting accurately that it would lead to a ruinous civil war, and the town surrendered twice to the Union army without a fight. The Natchez planters entertained Union officers in their mansions, and some homes were appropriated as military headquarters. The Union army departed without destroying the town, and that is why so many antebellum homes are still standing in Natchez today.

That night, in my comfortable four-poster bed, I was unable to sleep. My mind swirled with questions. How did Pilgrimage, when the ladies dressed up in hoopskirts and invited paying tourists into their antebellum homes, connect into the Royal Court, the Confederate uniforms, the children's maypole dances, and the social prestige of the mothers? Were any black people involved in this, except as servants?

And Regina had mentioned "the other club," in a disparaging tone of voice, and Doug had explained that there were two garden clubs in Natchez, and they had been feuding since 1935, although he didn't say why, or how such a thing might be possible. And flashing in and out, as my restless mind raced through the night, were phrases and images from those panels at the Forks of the Road, coffle songs and Negroes! Negroes! in top hats and calico dresses.

I kept coming back to Natchez, and staying at Twin Oaks, for two main reasons. The town is so singular, so fascinating, so richly stocked with bizarre tales, outlandish characters, contradictions and surprises. The mayor, for example, was an openly gay black man named Darryl Grennell. He was elected with 91 percent of the vote in a small, remote Mississippi town that is nearly half white and was once a hotbed of Ku Klux Klan violence. What is this place? I wanted to know. And how did it get this way?

At the same time, I came to see Natchez as a microcosm, or a barrel-strength distillation, of some much larger unresolved issues around race and slavery in America. In most of the country, especially if you're white, it's fairly easy to believe that slavery happened a long time ago and has nothing to do with the current racial situation in America. To sustain that belief in Natchez, however, requires strenuous denial and extra-large blinders because visual reminders of slavery are all over this racially divided town, whose marketing slogan until the 1990s was "Where the Old South Still Lives." These reminders are not just in the antebellum homes with their adjoining slave quarters, and the old slave-market site that you drive past on the way to buy groceries. Some African Americans here can look at their skin tone and know the white person whose ancestor lightened it.

Slavery and its legacy come up in almost every aspect of civic life in Natchez. It is heatedly discussed in meetings of the tourism department and the city council. It is addressed in local theatrical performances, historical reenactments and African American choir recitals. It is tackled at family reunions where black cousins fathered by white ancestors are being invited for the first time. After 150 years of denial and *Gone with the Wind* fantasy in the white community, a genuine effort is now underway to recognize the role of slavery in the town's history, as the necessary first step before any kind of racial progress can be made.

There was another question that I kept asking myself in Natchez: What was it like to be enslaved here? The local slaveholders left behind a vast trove of letters, diaries, books, and papers, nearly all of it reflecting their self-image as honorable ladies and gentlemen, trying their best to fulfill their paternalistic duties towards their frequently exasperating racial inferiors. But almost nothing exists from the tens of thousands of illiterate people whose labor they exploited and whose lives they essentially stole. A handful of ex-slaves in the area were interviewed by white people in the 1930s, but those interviews, while interesting, are brief and patchy, and many of them were doctored afterwards to present Mississippi slavery in a better light.

Ultimately, there is only one Natchez slave whose life story we know in detail, and that is because it was so extraordinary.

People interviewed him and wrote the story down. In Natchez he was known as Prince, and today his portrait hangs on the wall of the mayor's office at City Hall. When I moved into the upstairs rooms at Twin Oaks, I put a copy of the same portrait on the nightstand.

When he sat for the artist, his forehead was deeply lined and his white hair was grown out like a halo. Considering what he had gone through, his face was almost miraculously composed and self-assured, with a look of deep intelligence in the eyes. It's a portrait of dignity against all odds, with an air of royalty still discernible.

| 2 |

A British ship is anchored off the coast of West Africa in 1781. We might imagine gray-green waters, humid tropical air with a salty tang. The ship's surgeon, a one-eyed Irishman in his twenties named John Cox, climbs into a rowboat and goes ashore with some companions to hunt game. Moving through the unfamiliar vegetation and terrain, with its stifling heat and infernal biting insects, he becomes separated from the other men, who return to the ship without him. Dazed, sweaty and thirsty, as alone as a man can feel, Dr. Cox wanders inland until he collapses.

He is found lying facedown on the ground by a group of men from the Fulani people.[*] These Muslim warriors, traders, and cattle herders are tall and slim with delicate features and coppery skin. Their hair falls to their shoulders in long braids, which symbolize their Fulani identity and masculine pride. Dr. Cox is almost certainly the first white person they have ever seen. Unsure what to do with this strange being, who looks like a man dipped in milk, they take him to their king in Timbo, a

---

[*] One of the largest ethnic groups in the Sahel and West Africa, also known as Fula and Fulbe.

town of 8,000 people in the highlands of Futa Jalon, in what is now Guinea. The sick, exhausted Irishman arrives in a town of conical huts, hedged courtyards, thriving schools and markets, a mosque surrounded by orange trees, and a fortified citadel overshadowing everything.

The Fulani used to be nomads, following the seasonal rains and grazing with herds of cattle and sheep. Now they have mostly settled in towns, but they retain the old nomadic contempt for digging in the dirt. Farming in Futa Jalon is the allotted task of the Jalunke, a low-caste, non-Muslim people who some historians describe as serfs, and others as chattel slaves because they can be sold.

The king's name is Sori, and he has come through brutal wars and rebellions to consolidate his power. Following the Islamic code of hospitality to strangers, he gives Dr. Cox a house to stay in and a nurse to treat his wounds. Over the next few months, the Irishman recovers his health and forms a friendship with the king's favored son, a highly intelligent and capable young man named Abd al-Rahman Ibrahima. Earlier in the year, only nineteen years old and commanding an army for the first time, he won a great victory against 6,000 warriors of the Bambara people, a rival ethnic group. He tricked the enemy into entering a huge cane thicket and then set fire to it. One of the few survivors was the Bambara war chief. When he saw Ibrahima, he announced that he had been defeated by a boy and deserved to die for this disgrace. Ibrahima's men obliged by decapitating him with a sword.

The Irish doctor and the Fulani prince ride horses together and work at learning each other's languages. They are both well-educated, literate men. Ibrahima spent most of his teenage years at Islamic schools in the cities of Jenné and Timbuktu, studying geography, astronomy, mathematics, law, and the Koran. He can read and write Arabic and speak five African languages fluently.

Dr. Cox is a scientific rationalist with a warm, tolerant, slightly eccentric spirit. As an unbeliever, he sees Islam as no worse than Christianity, and he enjoys the company of these elegant, cultured Fulani Muslims, and the kindness and hospitality they show him. As an honored guest of the royal family, he is given a young woman to take as his wife and almost certainly fathers a child with her, before deciding to return to his own people. King Sori gives Dr. Cox enough gold to pay for passage on a ship, and clothes to wear for the journey.

After saying his heartfelt goodbyes, the one-eyed Irishman heads back down to the coast with an escort of fifteen Fulani warriors. Sori has instructed these men to leave Dr. Cox if a ship appears, and to be careful not to get captured and sold into slavery. By outlandish coincidence, Dr. Cox gets aboard the same ship that brought him to Africa and sails away to Europe. He remembers his Fulani friends with great affection for the rest of his life.

———————

Over the next few years, Prince Ibrahima marries and has a son. It is a time of peace and prosperity in the turbulent, war-torn history of his people. The herds multiply and trade flourishes. The Fulani pack up caravans of hides, gold, ivory, and slaves that they capture in raids on other tribes. They trade them on the Rio Pongas to a cruel, drunken trader named John Ormond, originally from Liverpool, England, now living in a small fiefdom with many African wives.

In return for their goods and captives, Ormond supplies

the Fulani with red silk and other luxury items, and guns and ammunition, which have become essential tools for survival. An arms race is taking place across West Africa, financed by the trade in gold, ivory, and slaves. Those who lag behind risk being annihilated or sold into slavery by their enemies.

The Rio Pongas is a deep river with a long estuary. Slave ships sail upstream to Ormond's station, bringing guns and other trade goods, then sail back down to the coast with their miserable human cargo bound for the Americas. In 1787, this trade breaks down because the Susu people, and what Ibrahima calls the Hebohs,[*] start attacking and plundering the ships. In early 1788, at the age of twenty-six, Ibrahima leads 2,000 warriors, including 350 horsemen, down from the highlands to avenge these outrages and reopen the trade route.

The campaign begins with triumph after triumph. Ibrahima's army attacks and burns one Heboh town after another without losing a man, because the cowardly infidels run away and hide. He declares victory and rides back towards the highlands with his men—a decision that will haunt him for the rest of his life.

The Hebohs are not cowardly or defeated, but concealed in ambush at a steep, narrow pass. The Fulani horsemen dismount to lead their horses up the trail, and soon afterwards the Hebohs open fire with their guns. Looking around him, Ibrahima sees "men dropping like rain," as he later describes it. He jumps on his horse, but is immediately surrounded.

"I will not run from a Heboh," he declares, and dismounts with a sword concealed in his robes. He kills the first warrior

---

[*] Scholars have failed to identify them with certainty. According to Terry Alford, Ibrahima's biographer, it might be a corruption of *habe*, which the Fulani use to describe non-Muslim slaves, strangers, and pagans in general.

that approaches him. Then he gets whacked across the head with a rifle.

When he regains consciousness, Ibrahima finds that his hands are tied, his clothes and sandals are gone, and most of his army has also been taken prisoner. The Hebohs march them barefoot for a hundred miles to a group of Mandinka traders. These tall, slim, dark-skinned Muslims are specialists in trading captives to European slavers. Ibrahima, who speaks their language and shares their religion, makes a last-ditch attempt to halt the voyage of no return.

He announces his royal blood and status. He promises the Hebohs that his father, King Sori, will pay an exorbitant ransom for his freedom: one hundred cattle, as many sheep as one man can drive, and as much gold as one man can carry. The Hebohs, fearing Ibrahima's vengeance if he regains his freedom, sell him to the Mandinka traders for two flasks of powder, a few muskets, eight hands of tobacco, and two bottles of rum. The Mandinkas then drive Ibrahima and the remnants of his army to the Gambia River. Their usual method is to tie the captives together at the neck, forming a coffle, and then whip them along like livestock.

In the words of Henry Louis Gates, professor of African American studies at Harvard, the "overwhelming majority" of African slaves in America were originally sold into bondage by other Africans. Many black Americans find this difficult to accept or understand: How could our own people sell us into slavery like that? But there was no concept of "our people" in Africa at that time. Africans didn't think of themselves as black, Negro, or African. They were Fulani, Bambara, Mandinka, or whatever ethnic-linguistic group they belonged to. The idea that black people share a common identity was created by the experience of being enslaved together in the New World, on the basis of their skin pigmentation and the newly invented fiction of "race."

White people were similarly invented. Europeans coming to America boarded ships as Germans, Poles, English, French, and so on. They soon learned that in America they had a new privileged identity based on something they had scarcely considered before: the pale color of their skins. Coming to America transformed them and their descendants into white people, just as all the different African ethnic groups, as they crossed the Atlantic in those nightmarish slave ships, were being transformed into black people.

———

At a Mandinka village on the banks of the Gambia River, Ibrahima is sold again. The buyer is John Nevin, the tough, wary, heavily-armed captain of the slave ship *Africa*. He buys fifty captives to add to his cargo and immediately claps the men in irons. He knows that these are not slaves who will obey his will, but warriors who will seize any opportunity to attack their captors and take over the ship.

Ibrahima is chained by the ankle to another prisoner and packed into the choking, airless, brutally overcrowded hold. It contains 170 men, women, and children in cramped and poorly ventilated compartments, which are soon fetid and reeking with the smell of human excrement. Only the children are able to stand up, and certainly not Ibrahima, who is six feet tall.

The ordeal of the voyage seems interminable to him, but the crossing is faster than normal, with, miraculously, only a few deaths. Normally, losses of 15 or 20 percent are considered acceptable because the profits are so good, and it's a high-volume business. Roughly 14 million people are shipped during the transatlantic slave-trade era, which lasts from the sixteenth century to the nineteenth century, with approximately 11 million surviving the passage.

When the *Africa* reaches the Windward Islands, Ibrahima is sold for the third time. He is now the property of Captain Thomas Irwin, who speaks English with an Irish accent, like Dr. Cox, and packs fifty-seven human beings into the hold of a small schooner bound for New Orleans, 2,300 nautical miles away. Fourteen people die on this voyage, probably from disease.

Arriving in New Orleans, Ibrahima is greatly relieved to stand up, breathe fresh air, and walk around a little, but he is thoroughly unimpressed by his first look at American civilization. With only 5,200 inhabitants in 1788, New Orleans is considerably smaller than Timbo and has recently suffered a devastating fire. Only two hundred houses on the outskirts are still standing, and the rest is a carpet of ashes and mud. Ibrahima spends a month here with the other captives, including Samba, one of his former military commanders, who has been with him since the ambush.

Then Captain Irwin loads them onto another boat, and they travel three hundred miles up the wide brown Mississippi River in the midsummer heat and humidity. The riverbanks are lined with a vast, dark primordial forest. Strange beards of moss hang from the trees. Creatures that look like crocodiles slip off the banks into the murky water. Except for the occasional small farming settlement, hacked out of the forest, the land appears almost uninhabited by people.

Then a verdant bluff comes into view on the right-hand side of the river, and the wooden towers of a fort. This is Fort Panmure de Natchez, the Spanish headquarters of the Natchez district. The town itself is minuscule, with maybe two dozen buildings. Most of the district's 1,926 residents live out of town on plantations along the creeks.

As the boat comes into the muddy landing under the bluff, Ibrahima, the favored son of King Sori, sees a small group of sweaty, pale-faced, bearded men. They size up the Africans like beasts of burden. Strong backs are at a premium with the tobacco harvest coming in.

3

Natchez today has a dwindling population of 15,000 people, approximately 55 percent African American and 44 percent white. Its factories have closed down, the local oil industry has declined, the school system is dysfunctional, prompting residents to leave, and the tourists don't come the way they used to. The old river town—two years older than New Orleans and proud of it—used to have a strong and well-respected Jewish community, but that is almost gone now. The garden clubs have declined in power from their heyday in the mid-twentieth century, when they were dubbed the Hoopskirt Mafia, but they still dominate the social life of white high society and control a large share of tourism, which is the biggest industry in Natchez. And the two garden clubs are still feuding with each other, as bitterly and irrevocably as ever.

When I arrived, the conflict between the Pilgrimage Garden Club (PGC) and the Natchez Garden Club (NGC) was in its eighty-fourth year. Regina Charboneau, as president of the PGC, the bigger, richer, more powerful and aristocratic club, was both embarrassed by the feuding and exasperated with the behavior of what she called "the other club," as if its name were too foul to pronounce and might cause an outbreak of boils and string warts.

As she explained it while venting in her kitchen one morning, the other club represented a lower stratum of the class hierarchy, and it was poisoned by jealousy and feelings of inferiority. Regina also accused the NGC of being more racist than the PGC, although she readily admitted that her own club contained plenty of racists as well. Neither club had a single African American member. Until recently, it would have been unthinkable to invite one. Regina was now trying hard to recruit black members, but every woman she had approached had turned her down.

The ladies of the NGC tended to see Regina and her club as arrogant, divisive, and domineering. Some of them referred to members of the Pilgrimage Garden Club as Pills—bitter in the mouth, and hard to swallow. In many cases, the enmity was passed down from mother to daughter to granddaughter, like a family heirloom. In addition to vicious rumor-mongering and snubbing each other in social settings, the two clubs had deployed lawsuits and financial chicanery against each other. They had padlocked mansions so tourists couldn't gain access during Pilgrimage. They had carved insulting graffiti into furniture and used laxatives to ensure that the other club's King and Queen would be presented on a stage covered with fresh dog excrement.

With Spring Pilgrimage fast approaching, and rehearsals underway for the controversy-racked Tableaux, which required the two clubs to collaborate, Regina's kitchen was a vortex of rumor, intrigue, and drama. It came pouring in by text, phone call, and email. It burst through her kitchen door as wide-eyed, immaculately coiffed women arrived to vent their frustrations, sob and weep, or impart some smoking-hot piece of gossip: "The poor woman is about to lose her mind because her daughter was removed from the Court, but what she did expect after those topless photographs in the tavern?"

And Regina was always cooking, managing the crises and sifting the gossip for truth while stirring a pot of gumbo, or a veal-stock demi-glace, or pulling out a batch of her famous biscuits. Natchez is the self-proclaimed Biscuit Capital of the World, with an annual Biscuit Festival, and Regina was recognized by the *New York Times* and most local opinion as the town's Biscuit Queen. Her biscuits were delectably flaky and fluffy with a golden-brown crust, and she would serve them to me with homemade jams and preserves when I came down the old creaking stairs for breakfast.

"I believe about thirty percent of what I hear," she said during a brief lull one morning. "The Natchez gossip machine is really a phenomenon. We should have anthropologists down here studying it. Some of the worst stuff comes out of a Pilates class that the over-eighties ladies go to. They have a saying that what goes on in Pilates stays in Pilates, but it never does. It comes roaring out of there like a tornado and causes all kinds of damage. Then there's prayer gossip, which is even worse."

I had never heard of prayer gossip, so I asked Regina to explain it. "Okay," she said, putting her palms together. "So you're sitting there in a prayer group with your friends, and you go, 'Jesus, I'd like to pray for a dear, dear friend of mine, because I'm just worried sick about her. She's been seeing a married man, and I mean every day. What if her husband finds out?' That was me they were talking about, and all I was doing was having coffee with the guy, in a group of people, at the Natchez coffee shop. By the time they'd finished praying about it, I was having a torrid affair and my marriage to Doug was on the rocks."

I asked her for another example. Assuming a more high-pitched, feminine, and exaggeratedly Southern voice than her own, she pressed her palms together and said, "Lord, I'd just like to pray for someone who is so dear to my heart. Her drinking has gotten so bad and I'm worried sick about those two poor children, the boy twelve years old and the girl just turned nine."

The prayer gossipers never mention anyone by name, Regina explained, but they drop clues, and the town was small enough that the others could guess who they were talking about. "The guessing probably makes it more fun," she said. "You're sitting there pretending to pray, and you're thinking, 'Now, who could that be? I bet she's talking about so-and-so.'" Then Regina's phone went off again with its piano-trill ringtone, and another woman came bursting through the kitchen door: the other club was threatening to sabotage the Tableaux by kicking out the African American performers, and one of them had compared Regina to a Nazi. "I have a secret weapon," said Regina when the woman left. "I don't care what anyone thinks of me. I know a lot of people say that. But I actually don't care."

One Friday morning, I came downstairs to find Regina cooking for 24 dinner guests that evening, and 140 wedding guests the following morning. Renting out Twin Oaks for wedding receptions, and doing the catering herself, was one of the income streams she had created from the house. She didn't seem flustered by this enormous culinary workload, even though Janet was absent and Regina had no one else to help her, and the gossip and the drama were pouring into the kitchen at the usual pace. Eight courses of gourmet Southern food with a strong Louisiana influence were beautifully presented at both events with souvenir printed menus, beautiful flower arrangements, and a limitless supply of wine and liquor.

Somehow she also managed to run the bed-and-breakfast,

King's Tavern, and the Pilgrimage Garden Club, an organization with 650 members, interminable meetings, and an annual operating budget of $1.2 million. As president, her responsibilities included the renovation and upkeep of Stanton Hall, and the spectacular octagonal mansion known as Longwood. She oversaw the Carriage House Restaurant at Stanton Hall, the annual Antiques Forum, the ticketing and promotion company Natchez Pilgrimage Tours, and Pilgrimage itself. Twenty-four antebellum homes were "on tour" this spring, and something always had to be dealt with or improved upon. Some of the ladies would lead the tourists into deep thickets of family genealogy and keep them there interminably. And several tourists had complained recently that a gay man in one of the mansions was throwing the N-word around.

Then there was the Historic Natchez Tableaux, which was generating more stress than everything else put together. Whenever Regina's phone rang close to midnight, it was almost invariably someone having a weepy crisis over the Tableaux. "It's always stressful," Regina said, while making a batch of crème-brulée ice cream. "Tableaux is an amateur theatrical production with children, live beagles, and overbearing mothers, and it requires us to work together with the other club. Some of the NGC women are wonderful to work with, and some of them are automatically suspicious of everything I want to do. I've been accused of siphoning off money, deliberately ruining other people's lives for my own satisfaction, spreading false rumors, and acting like a dictator, all of it completely untrue."

In the small, shrinking, isolated world of the Natchez garden clubs, which nonetheless considers itself to be the center of the universe, a fantastic degree of importance is attached to the Tableaux. It's a vital affirming ritual of this matriarchal society, a primary engine of advancement within it, and a vital mechanism for the garden clubs to secure volunteer labor. Pilgrimage, Antiques Forum, balls, social events, and ultimately the preservation of historic buildings, all depended on unpaid women volunteering their time, and knowing that the more time they gave, the more likely it was that their children would get into the Royal Court and hopefully become crowned King or Queen, whereupon their mothers could bask in the reflected glory. Without that incentive, the whole system would fall apart. A local attorney confided to me that several women had approached him over the years about suing the Tableaux committee because their children weren't chosen for high-prestige roles. "I declined to get involved in that catfight," he added. "Some of our ladies have mighty sharp claws."

The production is a series of skits and dances celebrating Natchez history and its white antebellum culture. Children begin performing at the age of three, with the girls dressed in pretty hoopskirt dresses and the boys in ballet slippers and velvet knickers, dancing together around a maypole. As they grow older, the children work their way up through a series of scenes and roles until, their mothers hope, they make it into the Royal Court with its uniformed Confederate generals and King and Queen. Each garden club has its own King, Queen, and Royal Court, and when they're announced for the year, it's a big front-page story in the *Natchez Democrat*, with the prior accomplishments of each member listed in detail: "Little Maypole, Big Maypole, Polka, Soirée, Page . . ."

The Tableaux contains elements of Mardi Gras and elements of a debutante ball, but it's a unique Natchez tradition that has been soaking in isolation, nostalgia, and liquor for eighty years. "The King and Queen register for gifts, as if they were going to get married, and they get a lot of nice stuff," said Regina. "For the parents, it's a very proud moment to see their children as King and Queen, but they also have to pay for a black-tie Royal Ball for five hundred people with a band and an open bar, which can cost $25,000. And there's also a month-long series of cocktail parties for the King and Queen. The ability to hold your liquor is absolutely vital."

Outside observers were usually baffled by the Tableaux or stunned by its political incorrectness and amateurish production values. I had heard it compared to the Mel Brooks farce *Springtime for Hitler*, with Confederates instead of Nazis. "That's what we're trying to change, and we're getting there," said Regina. "We have African American performers now portraying black history. We're finally addressing slavery in an honest way. We're trying to get away from glorifying the Confederacy and the Civil War. This is touching all our most sensitive nerves about race, slavery, history, and the South, and some people are losing their minds. It's making them furious. It's making them crazy. They want it all just like it used to be."

The production began in 1932 as the Natchez Confederate Ball. The garden club ladies had just invented Pilgrimage, which enabled them to dress up in their great-grandmothers' hoopskirts and charge tourists to parade through their antebellum homes. The main purpose of Pilgrimage was to make money and bring people to Natchez. To entertain the visitors in the evenings and make more money, the ladies came up with a theatrical production that portrayed antebellum Natchez as a gorgeous fairy tale, culminating in a heroic celebration of the Confederacy on the eve of the Civil War.

It made no difference that in reality Natchez had voted against secession and surrendered twice to the Union army. In the decades after the War, white Natchez had steeped itself in the romantic mythology of the Old South and the Lost Cause, which held that slaves were happy and grateful, and the Civil War was purely about states' rights. The garden club ladies didn't design the Pageant to advance this delusional view of Southern history. They believed in it utterly, like most white Southerners, and they simply wanted to show the visitors how wonderful and charming antebellum Natchez had been.

The production featured white teenagers in hoopskirts and military uniforms waltzing against Old South backdrops, while "happy slaves" sang Negro spirituals and pretended to pick cotton. Small African American boys were positioned onstage and given slices of fake watermelon to eat. Young men waved the rebel flag, and then the King, Queen, and Royal Court of the garden club were presented, wearing Confederate generals' uniforms and shimmering tiaras and gowns. The climax was a rousing chorus of "Dixie," with all the audience members, Yankees included, required to stand for the old anthem of the Confederacy.

The tourists, mostly from the Northern states and Europe, ate it up like ice cream, especially after *Gone with the Wind* came out in 1939 and became the biggest film in motion picture history. In the late 1940s and 1950s tourists thronged to Natchez by the tens of thousands. Selling tickets to the nightly performances of the Confederate Pageant became an important revenue stream for the garden clubs.

In the 1960s, the African American cast members refused to carry on portraying happy field hands, mammies, and pickaninnies. The garden club ladies found this regrettable and misguided, but the show had to go on. At first, white performers dressed up in blackface to re-create these scenes, but that proved inflammatory in the black community. For the next five decades the Pageant was an all-white production that made no mention of slaves, happy or otherwise. In 2002, bending a little to the changing winds of public opinion, the Natchez Confederate Pageant was renamed the Historic Natchez Tableaux, but the content remained largely the same, an unapologetic celebration of the old slaveholding white South.

Then, in 2015, the Pilgrimage Garden Club chose Madeline Iles as its Queen. Madeline is the daughter of Greg Iles, the bestselling thriller writer and Natchez's most famous resident. Like her father, Madeline is a liberal, and she balked at the prospect of appearing in a crown and gown at the Tableaux, which she had come to see as horribly insensitive to African Americans and an embarrassment to her hometown. She thought about refusing the honor, but that would have upset her grandmother. So instead she leveraged her power. Essentially, she told the garden clubs that she would only be Queen if they made the Tableaux less racist.

The production was suffering from slumping attendance and falling revenue, and this made the clubs receptive to modernizing and revamping it, especially when Greg Iles offered to write and direct it for free. He brought in local black performers, including two superb vocal talents: Tony Fields, the principal of Natchez High School, and Debbie Cosey, who was planning to open a bed-and-breakfast in a former slave quarters.

Greg Iles was determined to tackle slavery honestly and directly, so he wrote a scene where a slave in chains is led to the auction block, and another scene portraying a secret slave wedding under threat from slave catchers. But he also had to include the traditional tableaux of little white girls dancing in pretty dresses, and waltzing white teenagers, which made for some jarring contrasts. As a compromise with the traditionalists, he left in the Confederate uniforms and flag, but added a new ending to unglorify the Civil War. Broken wounded Confederate soldiers returned to a ruined plantation and raised the American flag, saying that too many sons had died for nothing.

Now, after two seasons of hard work without pay, and a hailstorm of criticism from local conservatives, who preferred the old Tableaux, Greg Iles had bowed out. "I hope this will be a model for racial cooperation," he said to the newspapers. The new writer-director was Chesney Doyle, a local documentary filmmaker and NGC member. She intended to build on the progress that Greg Iles had made, and also hoped that the production would help bridge the racial divisions in Natchez and bring the town together.

———

Regina sat down with a glass of wine after another extremely hectic day. Although Chesney Doyle belonged to the other garden club, Regina found her excellent to work with. But a group of women in Chesney's club were fighting progress and making things difficult. "They're not happy about slavery being included," said Regina. "They're not happy about having black performers, and they're really not happy about paying them."

Greg Iles had insisted on paying the African American performers, and Regina and Chesney both agreed that it was the right thing to do. White performers and their mothers were deriving social benefits from the Tableaux, they reasoned, but the reverse was true for black performers. They were catching withering criticism in the black community because the production had such a long history of glorifying the white antebellum

South, stereotyping African Americans, and completely ignoring their suffering under slavery.

In the garden clubs, it wasn't the grandes dames who were arguing for a return to tradition, as one might expect. The older ladies, with a few exceptions, welcomed the changes and thought it was high time that the Tableaux was brought more up-to-date. Most of the criticism and complaints were coming from younger women with less privileged backgrounds. "They're saying it's unfair that 'the blacks' are getting paid, while everyone else is a volunteer," said Regina. "And there's a definite undercurrent that 'the blacks' are looking for special treatment and a handout as usual, and they shouldn't be in the Tableaux because it's not part of their 'cultural tradition,' and some of them are still mad at Chesney for bringing an African American child to their swimming pool. But anyway, we're going to push on."

The situation was fraught and stressful, but Regina, Chesney, and many other people in town, black and white, also had a sense that progress was finally being made. Natchez had integrated its Tableaux. The essential wrongness of slavery was now being acknowledged in the former Confederate Pageant, along with a celebration of the town's African American history after slavery. And for the first time, some of the local black activists had agreed to participate. "This is huge," said Regina. "Ser Boxley used to stand outside the city auditorium wearing his Union army uniform to protest the Tableaux. Now he's agreed to give us a voice-over."

Ser Boxley, she explained, was one of the most passionate, committed, and effective African American activists in Natchez, and also something of an eccentric. In his late seventies now, he either wore traditional West African clothing, or the replica Civil

War uniform of a US Colored Troops infantryman. It wasn't just white people in Natchez who enjoyed wearing antique costumes and impersonating the dead. There was also a group of black living-history performers and historical reenactors, and Ser Boxley was their leader.

"For the longest time Ser Boxley wouldn't come into my house because it was built by slaves," said Regina. "But he wouldn't admit it. He would say that he liked being outside in the fresh air, even when it was August and a hundred degrees and we'd both be dripping with sweat. Finally I called him on it, and he said it was true. Now he comes inside the house, but first he says a prayer for the people who were enslaved here. He used to be called Cliff Boxley, but he changed his name. . . . Hold on a minute, it's a hard one to remember, and not the easiest to pronounce."

She swiped up one of his emails on her phone and showed me the Africanized name: Ser Seshsh Ab Heter-CM Boxley. A testy, uncompromising character, he had agreed to do a voice-over about slavery for the Tableaux, but he was still refusing to set foot in the auditorium, either as performer or spectator. Darrell White, the director of the Natchez Museum of African American History and Culture, had also agreed to record a voice-over, because the Tableaux was finally addressing black history in a way he could support, but he too was staying away from the auditorium. A young dreadlocked activist named Jeremy Houston was going a step further. He was going to appear onstage in the Tableaux and portray Abd al-Rahman Ibrahima, the Fulani prince who came to Natchez as a slave.

4

Among those watching Captain Irwin unload his Africans at the muddy landing under the bluff is a tall, dark-haired man named Thomas Foster. Twenty-six years old, the same age as Ibrahima, he is pious, solid and serious, with shrewdness and ambition, but very little education. He came to Natchez from South Carolina with his mother and three brothers, attracted by the land grants offered by the Spanish government. Soon after he arrived, Thomas married Sarah Smith, the daughter of a neighboring farmer, and two children followed in quick succession. Now, in the summer of 1788, his wife is pregnant again and he needs two slaves to work in the tobacco fields he has cleared and planted.

Ibrahima catches Foster's eye immediately. The long-haired, coppery-skinned Fulani has traveled six thousand miles in utterly degrading conditions, but he retains some of his aristocratic bearing and a look of obvious intelligence. Foster is impressed, in the same way that a buyer of horses is impressed by good breeding. After negotiating with Irwin, he settles on a price of $930 for Ibrahima and Samba, the former military commander captured at the same ambush. Putting up the one slave he already owns as collateral, Foster hands over $150 in silver and signs a promissory note for the rest. The deed of sale describes Ibrahima and Samba as *dos negros brutos*, two primitive untrained blacks. Leading them behind his horse, Foster takes the old Indian road to his farm, about six miles northeast of Natchez.

Every captive suffers through a kind of social death in enslavement. Everything that forms your identity—language, culture, social status, family ties, kinship ties, friendships, ways of dressing and adornment—all of it is ripped away in a place where you don't know how to survive and can't speak the language. It's always a brutal psychological shock, and for Ibrahima, it is particularly severe. He is the son of a great king and commander in chief of the kingdom's army, with a wife and son in the citadel. He is a highly educated man from a society with a constitution and laws, and a people who consider themselves superior to everyone else, including Europeans. Now he's led away behind a horse to a muddy little farm in the wilderness, with the stumps of cut-down trees poking up everywhere.

Ibrahima can scarcely believe that anyone lives in such primitive conditions, let alone that such people are able to own him as a slave. Foster's home, which he shares with Sarah and the children, is a crude log cabin chinked with mud and moss. Why do they live so far out in the forest by themselves? Why are their houses so poorly constructed?

Soon after he arrives, Ibrahima makes a speech in which he identifies himself as a Fulani prince and offers Thomas Foster a ransom in gold to be paid by his father, King Sori, in Futa Jalon. Presumably, he gives the speech in Mandinka, which is then translated into English by one of the Mandinka slaves living on the neighboring farms. Foster listens with mounting skepticism to this fantastic tale. He has never heard of Futa Jalon, which does not appear on most contemporary maps. Perhaps mockingly, perhaps not, Foster gives his new slave the name of Prince. Then he fetches some homespun clothes and a pair of shears.

When Ibrahima realizes that Foster intends to cut off his hair, a violent struggle ensues. In Futa Jalon, a man will only part with his hair if you kill him first. Foster eventually overpowers Ibrahima and ropes him to a tree. Then the long braided tresses, the fetishistic representations of Fulani pride and manhood, are sheared off into the Mississippi mud. Thomas Foster, although he has no way of knowing or understanding it, has given the commander in chief the haircut of a little boy and delivered a devastating psychological blow. For resisting his haircut so violently, Ibrahima is locked up for three days. Then comes the next stage of his social death.

It's hard to exaggerate the contempt of the Fulani aristocracy for manual labor, and nothing is more degrading than farming, a humiliating drudgery performed by the lowly Jalunke. When Foster tells Ibrahima to start carrying freshly cut tobacco leaves from the fields, he refuses to do it. Foster brings out the whip, which is supposed to solve problems like this, but the whipping only deepens Ibrahima's resentment and hardens his refusal to work in the demeaning fields. The two young men are now locked in bitter, intractable conflict.

Foster has the option of whipping Prince three-quarters to death, which is known to break the spirit of most slaves. Castration is another popular remedy for intransigence, along with torture by fire or boiling water. But Foster isn't that cruel, and he is also acutely aware of the mortgage he owes on Prince. Ibrahima has only one way to break the deadlock, and he exercises it first. He runs away one night into the huge, dark forest to the north.

Notices of his escape are posted at the fort and in the taverns. Slave catchers are dispatched, but they find not a single track. As the days turn into weeks, Thomas Foster loses hope and various theories are advanced in the Natchez grog shops. Maybe an alligator or a panther got him. Maybe it was snakebite. Maybe he drowned in the river, or starved to death, or died of fever, or was killed by Indians. These are all highly plausible ways to die. No white man would even consider going into that wilderness alone and unarmed.

Meanwhile, Ibrahima stays close to Foster's farm, perhaps up a tree, racked with hunger and going through the greatest existential crisis of his life. He can think of nothing more abhorrent than being enslaved in the fields of a primitive infidel farmer, and if he goes back to Foster's place, an agonizing punishment seems certain. Runaway slaves in this land are routinely whipped to a bloody pulp, maimed, mutilated, sometimes roasted alive. But he cannot survive in the forest, and there is no way back to Futa Jalon, or any other kind of freedom. And the Koran says that suicides will not be admitted to paradise.

Religion guides his decision to return to Foster's farm. Islam is a fatalistic creed, in which each person's life is written in advance. Nothing happens to a believer unless Allah has willed it. By accepting his cruel fate as Foster's slave, Ibrahima decides, he is accepting Allah's will and fulfilling his duty as a Muslim.

Sarah Foster is sitting in her house sewing when she hears something, looks up, and sees Prince standing at the door with his clothes in rags and a wild, tortured look on his face. She assumes that he has come to kill her, and her survival instincts compel her to stand up, smile, and hold out her hand in welcome.

He touches her hand briefly. Then he lies down on the floor, takes one of her feet, and places it on his neck. In West African warfare, this is a sign of complete submission, usually followed by a spear-thrust to the heart. Lacking English, he is trying to communicate to the Fosters that they can have him back as a compliant slave, or kill him, torture him, do whatever they want to him.

5

The first time I saw Ser Seshsh Ab Heter-CM Boxley, he was sitting on a bench outside the Natchez Museum of African American History and Culture on Main Street. His eyes were closed and his broad, rugged, white-bearded face was angled upwards for maximum exposure to the spring sunshine. He still radiated physical power and strength of character in his late seventies, and he was wearing a kente-cloth dashiki and holding a traditional African fly whisk. There were brass rings on his fingers and beads around his wrist. Amulets and masks hung from his neck on leather cords. He had the air of a warrior in repose, and his battlefield was the intersection of history, memory, and tourism.

For most of the twentieth century, Natchez had marketed itself as a romantic vision of the Old South, with slavery so sanitized that it almost disappeared, and the rest of African American history ignored completely. You could still take tours of Natchez that hewed to this model—Pilgrimage was almost unchanged—but there was now a consensus among tourism leaders that African American history needed to be recognized and included. No one had fought harder for this cause than Ser Boxley.

I walked up to him and introduced myself. He opened his eyes, made some small talk, nicknamed me Ricardo, and then began firing out rhetorical questions: "Are you here to see the monuments to chattel slavery and the denied humanity of our ancestors that the white folks call antebellum *homes*? Will you stay for Pilgrimage, Ricardo, to see the white folks dress up like enslavers and go to great lengths not to mention the African-descent people whose stolen labor built this town?"

He asked if I was staying in one of the local chattel-slavery monuments.

I said yes, at Twin Oaks.

"Sure. Regina's house. Send her my regards. She can do her thing, and I'll do mine. I'm on a twenty-two-year campaign for equal history commemoration. The garden clubs will give you the idea that white folks did everything around here. Sometimes they get slick and talk about 'the servants' quarters,' but that's as far as it goes."

"Do you want them to talk more about slavery during Pilgrimage?"

"Aw, hell no!" he thundered. "As Dr. Runoko Rashidi says, 'You know you're in trouble when you allow the same people who have historically oppressed you to tell your history.' We'll tell our own story, whether the white folks like it or not."

This was the launching pad for a strident, impassioned monologue that went on for nearly two and a half hours. It poured out of him like a river and swept aside all my attempts to ask questions, challenge assertions, or seek clarifications. He made long declamations on the history of the slave trade, the innate superiority of traditional African cultures, the history of black resistance in America, the perfidy of his enemies, the Civil War, racism in Natchez, and the story of his life.

He was born and raised here as Clifton Boxley, but that sounded like a plantation name bestowed by an enslaver, so he had Africanized it. *Ser* is an Egyptian word meaning "highly re-spected person." He left Natchez as a young man and spent thirty-five years in California working as an anti-poverty cam-paigner and activist. In his spare time, he traveled extensively in Africa. On the coast of Ghana, he communed with the spirits of the ancestors in nineteen different slave dungeons, where they had been held captive by European flesh merchants before the horrors of the Middle Passage. He understood that Ghana was his true spiritual homeland, and he was planning to move there permanently when he started receiving communications from dead people who had been enslaved in Natchez.

"The ancestors said to me, 'Who is going to speak up for us? Who will tell our history and reclaim the humanity that was stolen from us?' So I came home. I started researching and writ-ing grants. I started protesting and battling the white-supremacy power structure, and I refused to quit like they thought I would. I sacrificed everything in terms of monetary or social benefits, or housing, but that's alright. I'm working for the ancestors, not for materialistic reasons."

His greatest accomplishment had stopped me and stunned me on my first visit to Natchez. Ser Boxley, more than anyone else, had succeeded in getting the Forks of the Road recognized and commemorated as a historic site. The fact that the second-largest slave market in the Deep South was in Natchez, by the Lemon Delight car wash, the muffler shop, and the custom-sidings place, had been almost completely forgotten in the local community, the state of Mississippi, and the nation at large.

His campaign included a national letter-writing drive to raise funds, repeated protests in Natchez and Washington, DC, and securing a grant from the Mississippi state legislature. But in the end, it all came down to pressuring a recalcitrant white man to sell a piece of property. "It was a whites-only beer garden from the Jim Crow days and a gravel parking lot. We fought tooth and nail over it. I don't know if the ancestors got on his ass or what, but he finally came up to me and said, 'Okay, I'll sell it if you find some land with timber on it for my son.' We found the land, he sold the site, and we commemorated it with a libation ceremony." This is an ancient Pan-African ritual in which drinks are poured on the ground to honor the ancestors.

Having commemorated the Forks of the Road, Ser Boxley turned his attention to the role of the US Colored Troops (USCT) in the Civil War and founded a group of historical re-enactors known as the Black and Blue. Dressed up as enslaved people and uniformed USCT soldiers, sailors, and nurses, they perform living-history presentations and once gate-crashed a Confederate reenactment. Since moving to Mississippi, I had become accustomed to the Civil War fixations of many white people, with battles and troop movements discussed in fanatical detail, and a general sense that it had all taken place in recent memory. In Ser Boxley and his group, I encountered the same phenomenon among African Americans for the first time.

Ser Boxley was convinced that the outcome of the War, and therefore the end of slavery, had been decided by the 178,000 African American troops (runaway slaves and free Northerners) who fought for the Union from 1863 to 1865. Most historians would give at least some credit to Abraham Lincoln for ending slavery, but Boxley was allergic to white saviors: "The Emancipation Proclamation wasn't worth the paper it was written on, except for that clause allowing enslaved people to become freedom fighters for the Union army. Lincoln wasn't no Great Emancipator. It was the US Colored Troops who turned the tide of the war and allowed African-descent people to emancipate themselves."

Ser Boxley had now moved from the sunlit bench to the front steps of the museum, and a small crowd had gathered. Two stoned young men lounged on bicycles, nodding along and saying, "That's right." Jeremy Houston, the dreadlocked young man who was playing Ibrahima in the Tableaux, listened with a respect bordering on reverence. Darrell White, the director of the museum, a slim, round-shouldered, scholarly-looking figure, stood there smoking a cigarette, looking defiant and proud. He too was a regular costumed performer at the Black and Blue events, and a leading activist for the cause of African American history in Natchez.

Boxley and White portrayed their campaign as a fierce ongoing battle against the entrenched power structure of white supremacy. This had been mostly true in the early days and was now mostly exaggeration. They no longer faced any resistance from the city government: Natchez had a black mayor and a majority-black board of aldermen. The list of institutions that had supported black history projects in Natchez now included the US National Park Service, the Mississippi state legislature, the Mississippi Department of Archives and History, the Historic Natchez Foundation, the Visit Natchez tourism bureau, and the Natchez Trails tourism committee. Even the garden clubs, in their promotional brochures for Pilgrimage, were now encouraging visitors to tour African American historical sites.

Natchez had a surprising number of white liberals, concentrated in the historic downtown area, and they all supported the commemoration of black history, in "telling the whole story," as the phrase went, although Boxley didn't trust them. "Liberals are the worst kind of white," he said. "They are phony, and all about their own guilt and feelings. They will express their white supremacy by telling you what should be done. Don't send me no white liberals. It ain't their call."

He was equally scathing about African Americans who disagreed with his views, or his confrontational methods. They were all "Uncle Toms" or "house Negroes." Perhaps overstating himself in the heat of a tirade, he derided all African American employees of the US National Park Service, in Natchez and all over the country, as "typical house Negroes, trying to ingratiate and cozy up, while the people in charge refuse to tell the truth about our history."

He attacked the Holy Family Catholic Church, where an all-black choir in Afrocentric costumes sang freedom songs about black history to predominantly white tourists during Pilgrimage. The spectacle disgusted him: "I don't promote singing and dancing for white folks. That's steppin' and fetchin'. It's that old 'Come on, boy, sing me those good ole gospel songs.' Well, fuck you, who do you think you are?"

Boxley was an old-school freedom fighter, forged by the black power movement of the 1960s and 1970s. "I'm not a compromising type of Negro," he liked to say. Pugnacious, belligerent, self-aggrandizing, he always needed a villain to battle against, and he hated to cede control or take advice. He pushed and shouted, then complained that he was not warmly received. His ranting made it easy for some people to ignore his message, and he was exasperating for others to work with, yet he commanded a lot of respect in Natchez, even from some of the people he had publicly scorned.

In the words of Kathleen Bond, the white superintendent of the National Park Service in Natchez, "His absolute dedication to the Forks of the Road and the USCT has been so instrumental in turning the battleship of this town's feelings about history and tourism. He is a prophet in the truest sense—pointing out how power has been abused, how shaky are the moral foundations of a town built on human trafficking, and how pernicious the racism that still runs through the veins of the community, running the gamut from hard-line neo-Confederates to the implicit bias lurking in the hearts of downtown liberals."

Ser Boxley was a flawed human being, like the rest of us, but his sense of commitment was pure and absolute, and the more time I spent in Natchez, the more convinced I became that he was essentially right. The town, and the nation at large, were still deeply wounded and deformed by slavery, and no healing or progress could occur unless this vital truth was recognized. But it was stubbornly resisted, and not just by whites. "Most black folks don't want to think about slavery because it's painful, and they feel ashamed, and this is where they go wrong," said Boxley.

I had to halt his monologue because I had another appointment. He shook hands, wished me well, and climbed with difficulty into a small, dilapidated pickup truck festooned with African artifacts and memorabilia. He rolled down the window and said, "The only way to transcend the pain, anger, shame, and sorrow of our history is to face the situation and experience it, to allow the humanity of the ancestors and their suffering to wash through us and settle into our spirit. Only then will we be free and begin to heal."

———

Ser Boxley and others had succeeded in making the moral case for commemorating African American history in Natchez, but it was proving a difficult sell to the vacationing public. So much of that history was harrowing and heart-wrenching, sickening and disgraceful. It forced you to face America at its worst, in one of its loveliest settings, and this produced a strange, uncanny, dislocated feeling, as if you were admiring a gorgeous sunset over Auschwitz, or eating a picnic at a massacre site.

Walking through the historic district one afternoon, almost intoxicated by the beauty of the buildings and the gardens in the honeyed light and soft, fragrant air, I stopped to admire a particularly handsome Greek Revival antebellum house. The Natchez Trails committee had placed a sign in front of it, helpfully describing its architectural features and the original owner, a banker named George W. Koontz. The sign also included a small newspaper advertisement placed by Mr. Koontz in 1850:

TWENTY-FIVE DOLLARS REWARD!

Runaway from the subscriber on the night of the 12th instant, a negro woman named MATILDA, about 30 years of age, medium structure, color a dark griffe,* has a large mouth, rather thin lips, high cheek bones, and wears false hair, and has with her a good supply of genteel clothing. She is very intelligent and talks much of having gone through the Mexican war.

So now the experience of being there was irrevocably altered. Not spoiled exactly—at least, not in my case—but made more sinister, difficult, complicated, interesting, and historically vivid. I was struck by the intimate detail of Mr. Koontz's description, and I wondered about Matilda's plan of escape. The Underground Railroad in Natchez was the Mississippi River. Did she intend to stow away or pass as a free person of color on a steam-

---

* *Griffe*: a common term of racial classification at the time, denoting the offspring of a mulatto and a person of fully African ancestry.

boat going to New Orleans, where she could blend into the free-black population? Or was she intending to go upriver to the free states? And how curious that she was in the Mexican War and apparently wouldn't stop talking about it? Was she caught or did she make it to freedom?

Natchez Trails, a biracial committee, included a number of slavery-related newspaper ads on its interpretive signs in the historic district. Along with reward notices for runaways, you could read job postings for overseers, and announcements of VALUABLE NEGROES FOR SALE and SLAVES! SLAVES! SLAVES! These little snippets brought home both the everydayness of human trafficking here—before the Forks of the Road was built, slaves were sold in downtown auction houses, on street corners and the courthouse steps—and the all-American sales-manship involved. The merchandise was described in glowing terms—"choice selections," "a very lively lot"—available at the "lowest possible prices." Other Natchez Trails signs featured period drawings and sketches: a girl being sold away from her mother on the auction block, two enslaved women with babies being whipped in a cotton field by a white man in a top hat. Coming across these reminders, as you strolled through the flower-scented streets, added to the impression that slavery still lingered here, as a haunt, an echo, a theme.

The Nachee, or Natchez Indians, were the first to build a civilization on the bluff overlooking the great river. Early French visitors noted that their lordly tattooed chieftains, or Suns, kept war captives from other tribes as their personal slaves. When a Sun died, his head slave was strangled to death, so he could con-tinue to serve his master in the afterlife. Further north and east, the Spanish explorer Hernando de Soto saw Native American slaves toiling in the fields of Native American masters. The slaves had their toes cut off, or their Achilles tendons severed, so they couldn't run away.

All over North America, when the first Europeans arrived, native tribes and nations were enslaving war captives. They exploited their labor with violence, inflicted cruelties, and bought, sold, and traded their slaves to other tribes. It was a traumatic experience to go through, but the offspring of these slaves were usually assimilated as full tribal members, and enslavement had nothing to do with skin color or physical characteristics. This was, broadly speaking, the normal form of slavery all over the world throughout human history. Race-based slavery, with children and grandchildren automatically inheriting slave status because of their skin color and phenotype, was far more unusual. It was practiced by some Muslim societies in North Africa and the Middle East, using black Africans as slaves, and on a grand new commercial scale by Europeans in the New World, also using enslaved sub-Saharan Africans.

The French were the first to bring African slaves to Natchez, around 1720. The bluff subsequently passed into British rule, Spanish rule, and American rule, with black slaves as a constant presence. They toiled in fields of tobacco, hemp, and indigo until King Cotton swept all other crops asunder in the early 1800s, and Natchez became the center of a frenzied economic boom. More productive strains of cotton were developed, and a longer, crueler whip was invented—ten feet of plaited cowhide with a weighted handle—which tore its way through human flesh and extracted harder, faster work in the fields.

In the 1820s and 1830s, new financial instruments were invented, enabling planters to mortgage their slaves for credit, and bankers to bundle these slave-backed mortgages into attractive packages for investors on the East Coast and in Europe—the ultimate commodification of human beings. Fantastic fortunes were lashed and levered into existence, and Greek Revival and Federal mansions proliferated in Natchez and its environs. In 1837, the slave-backed mortgage bubble burst and the price of cotton collapsed, but another wave of credit-fueled prosperity and mansion building followed in the 1850s.

A growing number of visitors wanted to know the full, unexpurgated history of the town, no matter how painful or difficult, but we were still in a minority. The romance of the Old South was still the prime attraction for most tourists in Natchez. They tended to be white American retirees with the normal white American views about slavery: it was a long time ago, you can't change the past, let's not talk about it, let's not think about it, don't you dare make us feel bad about it.

I talked with some senior citizens visiting from Louisiana and Illinois. They were complaining about their tour of Melrose, a 15,000-square-foot mansion operated as a house museum by the National Park Service. There had been far too much talk about slavery, and they had not enjoyed the tour of the restored slave quarters. They had also resented the black park ranger's suggestion that they visit the Forks of the Road. "We all know it happened, so why do they keep shoving it down our throats?" one man said. "We're on vacation," said his wife. "Can't they just let us enjoy the pretty old buildings?"

This was exactly why some white people in Natchez wanted to keep slavery quiet. They didn't want to upset the visitors. Talking about slavery was an offense against Southern hospitality, which requires keeping everything nice, and making sure that guests leave with the best possible impression. Of all the objections voiced against the inclusion of African American history in Natchez, this was probably the most common.

Kathleen Bond of the National Park Service described the opponents of black history as a hydra with many heads, including the following: "Those who don't want to examine the sources of their own family's wealth and privilege, those who are in denial about the horrors of human trafficking on which the town's prosperity is based, those who are unwilling to embrace a vision for the future that turns its back on the past 'glories' of Natchez, those who are trapped in the sanitized version of Southern history they were taught growing up."

Finally, there were those unrepentant bigots who thought that black history was as stupid and worthless as the race itself. They could be encountered drinking outside a saloon on the riverfront, in the comments section of the local newspaper, on social media, and in internet chat rooms, where they felt most unbridled and sometimes called for the re-enslavement of the N-words. Their rhetoric was loud and ugly, but they had no influence on the decisions being made about tourism in Natchez, and they were a small minority, judging by the fact that Darryl Grennell, a gay black man, had been elected mayor with 91 percent of the vote. There was white racism aplenty in Natchez, but most of it wasn't hateful, and it didn't preclude voting for a black man. It was subtler and more complex than that, and arguably more insidious because it was less easy to call out.

Jeremy Houston, who was playing Ibrahima in the Tableaux, had started leading African American heritage tours of Natchez, following Ser Boxley's idea that black people were the only ones who should be telling their history. Jeremy was tall, lean, handsome, athletic. He had served two tours in Afghanistan, come home with post-traumatic stress disorder, and, like thousands of other veterans, learned that he could function best on low doses of marijuana. I would never have guessed any of this unless he had told me. He could get riled up about racial injustice, but his core personality was kind and gentle. Most whites in the tourism business supported Jeremy, admired his entrepreneurship, and also hoped that his tours would become more polished and professional as time went on. It was true that Jeremy's presentations were a little ragged, and his punctuality could be erratic, but he was an engaging speaker, and his tours had a rawness and passion that made a powerful impact.

They began at the Forks of the Road, with Jeremy stepping out of his van holding a set of slave chains with a neck manacle at one end, and wrist and ankle manacles at the other. "This is the Natchez reality tour, what I'm about to tell you, and not the *Gone with the Wind* fantasy," he said. The chains made a sinister clinking-clanking sound. "White folks glorify these planters during Pilgrimage time. I guarantee you don't see no whips or chains on none of them house tours."

He pointed towards Natchez Exhaust, and the Solar Eclipse Window Tinting shop, which bordered the small memorial that Ser Boxley had battled for so doggedly. "Looka here. This is where Isaac Franklin had his office. He was the kingpin, probably the richest dealer of enslaved people in the whole country. Theophilus Freeman was right over here. He's the one that sold Solomon Northup out of *Twelve Years a Slave*."

Jeremy had the Natchez tendency to think of events that took place nearly two centuries ago as fresh, vivid, all-consuming, and he soon slipped into the present tense. "Now think about these planters walking around here shopping for an enslaved person like they buying a damn Ford Expedition, or a Ford Focus. That's the mentality. 'Hey, nigger, I need someone to iron my clothes.

You good at that?' Think about three hundred Donald Trumps walking around here shopping for niggers. 'Look at that one, didn't they shine him up nice? What if I buy that other one, will you make me a deal?'"

That was a difficult image to unthink, and I wondered if Jeremy made the same presentation to all the white tourists. I was his only customer on that bright spring morning. His phone rang, and he answered, "Hey, big dog, whassup? . . . Ah-ight. Cool. Lemme holla back. Peace."

Then he went into more detail about the haggling. The price went down if whipping scars were on a slave's back. This was taken as proof of a defiant, rebellious character, rather than cruelty on the part of previous owners, even though "clean backs" were rare. Males and females were separated into rows, then arranged according to height, with the smallest at one end of the row, and the tallest at the other. This meant that mothers were separated from their daughters and were more likely to be sold apart. Family separations were probably the most brutal, heartless aspect of American slavery, although many slaveholders claimed that blacks, being less than fully human, weren't particularly bothered by it. "Fifty percent of the slaves in the Natchez District were sold away from their wives or husbands or parents," said Jeremy. "Little kids, mamas wailing and crying, that's how cold they were."

Then it was 1863, the Union army had occupied Natchez, the slaves were running off the plantations, the slave traffickers had fled, and the US Colored Troops were now in charge of the Forks of the Road. Among them was the grandfather of Richard Wright, one of the all-time American literary greats. In *Black Boy*, Wright's shattering memoir about growing up under Jim Crow, he described how his grandfather ran away from his enslaver to join the Union army, for the express purpose of killing Southern whites, and managed to bag a few on his way to enlist.

"First they used the Forks for a barracks and slept in the slave pens," said Jeremy. "Then they got the order to tear it down and use the lumber to build a new barracks at Fort McPherson. Some of those guys had been here in chains, getting sold and whipped. Can you imagine how it felt to be a free man, wearing a United States army uniform, tearing this motherfucker down? They went at it all night long."

After the war came Reconstruction, those extraordinary thirteen years when emancipated slaves got the vote and elected black leaders to local, state, and national government; when black entrepreneurs started opening businesses, and black children started going to school. White Southerners have characterized Reconstruction as "the rape of the South" by invading carpetbaggers and corrupt, ignorant blacks, but among historians, only the neo-Confederates take that view. Eric Foner, the leading historian of Reconstruction, calls it "a stunning experiment—to fashion an interracial democracy from the ashes of slavery." Nowhere in the South was that experiment more successful than in Natchez.

We climbed into Jeremy's van and rode slowly down the old St. Catherine Street, which he described as the "black Wall Street of Mississippi, back in the day." He stopped outside the Zion Chapel AME Church and told me about its minister Hiram Revels, who was the first African American to serve in the US Congress, in 1870. He talked about John R. Lynch, born a slave on Tacony Plantation with an Irish overseer father and an enslaved mother. At the age of twenty-six, he too was elected to the US Congress and went on to have a distinguished career as a lawyer, writer, and military officer.

Many black leaders in Reconstruction Natchez came out of the free black population and were well educated, well-intentioned, and highly competent. "Louis Winston had a white father and an enslaved mother," said Jeremy. "He was phenomenal, but white folks don't talk about him. He was a police, a tax collector, a longtime clerk of court, an attorney, and a planter."

Robert Wood also lived on St. Catherine Street. "He was the first black mayor, and he had a white father too," said Jeremy. Hearing that sentence, my sense of logic once again rebelled against the deeply held American belief about race, that "one eighth of a specified kind of blood shall outweigh seven eighths of another kind," as William Faulkner put it. A nineteenth-century Yankee traveler saw a woman with pale skin and blond hair working alongside the other slaves in the cotton fields of a Natchez planter. He asked the planter what could prevent her from living as a white person in the North. The planter said it was a question of manners and accent. Whatever race might be, it is certainly not logical or scientific. In Haiti, it was explained to me that "one drop" of European blood defined you as white.

After Reconstruction came the backlash of Jim Crow, when white supremacy violently reasserted itself, aided by its white-robed enforcers in the Ku Klux Klan. African Americans lost the vote and all political power. They were subjected to a fanatical system of segregation and terrifying acts of violence—beatings, rapes, castrations, shootings, whippings—and public lynchings at which refreshments and postcards were sometimes sold, and human body parts severed for souvenirs. Mississippi had 656 reported lynchings between 1877 and 1950, more than any other state. "When I talk about this stuff to Europeans and other foreigners, it trips them out," said Jeremy. "They don't understand why white folks hated us that bad. They want me to explain it, and I don't even know. That's just the way it was, until we organized and fought back."

Jeremy was at his most animated when the time line of his tour reached the civil rights era in Natchez. He stood on a street corner, talking fast, gesticulating, pointing over there, pointing over here. "The Klan firebombed Mayor Nosser's house right over there because he wasn't racist enough. They blew up Wharlest Jackson, and there was pieces of his body all over my neighborhood, man! They shot and killed a black man named Ben Chester White who hadn't even did nothing! Only reason they killed him was to scandalize Martin Luther King. They wanted to lure him to Natchez so they could kill him. It was serious, man. We had a boycott of all the white stores downtown, and we had the Deacons for Defense. Those guys are my heroes, man. They didn't play."

I had never heard of the Deacons for Defense, and Jeremy was glad to tell me about them. They were local working-class black men who rejected the principle of nonviolence preached by Martin Luther King and the NAACP. They believed in armed self-defense and patrolled the black neighborhoods with pistols and rifles. Many of them had fought in World War II. They protected activists and civil rights workers from the Klan and the police, and they stopped and intimidated suspicious white motorists. They also beat up "Uncle Toms" who breached the boycott of the white stores downtown.

"Are any of the Deacons for Defense still around?" I asked, hoping to interview surviving members.

"I saw one at McDonald's this morning and gave him maximum respect. Natchez had one of the most successful civil rights campaigns in the whole South. The boycott hurt the white merchants real bad, and the Deacons backed down the Klan. The city agreed to all our demands, and that was the end of legal segregation."

The biggest racial problem now, he said, was economic segregation. "White folks got the money and the nice houses. All the development is happening downtown. Ain't no developing up in my neighborhood."

The tour ended at the African American history museum, housed in a fine old building on Main Street that used to be the post office. Like most of the African American tourism experiences available in Natchez, the museum was heartfelt, well-intentioned, short on funds, and amateurish. Darrell White, the director, didn't like to work weekends, so the museum was closed when most visitors were in town. The windows were dirty, and paint was peeling off the ceiling. The collection was jumbled and ramshackle, with a heavy reliance on blurred photocopies, curling photographs, piles of books and magazines, and newspaper stories glued to pieces of warped cardboard.

Ser Boxley had made a series of informative panels about the transatlantic slave trade, and a small display about the US Colored Troops. The collection included African masks and flags, and a replica of a typical African American house from 1930, with an old bed and an ironing board, and a mannequin in a long skirt. In the slavery section, another mannequin was leaning over a wooden cotton gin, and tucked away in a corner behind that display was a small exhibit about Prince Ibrahima—a blurry copy of his only portrait, another of King Sori's tomb in Futa Jalon, a folded map of West Africa clipped to a piece of cardboard, and a small color photograph showing some of Ibrahima's living descendants.

6

Sarah Foster, when her foot is suddenly clasped to the throat of this ragged, starving, blazing-eyed African, is at first shocked and confused. Then the symbolism makes itself clear. Prince has prostrated himself before her in an attitude of complete supplication. She feels flattered and empowered. She will enjoy telling the story of this moment for many years to come.

When Thomas Foster arrives, his overwhelming emotion is relief. He no longer owes money on a slave who everyone assumed was dead. So powerful is his relief that he forgoes punishing Prince, despite the bad example that this sets to the other slaves. Ibrahima, seeing that renewed enslavement rather than torture or death will be the outcome, vows to accept his fate with as much grace as he can muster.

Laboring in the tobacco fields, on his knees much of the time, transplanting seedlings, hoeing, cutting, curing the wretched leaves, is the most demeaning and monotonous toil that Ibrahima can imagine. In Futa Jalon, the Jalunke only work for their masters until noon. Then they are free to worship and work for themselves, growing cotton, raising livestock, and they have plenty. Here the slaves work from sunup to dark and have nothing.

When spring arrives, Ibrahima is offended by the sacrilege of using a horse to plow a field. Allah intended the animal for nobler pursuits—riding, racing, nomadic herding, and war. But Ibrahima can't help being impressed by the efficiency of a horse-drawn plow, and other tools and technologies in this new world. The wheel, for example, is unknown in West Africa. The only farm tools in Futa Jalon are a small hoe and a sickle. Seeing a watch for the first time, Ibrahima is astounded that such a contraption can be made by men.

Thomas Foster works in the fields alongside Prince, Samba, and his original slave, Jesse, wishing he could afford to buy more hands, but pleased with these three, and Prince in particular. His behavior has been exemplary since his escape and dramatic return. He follows orders and works hard and efficiently. For months, he was completely silent, but now he has started talking to Samba in some guttural language. Most of the time his face is blank and expressionless, as if his mind is elsewhere, and he never smiles.

In 1791, the third year of Ibrahima's enslavement on Foster's farm, the price of tobacco falls, so Foster plants cotton instead. Ibrahima is familiar with the plant and is perhaps able to pass along some knowledge about its cultivation, but cotton emasculates him, crushes his pride, drags him down to a new level of humiliation and misery. In Futa Jalon, growing cotton, and working with cotton, is a job relegated to the Jalunke women, the lowest of the low in the caste hierarchy.

The following year, Foster sells 1,600 pounds of cotton and is able to buy a twenty-five-year-old man named Dublan. Three years later, he buys a twenty-five-year-old woman named Isabella, and three children under the age of ten that are presumably hers. Foster intends to get some more children out of her. It's an obvious way to increase his labor force, and his assets, without capital outlay. It's also well-known that a woman can pick as much cotton in a day as a man, and sometimes more. Moving down the rows, plucking the white bolls from their spiky casings, requires dexterous fingers and stamina, not muscle strength.

Isabella is American-born, perhaps from South Carolina, and is attractive, affectionate, easygoing, and quick-witted. She practices folk medicine and is a strong Christian, in the African-ized version of the faith developing among the slaves. Soon after her arrival, she marries Ibrahima in a formal ceremony presided over by Thomas Foster, and not the usual jump-over-the-broomstick event in the slave quarters. Masters do sometimes control the breeding of their slaves, as if breeding their best mares to their best stallions, but there is no hint of that here, and every indication that the couple are attracted to each other.

Isabella makes it easier for Ibrahima to endure his degrad-ing, exhausting, impoverished new life. Children arrive and the joys of parenthood are tempered because the children can be sold at any time and are doomed to a life of enslavement. Simon is first, a year after the wedding, then another son, who they name Prince, followed by three more sons and three daughters.

Having an American family strengthens Ibrahima's reluctant attachments to the land and accelerates the dying of his own culture within him. Afraid of losing his literacy, with no access to books, pens, or paper, he takes to drawing Arabic letters in the dirt during work breaks. Isabella improves his English, but it never becomes as fluent as the six other languages he used to speak. Perhaps he can't be bothered to put in the effort.

Meanwhile, the cotton gin has been invented, the price of cotton is rising, the textile mills in England are thirsting for it, the Natchez District is booming, and Thomas Foster is able to buy more land and more slaves. This enables him to grow more cotton, and to buy yet more slaves. He notices that Prince is the one they turn to when a problem arises, and Prince obviously thinks of himself as superior to the others. Even as he humbles himself in a cotton field, plowing, planting, chopping weeds and picking, he still retains an air of authority, and Foster sees a way to turn it to his advantage.

———

Apart from the slaves themselves, whose many forms of resistance include stealing, lying, breaking equipment, working slowly, running away, burning barns, and sabotaging crops, nothing gives Southern planters more trouble than overseers. One of the Natchez millionaires, Haller Nutt, who builds the great octagonal mansion known as Longwood, is driven to distraction by his overseers. They keep killing valuable slaves out of pure cruelty and ruining morale with rape. Nutt is compelled to write a book of rules for his overseers, and the most important one is this: "Above all things avoid all intercourse with negro women. It breeds more trouble, more neglect, more idleness, more rascality, more stealing and more lieing [sic] up in the quarters and more everything that is wrong on a plantation than all else put together."*

Many planters decide that overseers aren't worth it; almost two-thirds of the slaves in the South work without one. They are supervised instead by enslaved black men known as drivers,

---

* According to an interview with an ex-slave named Isaac Throgmorton, Haller Nutt fell prey to the temptation himself on his Winter Quarters plantation.
· When the woman's husband objected, Nutt had him tied up by the thumbs and "whipped awful, the next morning he was dead."

who take their orders directly from the planters and have the power to whip and punish. Even when a plantation has a white overseer, it usually has a black driver as well, working as second-in-command.

Drivers are the foremen of the labor gangs, and the authority figures in the slave quarters, responsible for solving disputes and keeping discipline. The bad ones are worse than overseers for cruelty, overwork, and rape. The good drivers are compassionate leaders and capable of running a plantation by themselves, except for the sale of the crop and other financial arrangements. Solomon Northup, a free black man kidnapped in Washington DC and enslaved on a Louisiana cotton plantation, is made a driver and given a whip. Like many drivers before him, he learns the fine art of delivering a fake whipping. The end of the whip cracks just short of the skin, and the slave completes the illusion by howling in pain, and complaining to the master about the severity of his punishment, and the horrible cruelty of the driver.

Thomas Foster decides that Prince will make an ideal driver. He never drinks alcohol, gambles, lies, shirks, or steals. The other slaves respect him. He understands how the plantation works. He appears happily married, although that is hard to determine. Despite his loving, affectionate, quick-witted wife Isabella, despite the playful antics of his children, despite his participation in the annual Christmas dances and feasts—the highlight of the year for slaves across the South—Prince is still known as a man who never smiles.

7

On the opening night of Tableaux, Regina Charboneau ordered a cocktail at King's Tavern to fortify herself for what lay ahead. She hoped that the production had now found the right balance of tradition, entertainment, historical accuracy, and racial inclusivity. But the rehearsals had been ragged, there were rumors of sabotage, and she had to be prepared for the possibility of a horrible, cringing catastrophe, for which she would be held largely responsible.

We were joined at King's Tavern by Layne Taylor, the director of the Natchez Little Theater, a slim gay man with horn-rimmed glasses and blond hair. Something about the shape of his mouth reminded me of the actor John Malkovich. "It's opening night, honey," he said to Regina. "Whatever can go wrong, will go wrong. That's just an ironclad law."

Regina summarized the new show for him: "We're grounding everything in real history this year. We're quoting from letters and diaries, and other original source material. We're acknowledging the importance of slavery, but we're trying to present it in a way that doesn't leave people covered in shame or anger. I love Greg Iles, he's a dear friend, but those clanking slave chains, people getting ripped away from their families on the auction block, it was just too much."

"We're not denying or excusing anything," said Doug, "but we also want people to buy tickets and enjoy the show."

Layne Taylor, in his theatrically expressive Southern drawl, told a story about bringing a group of friends from New York City to the old, unreconstructed Tableaux. They were bewildered by the maypole dancing, and the crowns and scepters, and genuinely alarmed when young men began charging around the auditorium with Confederate flags, aggressively whooping and howling.

"My friends asked me what they were doing," said Layne. "I told them they were looking for Negroes. They want to string them up, but don't worry. The Negroes are smart and don't come here. So they're looking for Yankees and Jews instead. They freaked out completely. They were all Yankees and Jews."

Layne grew up on a plantation in the Mississippi Delta and went to a liberal arts college in Jackson in the 1970s. I asked him if it was difficult growing up gay in Mississippi at that time. "I never had a problem being me," he said. "Mississippi was wonderful in the 1970s. We were expanding our minds with drugs and listening to great music. There was so much freedom because most people had no idea what we were up to."

After college he moved to New York City and enjoyed success as a waifish, innocent-looking underwear model, working for Calvin Klein and Ralph Lauren. He went to some of Andy Warhol's parties and was "glad to get out of there without catching some horrible disease." He took a lot of drugs and hung out at the legendary nightclubs Max's Kansas City and Studio 54, where he switched from downers to uppers and embraced the disco revolution.

Then he burned out on New York, came back to Mississippi, and chose Natchez. Why? "Obviously it's beautiful here, and the old homes are fabulous. I get to work in theater, and it's a very easy, accepting place to be gay, although the scene has been ruined by all the married Baptists who come out of the closet when they're drunk and behave like beasts. The worst thing about Natchez is the lethargy. This whole town needs amphetamines. My friends are nearly all straight married women because they're the ones who have the energy."

Regina ordered a second cocktail and told Layne about some of the difficulties with the Tableaux. A hardening faction of Chesney's garden club resented her inclusion of black history, and some were now describing the paid black performers as "mercenaries," or so the rumor mill said. Meanwhile the unpaid amateurs kept spacing out and missing their cues, which was excusable in the small children, but not in the young adults, no matter how much they were drinking backstage. The computerized audiovisual system—the backbone of the whole production—was either glitchy as hell or being incompetently operated by someone they couldn't fire because he had a powerful patron in the other garden club. Layne sympathized. He said, "Honey, I would have cut so many throats by now that we'd all be in prison."

We finished our drinks and walked the few blocks to the city auditorium. Regina, as president of the Pilgrimage Garden Club, was staging a radical breach of protocol by not wearing a hoopskirt to opening night. They were just so heavy and cumbersome, "like trying to balance a dinette set on your hips," as one woman described it. Regina was wearing a long black brocaded dress, which her enemies would see as a typical piece of arrogance, and an insult to a hallowed Natchez tradition.

She led us through the front doors of the auditorium into the President's Box, which was a partitioned row of folding chairs in front of the bleachers. Similar seating arrangements on the other side of the room championed themselves as the King's Box, Queen's Box, and Pages' Box. A harried-looking Chesney Doyle came over to welcome us. Regina asked her how things were going. Chesney sighed, rolled her eyes, said nothing, and rushed back into the fray.

We were fifteen minutes early, so I took a quick walk behind the scenes. There were long echoing corridors and many rooms with doors that kept opening and closing. It was a parade of glimpses: ladies pouring vodka into red plastic cups, young men throwing back shots and climbing into costumes and uniforms, a group of African Americans keeping to themselves and talking in low voices, an elderly woman fastening her granddaughter into a hoopskirt dress that the woman had probably worn herself as a little girl. It occurred to me that the cotton-slavery-mansion boom in antebellum Natchez lasted no more than sixty years. And these theatrical celebrations of that era had now been going on for eighty-five years.

Stagehands marched through the corridors. Little boys milled around in velvet suits, like a herd of Little Lord Fauntleroys. The back entrance to the building opened, and in came two men with a pack of hunting dogs, including a gigantic basset hound. Walking back to the President's Box, scanning the audience, I saw a lot of empty seats, very few tourists, and not a single African American. I had assumed that the family members of the black performers would be here, at least, but apparently they had chosen to stay away with the rest of the black community. This was a disappointment for Regina and Chesney, and the other white liberals, but not a surprise.

The mistrust and resentment of whites ran so deep and was so well-founded, especially for the generation that had fought through the civil rights era. Despite the recent changes, Tableaux was still an enduring symbol of white privilege and Confederate-worshipping racism in the black community. Staying apart was also just a habit that people of both races had inherited, and most preferred it that way. It was easier and more comfortable to stick with your own.

The auditorium darkened, then the lights came up slowly. A spotlight illuminated a young black man, who began singing "Ol' Man River" in a rich, resonant baritone. The impressive vocal performance set off an argument in my head. He was portraying a stevedore on a steamboat, resigning himself to a life of servile toil—"Body all achin' / And wracked with pain / Tote that barge! / Lift that bale!"—in a song taken from a mildly antiracist 1920s musical.

Paul Robeson had managed to infuse "Ol' Man River" with black pride and protest credentials in his famous rendition, but the song had also been attacked for promoting a demeaning, humiliating stereotype and nostalgia for the Old South. I was disappointed by my own reaction to the song. Here was a talented young man singing his heart out, and all I could do was judge, criticize, nitpick, and argue with myself, rather than listen with open ears.

Now well-dressed African American couples were promenading around the stage. The women were holding parasols. It was Natchez in the 1930s. Regina whispered that whites and other ethnicities were supposed to be in the scene as well; there must have been a mix-up backstage. A male voice-over started narrating the history of Natchez through the PA system, as images and quotations followed each other on big screens mounted around the auditorium. I wrote down a quote from Greg Iles: "Natchez is unlike any place in America, existing almost outside time."

Traditionally, when representing the Native American history of Natchez, the garden club ladies have shellacked a white boy in reddish-brown paint and sent him onstage with Davy Crockett pants, a feathered headdress, and a peace pipe. Chesney Doyle had attired two white teenage boys in faux-buckskin costumes and dispensed with the paint and feathers.

One boy portrayed a famous chief called the Great Sun. He moved his arms from east to west, setting the rising sun (a blood-orange spotlight) on its course. Then his brother, the Tattooed Serpent, handed him a document—a treaty with the French. In voice-over, a historian explained that foreigners had invaded their lands, and the Tattooed Serpent was trying to make peace. The destruction of the Natchez people and the theft of their land was dealt with succinctly: "The foreigners would prevail."

Now came the colonial era. Teenage boys marched around in French military uniforms, then British uniforms. Boys in Spanish military uniforms were ready to march when the audiovisual system froze up and all the screens went blank. The teenage soldiers stood there, uncertain what to do. The entire production ground to a standstill. "Rats," said Regina, showing impressive restraint with her choice of expletive. "The files are too big, they're overloading the computer. This is exactly what we've been saying to Floyd."

Floyd was the man operating the system, and he was a nervous wreck from all the last-minute changes that came raining down on him. What happened next was bizarre. After a painfully long wait, the blank screens came back to life, and they all displayed the same unsettling image. It was a jumble of white plastic heads with rectangular green eyes, and laughing mouths with teeth and pink tongues. Between the heads, cartoonish feet stuck out. They looked like goblin robots, or plastic doll babies with teeth, and they stayed there for many long minutes. Everyone sat stunned for a few moments, then began talking all at once. Was it malware? Was it a screen saver on Floyd's computer? If so, why he would choose such a creepy one?[*]

Finally, the system rebooted, the show resumed, but Ibrahima's scene had been skipped over, leaving Jeremy Houston high and dry backstage, and so had other African American scenes. Instead, we went straight into the traditional Tableaux dances. White children skipped around a maypole. Young men in antebellum costumes pretended to go hunting with real live dogs, including the giant basset hound I had seen earlier. Regina assured me that all the young huntsmen had observed tradition by drinking heavily before their performance. "They've been drunk for eighty-five years," she said.

Now came the portrayal of slavery. In voice-over, it was described as a trade in "humans." The forced migration to Natchez was a "thousand-mile river of people in chains." Right as Ser Boxley began talking about the Forks of the Road, the glitch struck again, another group of black performers was left waiting in the wings, and then everything fell apart. I got up and walked around. I found poor Chesney Doyle standing in the foyer, peering through a small window at the wreckage of her production. "I can't bear to go in there," she said. "How's Regina holding up?"

---

[*] I later found out it was a Windows 7 desktop background.

I went back to the President's Box and found Regina more suspicious than upset. "Our key black actors, and our key black scenes, got cut," she said. "That won't sit well in the black community, at all, and Floyd's such a Baptist that it wouldn't surprise me if he did it deliberately. The other club never wanted those scenes in the first place."

The production limped and stuttered on, plagued by technical difficulties, missed cues, and confusion, but you could sense Chesney's earnestness, thoroughness, and professionalism bleeding through the mess. The script was meticulously researched and scrupulously accurate. The writing was sharp and stylish. She had interviewed experts for the various voiceovers. I felt nothing but sympathy for her. She had worked so hard without pay, under such fraught circumstances.

Somehow the audiovisual system started working again, and the latter stages of the production went off better. Natchez-born Varina Howell was married in a wedding scene to Jefferson Davis, the future president of the Confederacy. The approach of the Civil War was heralded by a young Confederate soldier racing around the auditorium. He was making the traditional bloodcurdling rebel yells, but instead of the Confederate battle flag, he was holding the Bonnie Blue flag of secession. This flag was also a symbol of white supremacy, and Confederate determination to keep blacks enslaved, but it had the advantage of being obscure. Unlike the Stars and Bars, it had never been waved at a Klan rally or flown from the back of a pickup truck.

On-screen we were informed that Natchez had voted heavily against secession, 1,072 to 233, but once hostilities broke out, many Natchezians did support the war with money and sons. Moving swiftly through surrender, occupation by the Union troops, and slaves running away to join the army, we arrived at

Ser Boxley's favorite moment in Natchez history. A regiment of the US Colored Troops, the Forty-Fifth Black and Blue, were ordered to take down the slave pens at the Forks of the Road.

Uniformed black actors dismantled a wooden pen onstage, and in voice-over we heard a letter written by an eyewitness, a soldier from Wisconsin: "This order was received just at evening and was hailed with the wildest enthusiasm by these men who had been chained, gagged, and whipped, and suffered tortures unimaginable within these same walls, and through that long night they worked with a terrible earnestness. . . ." Then a live black choir from nearby Alcorn State University sang, "Joshua fit the battle of Jericho / And the walls came tumbling down."

Chesney had added a new section to the Tableaux titled "Reconstruction to Ragtime." This enabled her to celebrate John R. Lynch, Hiram Revels, and other black leaders during Reconstruction, plus Bud Scott, the Dixieland jazz musician, and Richard Wright, the author. Jim Crow was briefly mentioned, then it was time to present the Pilgrimage Garden Club's King, Queen, Pages, Maids, and Generals.

The lights went dark. A spotlight fell on an African American drummer. Then the house lights came up and the curtains opened to reveal the quintessential Natchez spectacle: Confederate uniforms and shimmering gowns, small boys with sabers, a young King who had clearly been drinking, the Queen with her glittering tiara and scepter, smiling bravely through her stage fright as she walked out with a fifteen-foot-long train behind her ivory gown, and somewhere in the audience a mother's heart threatened to burst open with pride and joy.

Afterwards came the postmortem at King's Tavern. Regina ordered a glass of red wine. "Opening night is always tough, and it'll get better," she said. "We had major technical difficulties. What bothers me is how many of our African American actors got cut out. Ibrahima, the Forks of the Road, the slave song. And the whites didn't show up in the opening scene. Am I crazy? Or is something going on here? Were we sabotaged?"

Jeremy Houston, when I reached him on the phone, sounded gloomy and faraway. People had told him not to get mixed up with the Tableaux. He had countered that it was a chance to promote black history, and now, on opening night, they had sliced most of the black history out of the show. He found it impossible to believe that it was accidental. "A black man praying to Mecca in the Natchez Tableaux was just too much for some of those white people," he concluded. He said he was going to quit the production, and he did for a while. Then he came back and delivered a few performances as Ibrahima.

Greg Iles had also been convinced that his Tableaux was sabotaged because controversial scenes kept going wrong, but ultimately he decided it was just incompetence, and he made the same case to Regina in a long, late-night phone call. Before the next performance, a new computer was purchased, loaded with the audiovisual files, and presented to Floyd. After that, the technical glitches disappeared, and the show began to run more smoothly, although ticket sales remained disappointing, and the auditorium was never more than half-full.

Chesney portrayed slavery using three elements: a brief voice-over from Ser Boxley about the Forks of the Road and the healing power of absorbing painful history; a line of black performers portraying slaves, being led across the stage by a white slave trader; and a live African American choir singing "Deep

River." I thought it was a decent attempt to do the impossible—there is no good way to portray slavery in an entertainment with crowns, gowns, and maypoles—but some white people were outraged that slavery was mentioned at all.

In one of the downtown antique shops, I got an earful of venom from an older couple. "I am so sick of hearing about slavery," the man vituperated with quivering jowls. "It's supposed to be about pretty dresses, gorgeous stage sets, dance numbers like a Hollywood musical. They've turned into a politically correct history lecture and blah-blah-blah, now we're all supposed to feel bad about slavery. How is that entertaining? Why would anyone buy a ticket for that?"

His wife was equally enraged. Referring to black people and slavery, she snapped, "They started it. Now they want to blame us for it. It's ridiculous."

He said, "And what's the point of having blacks in the show if they're not going to sing Negro spirituals? Everyone loves a Negro spiritual. They need to take it back to exactly how it was. Oh, it was gorgeous. The costumes! The dances! People would come by the thousands. They've destroyed it with their political correctness. And they wonder why people aren't showing up. It makes me sick."

There were errors of fact here, as well as overt racism. Ticket sales had been declining long before Greg Iles made the first "politically correct" changes. This was because fewer and fewer tourists were coming to Natchez as the *Gone with the Wind* generation aged out, and because the Tableaux had declined from its glory days and had the production values of a seventh-grade play. Yet socially and culturally, it was still a powerful force in Natchez, capable of roiling the town into conflict, and shaping children's minds. They absorbed the glamour and romance of the past, and performing in the city auditorium every spring gave them confidence in public situations. Tableaux marked them indelibly as Natchezians—people who thought it was normal to dress up as plantation belles and Confederate generals and be hailed as royalty.

———————

The morning after opening night, Regina threw together an outdoor brunch for the Royal Court and its parents. Heavily syncopated New Orleans brass band music was playing through big Bose speakers in the back garden at Twin Oaks, as forty-odd white people tucked into biscuits, corn-bread muffins, pimiento cheese, fresh fruit, and grits with bacon, cheese, and onions. A poker-faced African American bartender mixed the Bloody Marys and mimosas, which were in high demand.

One of the biggest challenges for the King and Queen of Pilgrimage was the number of boozy brunches, cocktail parties, and late-night balls that they were required to attend—for a month straight—while also trying to attend college, maintain grades, and not get arrested for drunk driving. These realities were explained to me by Regina's son Jean-Luc, whose portrait in a Confederate uniform had startled me on my visit to Twin Oaks. Luc, as he was known, now worked in the rum distillery with his father and dressed like a hipster distiller with a vest, flat cap, and long, full beard.

When Luc was King, Doug and Regina had hired a chauffeur to ferry him between his social-drinking duties in Natchez and his classes at college in New Orleans. "I spent a lot of time passed out in the back of that car," he remembered. The parents of another Pilgrimage King had hired a small plane and a pilot to fly their son back and forth from Natchez to the University of Mississippi in Oxford. "You can't explain it to the professors," said Luc. "They just don't get it, how important this is, how much it means to the moms and the garden clubs, the excessive drinking, the constant parties, none of it."

This year's King was Charles "Chase" Brakenridge, a business major at Louisiana State University. I already knew from the big spread in the *Natchez Democrat* that his uniform was a replica of the one worn by Confederate brigadier general John Hunt Morgan, manufactured by a historical reenactors' clothing company in Corinth, Mississippi. His sword had a rebel flag on the blade, and the insignia of the Confederate States of America. "I've been doing this all my life," he said. "I was so freaking excited when I found out I was going to be King. It's such an honor, and I basically get to party for a whole month."

Chase was standing next to his mother, Georgeanne Brakenridge, the power behind the throne. "This path started before he was born," she said. "It started with me. I used to receive at Longwood and Stanton Hall. I was chairman of Flower Show for eight years. I was Big Maypole chairman for three years. I do Antiques Forum. The garden club has made me all my friends. My daughter, Lansing, lives and breathes this."

Lansing, a junior at Louisiana State University, concurred enthusiastically with this assessment. She had dramatic red hair and was wearing an orange dress and a pair of radically underslung wedge high heels. "I was the bride in the Jefferson Davis wedding," she said. "I danced Polka last night, and I was in the Court. This is my social life. I love all the brunches and cocktail parties. I just love it so much."

Her brother, the King, said, "I stay intoxicated a lot. You have to. I was in Little Maypole, Big Maypole, Soirée, Lead in Soirée, Ring Bearer, and in the Court last year." Now that I knew her children's credentials, Miss Georgeanne explained how she had got them these roles, or "spots," in the production: "You work for points. We have cards, and we write down everything we do as volunteers, and the Pageant Committee tallies them up. That's how children get spots. But to be chosen as Page or King, that's an honor from the board."

"The board, not the committee?" I was scribbling hard in my notebook and struggling to keep up.

"Yes." *Yay-uhss*. Speaking slowly and clearly, as if to a half-wit, she said, "The board of the garden club."

I asked if they thought there was anything racist about the Confederate uniforms and rebel flags. Miss Georgeanne gave me an icy glare. Chase said, "All that stuff is just tradition. It's what the King is supposed to wear."

Regina's younger son Martin, a left-wing progressive living in Brooklyn and working for Google, had gone through dark nights of torment over the Tableaux uniforms and sent me an essay about his conflicted feelings. Soon after marching in a Black Lives Matter rally in New York, he got on a plane, went back to Natchez, swallowed his disgust, and put on a Confederate general's uniform in the Tableaux. He considered sewing a swastika on the back of it. He experienced doubt, depression, and self-hatred during the rehearsals. Martin describes slavery as "an atrocity" that makes him feel "physically ill," and he lives painfully with the fact that some of his ancestors owned slaves and fought for the Confederacy.

But he's also an eighth-generation Natchezian who began performing in the Tableaux when he was seven years old. When he was asked to join the King's Court, it seemed churlish and socially difficult to refuse, so he put himself through it. It was the first year of the Greg Iles Tableaux, which helped. Talking to the African American performers, he understood that it was much tougher for them to portray slaves than for him to portray a Confederate general. "I realized I needed to separate myself from the symbol, and step into a role," Martin wrote. "That is not to say it was comfortable."

I showed this interesting, thoughtful, well-written essay to various editors in New York and San Francisco. None wanted to publish it. They couldn't get past the Confederate uniforms or understand why anyone would care so deeply about such a hokey old tradition. It was a postcard from a world that was completely foreign to them. In the Natchez garden clubs, mothers and grandmothers were still passing down the tiaras they had worn as Queen as treasured family heirlooms. Anything to do with Tableaux was front-page news in the *Natchez Democrat*, rehashed in the coffee shop, and swirled together with gossip and rumor. But even in the neighboring towns, no one gave a damn. It was just some weird old thing in weird old Natchez.

| 8 |

The summer of 1807. Ibrahima has been enslaved for nineteen years, and despite the strength of his character, and his religious faith, it has exacted a heavy toll. The once-proud Fulani prince no longer takes any interest in his appearance. He neglects his hair and often looks weathered and dirty. Even fleeting moments of joy seem unavailable to him, such is the burden of his enslavement, and smiling remains an impossibility. His behavior remains obedient, however, and the cotton plantation runs smoothly and efficiently under his foremanship, piling up wealth for Thomas Foster and his thirteen children.

Foster now allows Ibrahima to grow vegetables in a small garden by his cabin and sell them at the market in the nearby town of Washington. He also gathers and sells Spanish moss, which is used in the area as a cool summer mattress. Ibrahima spends most of the gains from this small enterprise on better-quality clothes for his wife and nine children than the rough-spun garments that Foster provides.

Going to the market in Washington also allows him to meet other Africans and occasionally pick up news of his homeland. This is where he learned that his father had died, soon after

Ibrahima's own defeat and capture by the Hebohs. King Sori was succeeded by Ibrahima's brother Saadhu, who reigned well until he was knifed to death by the leader of a rival faction. Many of Saadhu's supporters and family members were also killed. Had Ibrahima remained in Timbo, chances were good that he would have been killed too, not that living as Foster's slave was a better option.

One morning, Ibrahima makes the hour-long walk to market with a basket of sweet potatoes balanced on his head and Samba walking alongside him. A middle-aged white man riding past on a horse looks strangely familiar. "Go see that man," Ibrahima tells Samba. "If he has but one eye, I have seen him before."

Samba goes up for a better look and confirms that the man is one-eyed. Ibrahima rushes up to his horse and says, "Master, you want to buy some sweet potatoes?"

The rider studies him with his good eye. He asks Ibrahima if he was raised in this country.

"No, I came from Africa."

"You came from Timbo?"

"Yes, sir."

"Is your name Abd al-Rahman?"

"Yes, that is my name."

"Do you know me?"

"I know you very well. You be Dr. Cox."

The Irishman jumps down off his horse, grabs Ibrahima in a bear hug, and whirls him around. Both men are giddy with shock and joy, and Ibrahima's face, for the first time since his capture, breaks open into a big smile. The two men go to Dr. Cox's lodgings. Ibrahima tells him about the Hebohs, the ambush, the Mandinka slavers, the Middle Passage, the grimness of his enslavement on Foster's plantation. Now it's Dr. Cox's turn. He gave up the sea after his second shipwreck, went back to Ireland, married a fifteen-year-old, emigrated to America, and lived in North Carolina for seventeen years, where he raised five children and financially ruined himself through land speculation. He is here in Washington, the capital of the Mississippi Territory, because his friend Robert Williams has just been appointed governor.

A message is sent, and Governor Williams comes over to meet Ibrahima. Dr. Cox says, "I have been to this boy's father's house, and they treated me as kindly as my own parents." The Irishman has been in the American South long enough to know that you never use the word *man* to describe an adult Negro male, even if he's an African prince and the former commander in chief of an army.

The following morning, Dr. Cox rides out to see Thomas Foster. He tells the planter about his adventures in Futa Jalon, the extraordinary kindness and hospitality of King Sori, the friendship he formed with Ibrahima, and now the whole insane, marvelous coincidence of meeting him again halfway around the world twenty-six years later. Dr. Cox intends to purchase Ibrahima's freedom and enable his return to Futa Jalon. What would be a suitable price?

Cox keeps making more and more generous offers. Foster keeps shaking his head. When Cox reaches $1,000, which he probably doesn't have and is double the going rate, Foster says that he's not selling Prince at any price. Why? Foster says that Prince will be more comfortable here on the plantation with his family than anywhere else, that freedom would not improve his happiness, and that it's foolish to talk about returning slaves to Africa.

Foster does not find it particularly interesting or significant that Prince really is a prince. It's far more important that he is an exemplary slave and a first-class driver. He sets a fine example to the other hands and commands their respect and obedience, which translates directly into high yields from the cotton fields, weather permitting, and the maximum number of dollars in Foster's bank account.

Ibrahima's downfall, as he and Dr. Cox now realize, is that he has made himself invaluable. If his character had been weaker and less shaped by the mosque, madrassa, palace, and military, if he had succumbed to the usual temptations of drunkenness, deception, shirking, insolence, breaking tools, or taking what was owed him in chickens because his life had been stolen, Thomas Foster would have almost certainly sold him after a brief negotiation.

In the span of twenty-four hours, Ibrahima has experienced his first moment of unbridled joy since the ambush, closely followed by bitter disappointment and a brutal reminder that his life is owned by another man. He withdraws again into steadfast fatalism, concentrating on his work and family, his position of dominance in the slave quarters, his small plot of vegetables. But things are different now. He has a friend among the white people, and he is famous. Everyone in the area, black and white, hears Dr. Cox's story and accepts his confirmation that Prince comes from African royalty in the kingdom of Futa Jalon.

Cox stays in Washington and buys a house and eighteen acres. He establishes himself as a highly respected physician and continues his friendship with Ibrahima. The two men see each other often, with Cox providing companionship and small favors, such as a pen and paper, which enables Ibrahima to revive his literacy. He makes Ibrahima feel less isolated, forgotten, and severed from his past. For the rest of his life—he dies of an unknown sickness in 1816, nine years after his arrival in Natchez—Dr. Cox continues to offer Thomas Foster large sums of money for Ibrahima's freedom, but they are always stubbornly refused.

Now that Ibrahima's royal blood is an accepted fact in Adams County, the possibility arises that other white people might help him obtain his freedom, or send word to Futa Jalon, or publicize his story. A sympathetic newspaper editor has taken an interest, but Ibrahima chooses the path of passive endurance and stoic fatalism. He makes no effort to change his circumstances until he's forced into an emotional crisis involving his daughter Susy and one of Thomas Foster's deranged sons.

9

On the first day of Spring Pilgrimage, Regina Charboneau sat me down in her kitchen with a plate of biscuits. I was now a semipermanent resident in the upstairs rooms of her house, and she enjoyed telling people that she kept an Englishman in the attic. To understand the phenomenon of Pilgrimage, she said, I needed to understand its origins.

"So it was 1931, in the Great Depression," she began. "Times were really hard in Natchez. The soil was exhausted, the boll weevil had ruined the cotton, and the railroads were taking over from the river, which had always been the lifeblood of the town. The old families were barely hanging on in their antebellum homes. Some of the ladies were selling eggs and vegetables to make ends meet. But they still had their maids, who were probably working for almost nothing, and they had kept up their gardens."

She was interrupted by the piano-trill ringtone of her phone. Someone was freaking out about criticism of the Tableaux on Facebook. Regina listened for a minute or two. Then she said, "Do they want us to have small black children eating watermelon on the side of the stage again? What is *wrong* with people?"

She told the woman not to worry, it would all work out, and

they would speak soon. She set down her phone. "Okay, where was I? Oh, yes, so there was a convention of Mississippi garden clubs in Natchez that year. It was scheduled for mid-March, when the azaleas are in bloom, but there was a late frost and it killed all the flowers. So now what are they going to do with these hundreds of people coming to Natchez? Katherine Miller, the president of the garden club, decided to tour them through some of the antebellum homes instead. I think the club had already been discussing it as a way to generate some income."

Ping. Ping. Ping-ping. Texts were coming in, but Regina ignored them. "So the ladies rushed around with their maids, moving furniture to cover holes in the floor, and rehanging paintings to hide stains on the wallpaper, and that sort of thing. A lot of the homes were in serious disrepair because people couldn't afford to maintain them. One reason why they still had all the original antebellum furniture, and silver, and china, and drapes, and all the rest of it, was because they couldn't afford to buy any new stuff. So the visitors arrive, and the ladies show them around their homes and talk about their family histories and point out things that might be of interest, and to everyone's surprise, the visitors absolutely love it. They rave about it."

The next year, Katherine Miller, a demanding, dramatic, brilliant, exasperating, motor-mouthed matriarch who was impossible to ignore, sent out invitations all over the country for a "pilgrimage of houses" in Natchez, and she persuaded the owners of twenty-six antebellum homes to "receive guests" for an admission fee. To enhance the theme of Old South nostalgia, the ladies dressed up in hoopskirts, and maids were outfitted like mammies. Black men, some of them wearing liveried uniforms retrieved from attics, were required to bow to the visitors as they entered the homes, like antebellum butlers, and small black children were hired for a few coins to fan the tourists and polish the mud off their shoes as they left the grounds.

Despite widespread skepticism among the local business-men, it was an overwhelming success. Visitors from thirty-seven states found their way down the long, slow country roads to Natchez, Mississippi, and they spent $50,000 that the town badly needed. A new industry was born. The redoubtable ladies of the garden club had saved the town.

"They were extremely savvy when it came to marketing," said Regina. "They traveled all over the country talking up Pilgrimage. There was a promotional film, and a national advertising campaign. They got a ton of media coverage. They got perfumes and china patterns and wallpaper designs named after Natchez. Eleanor Roosevelt came to Pilgrimage, and Douglas MacArthur. After *Gone with the Wind* came out in 1939, it got even bigger. In the 1940s and 1950s, we were getting tens of thousands of visitors. Now we're down on those numbers by about seventy percent. Other Southern towns with antebellum homes copied our idea. Times have changed. But Pilgrimage hasn't, and that's something I'm working on."

I asked Regina what she was going to do at Twin Oaks, which was coming "on tour" in a few days.

"A friend of mine is wearing a nun's habit to play Cornelia Connolly, who lived in this house before she went off to a convent. I'll serve cocktails and do a quick cooking class on how to make biscuits. I think what people really want nowadays is to eat, drink, and socialize in these old homes, and hospitality is what we're really good at. I may not even wear a hoopskirt. Oh, God, even saying that, I can hear Katherine Miller climbing out of her grave to come and shoot me."

Pilgrimage had gone through some changes over the decades.

African Americans had quit portraying servile mammies, butlers, and pickaninnies. The drinking while receiving was greatly reduced, although some of the ladies and docents still enjoyed a covert cocktail known as a Mr. Clean. "It looks like a glass of ice water, but it's straight vodka with lemon juice," said Regina. "Very refreshing, apparently."

There was also less embellishing and inventing than there used to be, partly because visitors were now in the dreary habit of checking things on their phones. Layne Taylor had told us a story about the actor Kevin Kline coming to Natchez for the fiftieth anniversary of *Gone with the Wind*. Layne took him to Monteigne, a stunning Italianate mansion on twenty-three acres. The owner, Mary Louise Shields, a steel magnolia who lived to be 109, showed Kevin Kline a quilt and said, "Now this belonged to Scarlett O'Hara."

Layne is no stickler for factual accuracy, but this was too much for him. He said, "Honey, she's a fictional character."

Miss Mary Louise said, "We do believe that to be true."

Layne lost his temper. "She's from a fucking movie!"

She said, "Honey, if you're not enjoying the tour, why don't you step off the back porch?"

My first experience of Pilgrimage took place at Linden, which has been occupied by the Conner-Feltus family since 1849. This longevity of ownership is unusual. Most of the antebellum tour homes have changed hands several times since the Civil War, and an increasing number are now owned by out-of-towners keeping the local tradition alive. Linden is just a short drive from downtown, but its grounds are so serene that it felt like a trip out into the country. At the end of a gravel driveway, an old black man took my ticket, showed me where to park, and rumbled a welcome from somewhere deep in his rib cage.

The house has a long colonnaded front gallery, partially shaded by big trees with hanging beards of Spanish moss. A matching gallery is on the second story, with four columns rising up to support the portico. It struck me as a classic example of the grace and beauty achieved by antebellum architects and enabled by chattel slavery—a subject that was not mentioned at any point during the tour.

At the front doorway, I was received with tremendous good cheer by Mrs. Jeanette Feltus, who was known as Miss Jeanette at Linden and didn't mind telling me and everyone else that she was eighty-four. She was wearing a green hoopskirt with a white blouse, and a long silk scarf with the two ends hanging down like a bishop's stole. The twelve other visitors were all white and nearly all Southern women eligible for Social Security. One of them, a small, determined-looking woman from New Orleans, wore a purple T-shirt that announced in bold capitals WORLD'S HOTTEST GRANDMA.

Miss Jeanette gave us a brief history of the house and directed our attention to the decorative work around the front door, which has a fanlight window and its own set of four columns. "The doorway of Linden was copied for Tara, the fictional home in *Gone with the Wind*. The fanlight is Federal, as you can see." She was referring to the Federal style of architecture, which was popular all over the country from 1790 to 1830.

Then we trooped inside, where three elderly hoopskirted women were receiving in three different rooms, all decorated exclusively with antebellum furnishings. "I'm Sybil," said one of the ladies with a sweet, gracious smile. "I'm a Natchez antique too." Could there be a deeper South? I wondered, taking in the hospitality and eccentricity, the sweetness and conviviality, the glorification of the antebellum past with the uncomfortable detail of slavery neatly snipped out and put away in a box.

Sybil directed our attention to a courting couch with a convex mirror that allowed the chaperone to "check on things," without interfering too closely, and an antique clear-glass fly-catcher that drowned the flies in water. "Some preferred a darker glass so you wouldn't have to watch the demise of the fly," she said, then pointed to a receptacle of some kind. "Southern ladies would never show their ankles, but they would chew tobacco. That's a lady's spittoon." Southern ladies, I thought to myself, had devised so many strategies to obscure the glaring fact that their men were screwing the slave women.

In the next room, we were greeted by a woman with an auburn bouffant. She was wearing a white hoopskirt with a salmon-pink blouse and a white shawl. In the slightly blurred photograph that I took of her, she looks like an antebellum ghost who has just floated down the staircase. She spoke with a deep, rich, raspy voice. She swiveled back and forth with her arms akimbo, gesturing to various paintings, items of furniture, and other artifacts—a Percy Faith album called *Gone with the Wind* with a photograph of Linden on the cover, a card table "attributed to" the famous furniture maker Samuel McIntire.

"We play bridge in this room, but do you think Miss Jeanette lets us play on this table?" She searched our eyes for an answer, then delivered the punch line: "No, she drags out the Walmart table." I wondered how long she had been telling this joke, and how many times she would tell it this year during Spring and Fall Pilgrimages. Regina said that some of the ladies had been using the same lines for fifty years and might have inherited them from their mothers.

We moved on through the immaculate museum of Miss Jeanette's bedroom, where a young blond woman told us all about the four-poster bed with its embroidered curtains. In the next bedroom, an earnest, lisping gay man in a bright blue sports coat described the architecture and the bed. By far the most exciting attraction for our group was a life-size cardboard cutout of Clark Gable as Rhett Butler.

"Ain't he fine?" one of them said. Another batted her eyes at him and said, "Ooh, let me kiss those sweet lips." A third said, "Oh, Rhett!"—drawing out the name in her breathiest bedroom voice. The World's Hottest Grandma gave him a big kiss on his cardboard lips, provoking shrieks of laughter, and requests to do it again so the others could record it on their phones.

Miss Jeanette poked her head through a door. "Would y'all like some coffee? I don't have any liquor out yet. Oh, the first day of Pilgrimage is always bedlam." A tour bus had just arrived, and it was full of women who urgently needed a bathroom. "Honey, cross your legs, we'll get you in as soon as we can," Miss Jeanette called out to one of them. Then she dispatched a black maid to clean the upstairs bathrooms and told her to hurry.

When the tour was over, I talked for a few minutes with Miss Jeanette on the front gallery. She had been receiving at Linden for sixty years, having married into the family, and she had read as much as she could about antiques and architecture to make sure she had her facts straight. "Was the doorway really copied for Tara?" I asked.

"Look it up and see for yourself. The resemblance is unmistakable."

Gesturing to the outbuildings, I asked if slaves had lived there.

"Why, yes, we had servants of course." She put on a half

smile that was like armored steel. "You couldn't possibly run a big house like this without servants."

———————

Regina described Linden as the classic old-school Pilgrimage tour, and she suggested that I drive out to Elgin, the home of Ruth Ellen Calhoun, to see a slightly different approach. "You hear a lot of nonsense about Southern ladies around here, but Ruth Ellen is the real thing," Regina said. "When I was growing up, I wanted to be Ruth Ellen so badly."

Elgin is seven miles south of Natchez, and to get there, I drove down Highway 61 to Mammy's Cupboard, the most startling work of local architecture. It's a twenty-eight-foot-high statue of a black woman dressed like Aunt Jemima, smiling and holding a serving tray. She has horseshoes for earrings, and a door opens through the front of her skirt into a restaurant. Built in 1940, the establishment has come in for some criticism over the years, as you might expect. Many local African Americans find it extremely offensive, although others are regular customers, putting aside the fraught racial symbolism because the homemade pies are so good.

The owners of Mammy's Cupboard responded to the criticism by the curious stratagem of repainting Mammy's face. They lightened her skin tone a few shades to a yellowish color. I struggled with the logic. Why would a lighter-skinned mammy with a door through her skirt be construed as less controversial? If anything, didn't lighter skin amplify the symbolism of slaveholder rape? I bought a postcard there, featuring the dark-skinned original mammy, and drove back across the highway towards Elgin.

A long, winding road led to a gravel driveway and two elderly black men sitting on folding chairs and showing visitors where to park. Half a dozen cars were there, and a tour bus was leaving. It was a warm, drowsy afternoon full of birdsong. The house was obscured behind trees, and as I walked up the driveway, it slowly and gradually came into view. Someone in the 1840s had quipped that Elgin looked like the "amen at the end of a long prayer."

The two-story plantation house had clean simple lines, and matching galleries above and below. Standing by the front door with a group of visitors was a tall woman in her eighties wearing a green satin dress with a hoopskirt. A sense of grace, elegance, intelligence, warmth, and decency radiated calmly from her person. When I told Ruth Ellen that I was a friend of Regina's, she exclaimed, "Oh, Regina is wonderful, the best president we've ever had. I love all the changes she's making. We simply can't go on pretending that slavery never happened, or that it wasn't awful."

Ruth Ellen talked openly about slaves in her tour, although she didn't dwell on it. Her main focus was the diary of Elgin's original owner, Dr. Jenkins, who came to Mississippi from Pennsylvania in 1835, married into a cotton-slave fortune, and established himself as a planter, doctor, and nationally renowned horticulturalist. Using his diary entries, Ruth Ellen took us through the history of the house until 1855, when Dr. Jenkins, his wife, and a large number of their slaves died in a yellow fever epidemic. The dreaded disease used to ravage Natchez regularly.

Ruth Ellen carried on into the Civil War, when three federal soldiers stole all the house's silver and were court-martialed for it. Then she skipped forward to 2012, when an African American woman named Janice Skipper, a lawyer from Washington, DC, showed up at Elgin one day and said, "My people were here." Ruth Ellen took Janice down to the old slave cemetery, where they found the grave of her great-grandmother. "She knelt down and rubbed the dirt," said Ruth Ellen. "It was a very emotional moment for her." *

"Did your ancestors enslave her ancestors?" I asked.

"No. My ancestors owned slaves, but I'm not a Jenkins descendant. My husband and I bought Elgin in 1975. He was a pediatrician."

The old house contained many old things, but it wasn't a rigorous antebellum time capsule like some. Ruth Ellen showed us some of the more interesting pieces, then she turned the tour over to Lizzie, her black maid, who stood waiting in one of the bedrooms in white pants and a white shirt. "I've been working for the Calhouns for fifty years," she said. She didn't look old enough for that to be true, as I pointed out. "I'm a health nut," she said. "I eat fish, vegetables, and fruit. That's it. And I exercise every day."

She went into her presentation about the furniture and the old photographs and the jib windows, which you could open and step through onto the gallery. She shared some observations on raising the Calhouns' children, and the importance of strictness. "I love those kids like my own, but love has an ugly side too. That's what I would tell them. 'If you break the rules, my ugly side will come out. Do you want that?'"

Lizzie managed the bed-and-breakfast in the old slave quarters behind the big house. An impressive building in its own right, it had two stories, thick columns, and an upstairs gallery. The richest planters would often house their "servants" in hand-

---

* Not all Natchez stories are fact-checkable, but Janice Skipper confirmed this one by telephone, adding that Ruth Ellen had given her a "warm, warm welcome," and that it had been a positive experience. "It made me joyful that my people have come so far."

some buildings, mainly as a way to advertise their wealth. Lizzie also managed three rental properties that Ruth Ellen owned downtown, and she was a confidante, a kind of family member, and an inseparable companion. The two women were completely dependent on each other, and inevitably they sometimes got on each other's nerves.

"After fifty years, you know when to shut up and know when to run," said Lizzie. "Sometimes I tell her, 'You want to fight, or you want me to do this work? I'm too old to do both.'"

Ruth Ellen laughed. "We are getting old, aren't we, Lizzie?"

"Mrs. Calhoun, do you remember when birds attacked the house that time? Wasn't that crazy?"

After fifty years of being woven so closely into each other's lives, Lizzie didn't feel comfortable calling her employer Ruth Ellen. She would always be Mrs. Calhoun.

Spring Pilgrimage was still the busiest, most lucrative time of year for the garden clubs, but the ladies yearned for the old glory days. Some could remember having hundreds of visitors packed into their homes and praying that the old floorboards wouldn't buckle and splinter under the weight. They had accepted a certain amount of pilfering as inevitable and minimized it by tying fishing line around the silverware, and other techniques still in use today.

"Oh, it was marvelous," said Miss Bettye Jenkins, in a resplendent yellow hoopskirt dress in the spectacular hallway of her home, Hawthorne. "It felt like the whole world was coming to Natchez." Now the ladies felt lucky to get eighty visitors in a day, and some were reporting a dismal twelve. One poor woman and her maid had spent weeks cleaning, polishing, rearranging furniture, hiring docents, preparing food and drinks, and then received only nine visitors on the first day.

Each home toured its visitors in a different way, reflecting the personality of its owner. At the Governor Holmes House, the emphasis was on costumed portrayals of historical characters. In the courtyard, I was pressured into dancing a jig with Layne Taylor as the gayest, flirtiest Andrew Jackson imaginable. Jackson moved to Natchez in 1789, traded in slaves and other commodities, and married the one true love of his life here.

At Elms Court, two elderly sisters took me deep into their family history. Twenty years ago, they never mentioned slavery in their tour. Now they addressed it openly, even though they found it difficult and agonized over one particularly cruel slave owner in their lineage. At Green Leaves, where enslaved Matilda with her high cheekbones and Mexican war stories ran away from George Koontz, and a sign now carries his runaway slave advertisement, I met some descendants of Mr. Koontz's. The family has been living in the house ever since and has accumulated a vast collection of memorabilia, including hundreds of antique dolls, a sword from the Battle of Waterloo with a Civil War bullet hole through its blade, and a moldering seventy-year-old wedding cake under a glass dome.

I had minimal interest in architecture, antiques, china, silverware, and other decorative arts of the antebellum South, which were a big part of Pilgrimage. What fascinated me were the costumed people who lived in these old museums, the stories they told, the things they omitted, the way they were so consumed by the past that the present seemed like an afterthought. Pilgrimage for me was peculiar, intriguing, often racially insensitive, largely in denial about slavery, although finally starting to grapple with it, much like the old town itself. Each home was a new voyeuristic adventure because you never knew what to expect.

Airlie, a genteel planter's cottage, was built on a farm outside Natchez in 1790. Now it was surrounded by a poor black neighborhood of old cars, loose dogs, peeling paint, men clustered on street corners, others sitting by themselves on front porches. They raised their hands in greeting as I drove past them and turned through the gates of Airlie. Once again, an elderly black man on a lawn chair showed me where to park. Walking back towards the house, I stopped to talk to him. His name was Charles and he had a quiet, thoughtful, still quality. He wore thick glasses, a camouflage hunting cap, and the tusk of a wild hog on a beaded necklace. I asked him if he'd killed the hog.

"No," he said. "I let other people kill the hogs. They eat every part of them, including the testicles. I don't eat the testicles. I don't want anybody eating on mine, so I won't eat on anybody's. I eat the hams, ribs, and shoulders. I enjoy them. Once you start eating testicles, it's like you've gone cannibalistic. I was reading about cannibals. They eat the heart and the eyeballs, so as to increase their prowess as a hunter, but I haven't seen where any of them eat testicles, so I don't know."

I said, "I had Rocky Mountain oysters once, which are fried cattle testicles. Something just feels wrong about chewing them up in your mouth."

"Mmmm-hmmm, that's right. Well, I'm pleased to meet you, and you can just go on up the house now." Then he sat back down in his lawn chair and picked up his ancient *National Geographic* magazine, as chickens walked about, and insects scratched their legs together in song, and the sun heated up the heavy humid air, and the sweat soaked through my shirt. I walked up to the house and reflected that it was only March.

Airlie, a long low cottage with many windows and doors for ventilation, was used as a hospital during the federal occupation of Natchez in the Civil War. Now it belonged to Katie Freiberger, a lawyer and PGC stalwart, who was standing on the front porch in a hoopskirt. "It's my family home," she said. "So you're going to see my big tacky TV and my kitchen sink."

In the front parlor, a young, hoopskirted woman, very pretty and badly hungover, as she later disclosed, was telling a group of tourists about some gold-colored antique chairs. They had belonged to the notorious Katherine Lintot Minor, also known as the Yellow Duchess. Originally from Pennsylvania, like so many of the slaveholding Natchez elite, she was a haughty commanding blonde who wanted everything in her world to match the color of her hair. She only wore yellow and gold, and that included the feathers in her hats and reputedly her undergarments.

She was married to Stephen Minor, the last governor of Natchez under Spanish rule, and they lived in gilded splendor at a vast mansion called Concord, where only the slave quarters still remain. The drawing room had yellow walls and yellow carpets, with gold mirrors and cornices, and gold sofas and chairs. She rode around Natchez in a golden carriage with a golden interior, drawn by four claybank horses, which were the nearest thing she could find to golden horses. As the young woman now explained, the Yellow Duchess also insisted that her house slaves and carriage drivers be yellowish-skinned mulattoes, so they matched the rest of the accoutrements.

When the tourists left, I introduced myself to the young woman and wrote down her name as Kerry Dix. She was forced to correct me: "No. *Dicks*, like the appendages." She was having a tough morning. "I woke up with a god-awful hangover, and I lost my pantalets." These are the ruffled leggings worn under a hoopskirt—essential garb when receiving because a lady never shows her ankles.

Kerry, who sometimes introduced herself as Rose, depending on her mood and the situation, was working part-time as a freelance archaeologist, a "shovel bum," and lately she had been digging in Italy and New Mexico. She was supposed to be digging in Tennessee right now, but the job had fallen through, so here she was back in Natchez again, going to cocktail parties and receiving in a hoopskirt, as if the town had refused to release her from its clutches. The homeowners paid her a small sum—it varied from house to house—but she wasn't doing it for the money.

She started receiving at the age of six. "I would stand by a ladies' fainting couch, and I had a music box with golden honey hives and tiny bees. They let me tell about the music box, and then I would pretend to swoon and faint on the couch. The tourists ate it up. Then I graduated to a pair of yellow slippers that belonged to the Yellow Duchess. I was in Tableaux, the Court. I've got my problems with it—this whole town is like a Southern *Twin Peaks*—but you get indoctrinated so young. I played hide-and-seek at Stanton Hall when I was a kid. I thought seventeen-foot ceilings were normal."

Her family's financial fortunes had dwindled away over the generations, but they had impeccably aristocratic Natchez blood, and that was enough to preserve their social status. Kerry was a direct descendant of David Hunt, who was known as King David because he owned twenty-five plantations and 1,700 slaves. She was also descended from the Surgets, another extremely prominent old family. "I must be related to fifty houses in Natchez," she said. "It's a miracle that I don't have webbed feet and eyeballs on the side of my head because all the old families are so inbred. It was quite deliberate. They married off their first cousins to each other, to keep the money and the homes in the family."

Given the depths of her Natchez roots, I found it odd that Kerry didn't have a Southern accent. Instead, she sounded vaguely like Katharine Hepburn and was sometimes mistaken for an Australian. "I promise you it's not deliberate," she said. "It's like I have a speech impediment. I can't even fake a decent Southern accent, even though I've been surrounded by them all my life."

"How does it feel to be descended from so many slave owners?" I asked.

"Hmm. I'm different from most people here, who are always trying to make excuses for it, or explain it away, or say it wasn't that bad. If I hear one more person say that the Irish had it hard, too! I assume my ancestors were either horrific bastards or somewhat horrific bastards, operating in an absolutely horrific system, and I avoid talking about slavery at cocktail parties because I want to be invited back."

When the tour ended, I stayed on for lunch at Katie Freiberger's invitation, and for the next hour I sat and listened as the women told Pilgrimage stories and gossiped about the dead, and the black maid prepared the food in the kitchen. Much was said about Katherine Miller, the founder of Pilgrimage and the great-aunt of Elodie Pritchartt, one of the lunch guests. Katherine's husband Balfour was a notorious womanizer, and Elodie told us about the time Katherine found him in flagrante with one of the maids. "Get that Negress out of my antique bed," she thundered, and that was classic Katherine, to reference the antiquity of the furniture at such a moment.

The women talked about hoopskirts, how uncomfortable they were, how dogs liked to get under there, and how a certain bold young woman had stashed a crouching boyfriend under her hoopskirt while receiving. When she started making "feminine noises," she told the tourists there was a ghost in the house, and apparently they fell for it. They talked about the word *receive*, and one woman mocked it unmercifully, going into exaggerated Southern-belle mode to satirize its pretentiousness and unwitting sexual connotation. It was easy enough for outsiders to make fun of Pilgrimage, but the real experts at it were the insiders.

The most outrageous tour home in Natchez was Choctaw Hall, a colossal downtown mansion recently purchased and extensively redecorated by a gay couple from Arkansas, David Garner and Lee Glover. David was the older one with the money. A tiny man with an immaculately trimmed white mustache, he had two wings of white hair that he swept up together and hair-sprayed into a kind of pompadour. He liked to pour bourbon on his ice cream and make colorful remarks in a slightly hurried, breathy drawl: "The South couldn't function without rouge," "I jumped on it like a chicken on a june bug." Referring to a diminutive ancestor, he said, "On a sultry Southern summer day, he could stand in the shade of great-grandmother's bosom."

Lee was tall, slim, and handsome, although he found himself wearing more makeup these days than he used to. He had dark hair and a bushy mustache, and when I arrived at Choctaw Hall, he was wearing a ruffled tuxedo shirt with a high collar and no tie, a gold bracelet on his wrist, and the gayest pair of black suede loafers I had ever seen. David liked to stir up trouble and be outrageous. Lee was the sweet, calm, rational one;

he worked in a nursing home and helped with the downstairs bed-and-breakfast business at Choctaw. Officially, he and David were "business associates."

David was an interior decorator and event planner who had restored and run the antebellum Marlsgate Plantation outside Little Rock. The same theme of lavish period-appropriate excess had been applied to the interiors at Choctaw Hall: crystal chandeliers, a piano made in London in 1830, candelabras, red velvet curtains from Paris, massive gilded mirrors, rococo porcelain figurines. The dining room table was permanently set with a stunning display of antique china, stemware, and silver.

David pointed to an oil portrait of his beloved grandmother. "She was the quintessential Southern grande dame, and ninety-three when that was painted. She told me, 'I'm going to give you Cornelius in my will.' Cornelius was her servant. I said, 'You can't do that. There was a war. Slavery is over.' She said, 'Nonsense, I'm giving you Cornelius.' Don't you love it?"

Before I could say, "Not really," he started denouncing the new Tableaux, "It was so gorgeous when I started coming here in the 1980s. They sang 'Dixie.' It was uplifting. Now they've taken out 'Dixie' and they're leaning towards this blackism. It's disgusting. History is history. I'm here to preserve it, not erase it."

A magnificent elliptical staircase led up through the four stories of the mansion, and we climbed it to the next floor. David talked about furniture that had belonged to Queen Wilhelmina of the Netherlands and showed me an ancient jeweled sword. "Many a slop jar has been sold for a soup tureen, but this is the real thing. It puts antique dealers in a quiver. They just lose all control. We have a few more little trinkets to show. The drapes are Scalamandré, by the way. The best."

A notable feature of David's interior decoration was the use of Venetian blackamoor sculptures, depicting African males in decorative servile poses, often with their torsos bared. One was holding up a table. "You couldn't buy a Negro after the War, but you could buy a miniature," David quipped. "We're not politically correct," he added redundantly.

Then he showed me a first-edition of Jefferson Davis's *Rise and Fall of the Confederate Government*, which was laid out next to an antique Bible in a kind of shrine. "You can tell we love the Confederacy. Our vice president of the Confederate States was Alexander Stephens. He was about my size, a miniature little guy." On the wall was a bust of Nathan Bedford Forrest, the former slave trader and Confederate general who became the first Grand Wizard of the Ku Klux Klan.

"What happens when you get black tourists through here?" I asked.

"We don't generally tell them who that is," said Lee.

"And of course they have no idea," added David.

I had met my first gay neo-Confederates, and they were not the only ones in Natchez.

10

Thomas Foster, greatly helped by Ibrahima's management, has ascended into a new income bracket. His plantation holdings, which he names Foster Fields, reach 1,785 acres, and he now owns more than a hundred slaves. He has built a fine two-story house and furnished it with imported mahogany and rosewood furniture.

He is considered prosperous, but well below the aristocratic "nabob" elite, whose members own multiple plantations and often banks and railroads too, whose butlers or "body servants" bring them mint juleps in silver cups before a leisurely breakfast on the gallery. Foster does not go on shopping trips to Paris or send his sons to Harvard or stock his library with thousands of volumes. Foster gets all the reading he wants from the Bible and agricultural journals, and his wife Sarah remains illiterate. Their thoughts are dominated by money, cotton, slaves, religion, and their thirteen children, who set out into adulthood with all the advantages of education, social status, and financial security that Thomas and Sarah lacked when they were young.

Their youngest daughter Caroline receives a full set of house slaves as a wedding gift from her doting parents. Another daughter gets two farms. Their son Levi moves to Louisiana, becomes a rich planter, and serves in the state legislature. James, "one of the finest-looking men in the country," according to an acquaintance, returns from visiting Levi in 1833 with a gorgeous fifteen-year-old Louisiana bride.

The following year, carrying his whip as planters do, James invites his wife to take a walk with him and suddenly starts whipping her about an alleged infidelity. He beats her and then stomps her to death. Ibrahima's family is instructed to dress the body and bury it in the Foster family graveyard. James is tried for murder in Natchez. Freed on a technicality, he is then seized by a lynch mob outside the courthouse. Stripped, whipped, tarred, feathered, partially scalped, and very nearly hung, he escapes with his life and is never heard from again.

The Fosters' daughter Cassandra marries a man who, in her words, "contracted those habits of excessive intemperance and debauchery" and spends days lying in bed with "lewd and dissolute" women. But none of their children put Thomas and Sarah Foster through more hell than Thomas Jr. By the age of twenty-five, he owns two plantations and is a notorious drunkard and gambler with a highly unstable temperament. All the racial and sexual tensions of Southern slave society seem to bubble up and corrode his youthful brain.

In 1820 he marries Susan Carson, the thirteen- or fourteen-year-old daughter of the Reverend James Carson, recently arrived with his family from New York. Three years later with two children born, Susan finds Thomas Jr. in bed with his slave Susy, who is almost certainly the daughter of Ibrahima and Isabella.

After an initial show of guilt and repentance, followed by a crazed episode in which he chases his wife out of the house with a sword and threatens to kill her, Thomas Jr. openly and brazenly conducts an affair with Susy, ignoring the admonitions of his parents, and the horrified disgust of his teenage wife. This is more than a young rake slaking his lust in the slave quarters. Thomas Jr. throws parties for Susy and showers her with gifts, including his wife Susan's clothes. In Susan's words, he treats the "base wretch" Susy "with all the kindness and generosity of a wife."

Thomas Jr. keeps promising to reform, but he cannot stay away from Susy. She becomes more important to him than his wife and children, his parents and siblings, and his good name in society. Thomas Jr. is unquestionably in love with Susy, but we have no way of knowing her feelings about him. Susan mentions her sneaking out of the slave quarters to meet Thomas Jr. one night, which suggests that she is willing, but certainly doesn't prove it, because she has no right of sexual refusal as his slave. It's possible that she is using her agency to stay out of the cotton fields, and it's not inconceivable that she is attracted to him or flattered by his obsession with her. Or she might be a helpless victim following orders.

The situation at Foster Fields becomes so fraught and over-heated that Thomas Senior sends Susan away to Natchez to stay with her father. When she returns to pack up some more clothes, Thomas Jr. stops her from taking a bonnet because he thinks Susy might like it. Then he shoves his wife out of the room and tells her that he wants nothing more to do with her. He just wants the children.

"What do you want with them?" she asks.

"To cut their throats," he replies.

The following day, feeling remorseful and unwell, Thomas Jr. changes his mind. He promises to sell Susy if Susan will come back to him. A bill of sale is drawn up at his bedside, passing Susy's ownership to Thomas Senior, who plans to sell her far away. Two days later, heartbroken over Susy, Thomas Jr. changes his mind again and tries to wrest the bill of sale from his father. Thomas Sr. refuses to let him have it and tells his wayward son that Susy will be placed in irons and removed from the county.

Thomas Jr. responds to this by going on a three-day drinking bender. Then he comes raging through the house with a knife, vowing to kill his family members if Susy is sold away. They manage to calm him down, and his father gives him an ultimatum: go home to your wife and children, or go off with your slave wench and say goodbye to your good name forever.

On Christmas Day of 1826, Thomas Foster Jr. reaches his decision. He goes off with Susy and the rest of his slaves to one of his plantations in Warren County. He never sees his white wife or children again. Nor do Ibrahima or Isabella ever see their daughter Susy again. The whole saga has been a horrible torment for them because of their complete powerlessness to affect the outcome. They watch their daughter Susy disappear into the distance as the owned property and sexual obsession of an unstable, alcoholic gambler. These wretched, shaming events in 1826 have a motivating effect on Ibrahima, and he decides to make one last desperate, long-shot attempt to gain his freedom and return to Africa.

He is sixty-four years old. On the plantation, he is no longer required to work as hard, and Foster has granted him more free time. One of his new, lighter responsibilities is to sell vegetables at the brick market house in Natchez, where he has become well acquainted with a local newspaper editor named Andrew Marschalk, a big, loud, talkative, energetic man with a swelling gut and voluminous chins. A few years before, Ibrahima went to Marschalk's office and saw Arabic script in a printer's grammar. Humbly requesting permission to copy it, he produced a perfect facsimile with pen and ink. Marschalk, who publishes strident defenses of slavery to keep his subscribers happy, but secretly detests it, became interested in Ibrahima's case.

The two men hatched a scheme for Ibrahima to write a letter in Arabic to his relatives in Africa. Marschalk knows the US consul in Morocco and suggested forwarding the letter from there. But Ibrahima never wrote the letter, maybe because he was ashamed of the decline of his Arabic, or maybe because he was resigned to his fate. Only now in 1826, after seeing what happened to Susy, does Ibrahima decide to put pen to paper.

Instead of a letter, which would challenge his rusty grammar, he inscribes the longest passage he can remember from the Koran. Marschalk puts it in an envelope and hands it personally to Thomas Reed, the US senator from Mississippi, with a cover letter attesting to the fine, dignified character of the "venerable old slave known as Prince." The letter also contains a major error, or misunderstanding: "He claims to belong to the royal family of Morocco, and the object of his letter, as he states it to me, is to make inquiry after his relations and with the hope of joining them."

Senator Reed himself carries the letter to the State Department in Washington, DC. Then it crosses the Atlantic and reaches the desk of the US consul, Thomas Mullowny, in Tangier, Morocco, who has little else to do and finds it intriguing. He secures a meeting with the emperor of Morocco, who listens carefully and reads the Arabic inscription. It is impossible to determine the nationality of the man who wrote it, but he is clearly a Muslim, and perhaps a Moroccan. The emperor makes his decision. The enslaved man must be freed, and he will pay whatever it takes.

Mullowny then writes a letter to Henry Clay, the secretary of state in Washington, DC, advising "most earnestly" that the slave known as Prince be sent to Tangier and "restored to his King and family." On July 10, 1827, the chief clerk of the State Department takes Mullowny's letter to the White House. President John Quincy Adams reads it and, mistakenly writing *Georgia* instead of *Mississippi*, instructs the State Department to write a letter to Andrew Marschalk, telling him to "ascertain the price for which he [Prince] could be purchased."

It's unclear if Ibrahima initiated, encouraged, or went along with Marschalk's belief that he is a Moroccan prince, but the misunderstanding works with almost miraculous power. The slave known as Prince, a part-time seller of corn and sweet potatoes at the Natchez market, now has Henry Clay and John Quincy Adams on his side, two of the most powerful men in the world.

11

On the evening of the Royal Ball of the Pilgrimage Garden Club, I put on a tuxedo and went with some of the ladies to see another performance of the Tableaux. The production was running more smoothly now, although the air-conditioning went out in the building, and a projector broke, and many of the performers made mistakes. Jeremy Houston's replacement as Ibrahima just stood there with his prayer rug, failing to kneel and bow towards Mecca. I wondered if he was frozen with stage fright, or if praying to Mecca offended his Christian beliefs.

I was surrounded in the audience by Pilgrimage Garden Club members, and I got out my notebook and started writing down what they were saying.

"She'll never make Court now her mama pitched such a fit."

"That sweet boy is gay as a maypole, bless his heart."

"Remember when they set a skunk loose during the Hunt Scene and the dogs went crazy?"

"Remember when they fed Ex-Lax to the dogs?"

"Not that those dogs need any help when it comes to pooping onstage."

"It's an important part of being Queen, being able to glide across that stage in your crown and gown, like there's roller skates under your hoopskirt, and avoid the dog poop at the same time."

"So they've done away with the amputees that Greg Iles put in. I think we all know the Civil War was bad."

"Is that the Bonnie Blue?"

"Yeah, every bit as Confederate as the rebel flag, but no one ever waved it at a Lynyrd Skynyrd concert."

"Aw, doesn't the Queen look so beautiful?"

"And look at the King, oh my Lord. Don't you love a drunk King?"

———————

After the performance, it was a short walk to Stanton Hall for the Royal Ball, an all-night party thrown for the King and Queen and paid for by their parents at an approximate cost of $25,000. Once again, the guests were all white, and the staff were all black, but this time I was expecting it. I would have been surprised to see a black guest or a white bartender. Once again, the grandes dames held court, and the younger women abased themselves in front of them, but now I knew many of these women as individuals.

Kerry Dicks was there, and our conversation found its way to her great-aunts in the 1930s. "You could make a very twisted sitcom about those women and their maids," she said. "Three of my great-aunts never married, and they all lived together at Airlie with their maids. You've seen how it is with Ruth Ellen and Lizzie, how they're basically devoted to each other. Well, this was the opposite end of the spectrum. My great-aunts and their maids hated each other's guts. They called each other 'darkies' and 'white old bitches' to their faces. My aunts later found voodoo dolls in the walls of the kitchen with hair tied around them."

Once again Regina was circulating through the crowd, following her antennae and instincts, picking up hints and information, dispensing reassurance and favors, gliding past some troublemakers and assuaging others, hardly bothering to talk to any men because they were irrelevant. The immense dining table in the immense dining room was heaped with Southern food in elegant tureens and serving dishes, and then demolished by hundreds of people in tuxedos and ball gowns. Alcohol flowed in prodigal quantities. People danced to an R&B band in a tent on the grounds, and a Southern breakfast was served after midnight. Chase Brakenridge, the King of the Pilgrimage Garden Club, was wobbling and wavering, stumbling and swaying, but still doggedly drinking and managing not to fall over.

Around one in the morning, Regina's son Luc called the only taxi driver in Natchez, a white man known as Pulley Bones. A group of us climbed into his taxi outside Stanton Hall. He drove us to the edge of the bluff, then made a steep descent on Silver Street to the Under-the-Hill Saloon, an old, battered, scarred establishment right on the edge of the Mississippi River. As we walked through the door, in our tuxedos and ball gowns, a group of musicians led by the tremendous Brint Anderson was playing a thick, swampy, gumbo-dripping version of Tony Joe White's "Polk Salad Annie."

Everyone else was dressed in casual clothes, or biker apparel. There was a short man in a cowboy hat who was rumored to have screwed a pony. No one batted an eye at our group, or fifteen more people who came into the saloon from the Royal Ball. I had read enough local history to know that we were participating in a venerable Natchez tradition. The sons of the antebellum aristocracy, dressed up in their tailored finery, would often round out the evening by "going down the line" to the rough saloons, brothels, and gambling dens in Natchez Under-the-Hill.

————————

Nineteenth-century travelers were almost invariably shocked by the squalid, depraved scenes they encountered in this part of Natchez, and the heaven-and-hell contrast to the life of colonnaded elegance up on the bluff. Captain J. E. Alexander published a typical description of Under-the-Hill in 1833:

> The lower town of Natchez has got a worse character than any place on the river; every house seemed to be a grog shop, and I saw ill-favored men and women looking from the windows. Here the most desperate characters congregate, particularly in the spring of the year, when the upcountry boatmen are returning home with their dollar bags from the New Orleans market. Dreadful riots occur—eyes are gouged out, noses and ears are bitten and torn off.

New Orleans boasted about the sinfulness of its waterfront, and Vicksburg claimed to be even more wicked. Memphis and St. Louis were no slouches either when it came to vice and violence. But for the boatmen, steamboat captains, professional gamblers, and travelers who decided these matters, Natchez Under-the-Hill reigned supreme for nearly fifty years as the bloodiest, wildest, most debauched place on the entire Mississippi River.

Picture hundreds of boats bobbing in the river next to a wide muddy shelf of ground covered with shacks on stilts, and buildings on blocks. Rough-looking boatmen yelled elaborate curses at each other as they tried to maneuver their crafts in and out of the landing. The flatboats were broad rafts with cabins on top, typically loaded with sacks of grain, barrels of whiskey, live pigs and turkeys, wagons, horses, sometimes shipments of manacled slaves. The keelboats were bigger and more elongated, with crews of twenty-five men or more, all thirsting for booze, women, and hell-raising action after long, isolated days on the river.

The culture among Mississippi River boatmen in those days was defiant, belligerent, individualistic, self-aggrandizing—an exaggeratedly masculine expression of the American frontier spirit. It is best recorded in the half-horse, half-alligator folk tales of Mike Fink, a legendary boatmen and brawler, and the descriptions penned by Mark Twain in *Life on the Mississippi*.

Rough-and-tumble fighting was the boatmen's recreation, a sport transplanted to the American frontier by the Scots-Irish. The object was to gouge out your opponent's eyeball with your thumb, tear off his ear with your teeth, rip off his genitals, strangle him to death—whatever it took to declare an unequivocal victory. Most opponents would quit after losing an eyeball, but some would just get mad and fight even harder.

Bragging was their art form, delivered at roaring volume, accentuated by swinging arms, a clacking together of bootheels, and claims to the body parts of various wild animals. "I am a Mississippi snapping turtle; have bear's claws, alligator teeth, and the devil's tail; can whip *any* man, by G---d," as one traveler recorded it. Contemporary observers were stunned by the virtuosic obscenities, but sadly, Victorian sensibilities prevented any of them from being accurately published. Mark Twain, who passed through Natchez many times as a cub steamboat captain and has a small guesthouse named after him on the riverfront today, left us a satirical account of verbal jousting between two boatmen:

Whoo-oop! I'm the old original iron-jawed, brass-mounted, copper-bellied corpsemaker from the wilds of Arkansaw— Look at me! I'm the man they call Sudden Death and General Desolation! Sired by a hurricane, dam'd by an earthquake, half-brother to the cholera, nearly related to the smallpox on my mother's side! . . . I take nineteen alligators and a bar'l of whiskey for breakfast when I'm in robust health, and a bushel of rattlesnakes and a dead body when I'm ailing! . . . Blood's my natural drink, and the wails of the dying is music to my ear! Cast your eye on me, gentlemen!—and lay low and hold your breath, for I'm bout to turn myself loose!

Then the Corpsemaker's opponent makes his declamation, cracking his heels together three times, and announcing himself as the "pet child of calamity":

Whoo-oop! Bow your neck and spread, for the kingdom of sorrow's a-coming! Hold me down to the earth, for I feel my powers a-working! . . . I'm the man with the petrified heart and biler-iron bowels! The massacre of isolated communities is the pastime of my idle moments, the destruction of nationalities the serious business of my life!

In addition to the flatboats and keelboats operated by these fierce characters, there were barges, skiffs, ships, and, from 1811, paddle-wheeled steamboats with filigreed balconies, chandeliers in the dining room, and champagne flowing at the bar, where sharp-dressed professional gamblers with diamond stickpins waited for their marks. George Devol, author of the shameless 1887 memoir *Forty Years a Gambler on the Mississippi*, was a card sharp, swindler, and three-card-monte man who went up and down the river fleecing cotton planters and other suckers. He rarely needed to draw his gun when they challenged him as a cheat because he delivered such a devastating headbutt.

Once disembarked from your boat at Under-the-Hill, you had to make your way through a filthy, reeking alley crowded with boatmen, cutthroats, dirty children, dogs and pigs. Then you emerged into the teeming chaos of revelry at the bottom of Silver Street. Drunks of all kinds staggered and strutted about— Choctaws, slaves with day passes, free blacks, fugitives from justice, slumming aristocrats with lace cuffs, white stockings, ruffled shirts, and enslaved valets or "body servants." Prostitutes of every skin tone were in the brothels, to suit every taste, with whispered claims of "special attributes" in the women imported from Paris and New Orleans.

Topless women leaned out of windows and beckoned. Musicians sawed on fiddles. There were peep shows, dance halls, gambling dens, a racetrack nearby. On one occasion, a naked sailor charged after a shrieking "mulatress" claiming he'd been robbed. The racket of tinny pianos, drunken laughter, shouting, yelling, and squawking parrots was constant, and the saloons were open twenty-four hours a day, seven days a week. The only thing cheaper than the body of a woman, they said, was the life of a man.

When the boatmen started fighting, it sometimes escalated into the "dreadful riots" described above by Captain Alexander. Broken jaws, gouged eyes, and knife fights were everyday occurrences. Several buildings were torn down during one free-for-all. Murders were commonplace, with the bodies shoved into the river, and no one had ever seen a thing when the lone constable, or after 1838 the Natchez police, came down the hill to investigate.

The toughest, meanest, baddest son of a bitch in Natchez

Under-the-Hill was a bearded, bullying riverman named Big Jim Girty, also known as No-Ribs. So many men had tried to stab him to death without succeeding that people thought he had an unnatural rib cage. They described a solid body-casing made out of bone as thick a man's skull, or thicker, with no gaps where a knife blade might penetrate. Big Jim's woman, Marie Dufour, was a strawberry blonde who ran a brothel and could reputedly open a beer bottle with her teeth and shoot off a man's nose from a hundred feet. She and Jim loved each other hard, "if only for their unchallenged strength and their cold scorn for the universe," according to Harnett Kane in his 1957 book, *Natchez on the Mississippi*.

One night a group of gamblers decided to test the prevailing wisdom about Big Jim's rib cage. They rushed him in the bar at Marie Dufour's place and stabbed him before he could reach for his knife or gun. This time he went down bleeding and gasping like a normal man. Marie shot down two of the assailants and stood over her lover with a smoking pistol. When she saw that he was going to die, she reloaded and shot herself through the head.

Another big character who frequented Under-the-Hill was John Russell, a fiery-tempered steamboat captain. He loathed the professional gamblers who kept fleecing his passengers. On one occasion, heading upriver from Baton Rouge, he stopped at Natchez with a delegation of preachers on board. A young minister, carrying all the delegation's money, succumbed to temptation and went into a gambling joint near the river's edge. The professional gamblers stripped him of every last dollar.

Captain Russell marched into the joint and demanded the money back. The gamblers laughed. He threatened to use his steamboat to pull the whole building into the river. They laughed again. The captain set his black crewmen to work, attaching ropes around the blocks at the base of the building. "All right, let her go!" he roared. The big wheels started churning, and the steamboat slowly pulled away. When the building started to crack and tear, the gamblers ran out cursing, and the young minister got his money back. Greg Iles put the story in his Tableaux, although in his version the whole building gets pulled into the river.

The upper-town folk would stage periodic clean-outs of Under-the-Hill, usually in response to some particularly bloody or shameless incident. Coming down Silver Street in a heavily armed mob, they would lynch people, burn shacks, run men into the river, or tie them up and set them adrift in canoes. But what really cleaned up Under-the-Hill was the passing of the frontier, and the changing course of the river. As it flowed past Natchez, the Mississippi began to scour away more and more of the muddy flats until great slabs of land calved away into the river. Silver Street is still there today, with a few restaurants and shops, and the one remaining saloon where the cutthroats and prostitutes used to drink, but now these buildings are at the river's edge.

One legacy of the old days is that bars in Natchez have no legal closing time. If the staff and customers are willing, the bars can stay open twenty-four hours a day, seven days a week. This would be unthinkable elsewhere in Mississippi, where religious fundamentalism is powerful, dry counties and blue laws are commonplace, and the sale and distribution of alcohol is controlled by a grasping, punitive state agency. Natchez is nicknamed the Little Easy because it has more in common with

New Orleans, the Big Easy, than the rest of Mississippi. After Hurricane Katrina, there was a migration of gay men from New Orleans to Natchez because you could buy a fabulous old house for not much money, and because Natchez has always been gay-friendly.

Perhaps the best example of the town's laissez-faire spirit is the long career of Nellie Jackson, an African American woman who ran a brothel in the middle of Natchez for sixty years, until 1990, without any attempt to disguise or conceal it. The local bars used to sell T-shirts proclaiming I GOT IT AT NELLIE'S, and FOLLOW ME TO NELLIE'S with a set of footprints.

At the annual Natchez literary-cinema celebration, I went to see the first screening of a documentary entitled *Mississippi Madam: The Life of Nellie Jackson*. At least 2,000 people were in the convention center, with dozens standing in the aisles, and dozens more crammed against the back wall. From the size of the crowd, the affectionate reminiscing about Miss Nellie before the film, and the opening few minutes, it became obvious that Natchez had not only tolerated this madam, but venerated her as a local treasure.

Former mayors, sheriffs, police chiefs, and priests talked on camera with obvious affection about a woman who ran an illegal and supposedly immoral business right under their noses for sixty years. Tony Byrne, who was mayor of Natchez from 1968 to 1988, said, "I just let her rock along. Then we became friends, basically."

David Armstrong, who succeeded Tony Byrne as mayor, heard a knock at his door one day in mid-December, soon after he had taken office. His administrative assistant came in and said, "Nellie Jackson's here." He was stunned, but asked her to come into his office. Miss Nellie was in a wheelchair, being pushed by two of her "girls," as they were always known. She had a white poodle in one hand, and a fifth of Jack Daniel's in the other.

She said, "I'm here to present you with your Christmas fifth of Jack Daniel's whiskey to not close Nellie's down."

Armstrong had never heard of this long-standing tradition at the mayor's office, but it didn't even occur to him to object. "Miss Nellie, I can assure you, as long as I'm mayor, you will not be closed down."

The chief of police also got a bottle of whiskey or brandy at Christmas, and she baked a cake every year for the sheriff's office.

No doubt these gestures helped, as did her financial generosity with the Catholic church and a local home for abused children. But her main protection, according to the film, was that so many rich, powerful married men frequented her establishment, and she was rumored to have all their names in a black book. So potent was the rumor that it didn't even matter if the black book existed or not.

She was born into dire rural poverty in the now-defunct community of Possum Corner, Mississippi, in 1902. Her first marriage was probably strategic. It enabled her to move to the bright lights of Natchez in 1930, but soon led to divorce and an income quandary. Rather than supporting herself as a housekeeper, laundress, or nanny, which were the main forms of employment available to black women at the time, she went down to the small red-light district that still remained Under-the-Hill. After a few years—maybe prostituting herself, maybe running a brothel, and possibly bootlegging too—she was able to come up the hill and purchase an ordinary-looking family house at 416 North Rankin Street, two blocks away from where Regina

Charboneau and her eight siblings grew up in a churchgoing Catholic family.

The house had red-and-white-striped awnings and a twin-gabled roof. Customers would come in through the back door into the kitchen, then into the dining room, which had a jukebox and a dining table, and "girls" parading through at regular intervals. "Ooh man, some of the finest womens you ever met," said Alonzo Green, a neighbor who ran errands for Miss Nellie and appears in the documentary. Another neighbor said, "She had the best, no rinky-dinky little old women."

Miss Nellie believed in variety for her customers, and her stable included white women, black women in a full range of skin tones, Vietnamese, Japanese, and the occasional German. But all the customers were white, and this was crucial to her survival. Even a rumor of a black man with a white woman would have got her closed down immediately, and almost certainly burned out by the Klan.

Most of the girls traveled a nationwide circuit of brothels that encompassed Las Vegas, San Francisco, Houston, Detroit, and New York. They would spend three weeks or a month at one place, then move on. There were also "weekenders": married women from the local area who turned tricks at Nellie's on weekends, or when their husbands were out of town. Nellie's accountant, who filed her taxes every year, described her business as a boardinghouse for young women, and Nellie would say that what the girls did in their rooms was their business.

But in reality it was also her business. She took half their earnings and charged them $10 a day to stay in the house, and $1 more for towels. With the considerable profits that she made, Nellie supported one husband, then another, and took herself on regular shopping sprees in New Orleans. She liked to dress well and had a mink coat with her name embroidered inside. She drove a succession of white Cadillacs with a succession of white poodles on her lap, and she always carried a loaded pistol.

Very few people—especially on the white side of town—knew that she was heavily involved in the civil rights movement in Natchez. Not only did she bail protesters out of jail and get activists released by calling her friends in the police department. At tremendous personal risk, she also became an informant for the FBI on the activities of the local Ku Klux Klan.

The Klan was loudly and violently against the sin of prostitution and would burn crosses right outside Nellie's house. But Klansmen were also some of her most ardent and regular customers, and they invariably wanted her black girls. When I met Tony Byrne, the former mayor, he told me that all the Klansmen he had known in his life were sexually fixated on black women. It was an integral part of their racism and hearkened back to the sexual privileges of white supremacy during slavery.

After sex, feeling contented, confident, and incautious, some of the Klansmen would indulge in pillow talk with Nellie's girls and spill secrets about Klan activities. These activities, in the mid-1960s, included burning, bombing, raping, kidnapping, murder, and mutilation. When their Klan customers left the building, the girls would then tell Mama Nellie, as they called her, what they had heard. At three or four in the morning, every night at the height of the civil rights struggle, two FBI agents would sneak in through Nellie's back door. She would meet them in her lavishly decorated bedroom, give them beers, and relay everything she had heard from her girls that evening. Had the Klan ever found out she was informing, they would have burned down her house and probably killed her, too.

Growing up two blocks away, Regina Charboneau was always impressed by Nellie Jackson, and the girls sunning themselves out front, and never thought of the business as scandalous or even unusual. "She would come riding past in a long white Cadillac with a mink coat and a poodle on her lap, and I just thought, 'Wow, there she goes.' And Nellie's was the best place to go at Halloween. Everyone else would give you candy. Nellie would give you a roll of quarters."

"Your parents let you go trick-or-treating at a whorehouse?" I said.

"Yes. They were fine with it. But on Sunday mornings, we would have to walk around three sides of the block so we didn't pass Nellie's on the way to church."

When Regina was older, she and Nellie became friends. "She came out to see me in San Francisco when the World Series was played there. She was so proud of me, as a girl from the neighborhood, and what I had accomplished with my restaurant. And she loved baseball. The walls of her house were lined with pennants from all the World Series she had gone to."

Ron Miller, the now-retired director of the Historic Natchez Foundation, a charming man with gentle manners, remembers going to her house one night with a group of visiting dignitaries from Washington, DC. It was after midnight and drink had been taken, as the Irish say. The visitors just wanted to see the legendary establishment, without engaging its services. So Ron drove them over there and knocked on the back door. It was opened by a beautiful young black woman. Ron said, "We just thought we'd come in and maybe have a beer or something."

"Listen," she said. "We don't sell beer. We sell pussy. Now when you want some of that, you come on back."

On a hot July night in 1990, Nellie Jackson turned away twenty-year-old Eric Breazeale because he was drunk. Being drunk was against her rules. Furious with injured pride, he walked two blocks to the nearest gas station and purchased an ice chest. He took the ice chest out to the gas pumps and filled it up with gasoline. Then he walked it back up to Nellie's, with the gasoline sloshing around and spilling over the sides onto his clothes.

When he reached the door, he knocked. Miss Nellie opened it holding a pistol. He threw the gasoline on her, lit his cigarette lighter, and they both went up in flames. Breazeale ran across the street, looking like a ball of fire, as the brothel glowed orange in the night. A woman rushed over to help him as he rolled around on the ground. He told her, "Ma'am don't come down here. I used to be a nice-looking guy but I messed myself up now."

When the firefighters arrived, young women in lingerie were running around in the street, saying, "Miss Nellie's still inside!" A firefighter named Karen Moseley found her at the foot of her bed, with her hair and clothes burned away and her skin shiny and unreal looking. Moseley bent down and heard Miss Nellie still breathing. Both Eric Breazeale and Nellie Jackson died of their burn wounds. She was eighty-seven.

The house on North Rankin Street still stands, derelict and overgrown with vines, and there is talk of putting up a plaque to commemorate this historic Natchez landmark. "She was a very savvy businesswoman, to operate for that long as a black woman in an illegal business, especially during Jim Crow," said

Ron Miller of the Historic Natchez Foundation, over a glass of whiskey at his house. "She was also a kind, gracious lady, and a pillar of the community. She was much beloved here, although not without her detractors. As far as I know, that was the last establishment of its kind in Natchez. The long tradition of vice here is over."

12

August 1827. When Andrew Marschalk receives the letter from the US State Department, he immediately rides out to Thomas Foster's place. On the specific instructions of President John Quincy Adams, Marschalk asks Foster at what price Prince can be purchased, for his repatriation to Africa. The old planter refuses to sell, but he makes a proposal.

Some years ago, says Foster, he told Prince that he was free to return to his native land if someone was willing to take him there and pay for all the expenses. Since the US government is now offering to do this, he will give Prince his liberty, without taking any payment, if Henry Clay and President Adams agree to one vital condition. Prince will only obtain his liberty when he reaches Africa. He will not be free in any part of the United States, and if the attempt to repatriate him should fail, he must be returned as a slave to Foster Fields.

On this latter point, Foster says that Prince will be better looked after here than anywhere else in the nation—because of his own benevolence and feelings of gratitude towards his old driver, and because Prince's wife, children, and grandchildren will be here enslaved for the rest of their days. If Prince is allowed to enjoy freedom on American soil, Foster says, it might have an improper influence on his family members, and a troublemaking effect on other slaves.

Marschalk rides away and writes a letter to Henry Clay describing Foster's proposal. Ibrahima, now sixty-five, is exhibiting more energy than anyone has seen in him for many years. The man who hardly ever smiles is now "beaming with joy" at the prospect of finally returning home, according to one acquaintance.

Long, slow, frustrating months pass with no reply from Henry Clay. A disabled attorney named Cyrus Griffin, a newcomer to Natchez from the North, befriends Ibrahima and initiates a series of long conversational interviews about his life. Griffin, who takes extensive notes, realizes early on that Ibrahima is not a Moroccan prince, as President Adams and Henry Clay have been led to believe. He thinks this is a major problem that needs to be corrected, but Marschalk, its instigator, advises staying quiet since the wheels of power are turning. In his follow-up letter to Henry Clay, Marschalk makes no mention of Morocco and refers instead to Prince's "native land."

In December 1827, after four months with no reply from Henry Clay, Griffin writes to the American Colonization Society, an organization that repatriates freed slaves to the new colony of Liberia in West Africa, only three hundred miles from Futa Jalon. He suggests that Ibrahima, or Abduhl Rahhahman, as he calls him, would be a perfect candidate. Two months later, a letter finally arrives from Henry Clay, stating that he and President Adams have agreed to Thomas Foster's terms, and to please send Prince to Washington, DC.

Thomas Foster and Ibrahima ride into Natchez together for the last time, remembering the day they rode in the opposite direction forty years ago, when they were both in the prime of youth, and one had just become the enslaver of the other. What an immensely profitable investment Prince has been. Under his management, the plantation has run so smoothly with such excellent yields. Only one slave ran away, and he soon returned.

Now Thomas Foster signs a deed placing Prince in the custody of Andrew Marschalk, for the "sole and only purpose of his being transported to his native country by the government of the United States." Ibrahima is technically still enslaved, but he experiences the moment as a wild rush of joy, a bursting open of the gates of freedom. For the first time since his capture by the Hebohs, he does not have to obey another man's will.

The joy is short-lived, however, because Isabella, his loving wife of thirty-three years, the mother of their nine children, is in agony at the prospect of her husband leaving. Seeing her pain and desperation to go with him, Ibrahima is tormented. How can he exercise his new freedom without breaking his wife's heart, and living out the rest of his days in sadness and regret? He keeps asking Marschalk what he should do. Marschalk can't come up with a good answer and now regrets his involvement in the whole business. Separating the devoted old couple, he writes, will surely "accelerate the death of both."

Finally, Marschalk goes to Thomas Foster, who tells him that Isabella is essential to the running of his plantation because she is the head midwife and physician in the slave quarters. But Foster also can't bear the idea of separating the old couple, so he agrees to sell Isabella for $200. Ibrahima goes around Natchez asking for donations. He is so well liked and respected, and his story so well-known, that he raises $293 in a single day, with 140 people contributing. Thomas Foster then deeds Isabella to Andrew Marschalk under the same restrictions as her husband.

He calls himself Colonel Marschalk, honoring his brief military career, and one imagines that Mark Twain would have found him irresistible, for his thundering editorials, swollen sense of self-regard, supple sense of ethics, and natural-born huckster-ism. Marschalk becomes so consumed by his role as Ibrahima's savior that some people in Natchez, including Cyrus Griffin, the disabled lawyer, find him ridiculous.

When Henry Clay's letter finally arrives, Marschalk parades it around the market house, "boasting and gabbing from day light until breakfast, and up the street and down." He tries to throw a farewell public dinner for Ibrahima, a ridiculous idea that gets nowhere. White people in Natchez are happy to give money to Prince and write glowing letters of introduction and recommen-dation for him, but the idea of dining with him, or any other Negro, is grotesque and absurd.

Now, having booked tickets on a steamboat to Cincinnati and received authorization from Henry Clay to spend $200 on clothing for Ibrahima, Marschalk goes into a Natchez tailor shop and orders up a "Moorish costume." This consists of a white turban with a crescent, a blue coat with yellow buttons, billow-ing white pantaloons, and yellow boots. Somehow a scimitar is found to complete the look. For Cyrus Griffin and others, the "tawdry dress" is a cringing embarrassment, but Marschalk thinks Ibrahima looks splendid and princely in his new getup. The newspaperman also knows that it will be useful for publicity and fundraising, and that a "Moor," or North African, falls into an easier racial category for white Americans than a "Negro."

On the clear and unseasonably cool morning of April 8, 1828, Ibrahima stands at the landing Under-the-Hill and says goodbye to his children and grandchildren. He promises to buy their freedom as soon as he can. An atmosphere of dignified formality prevails. The sons say how pleased they are to see their parents freed, and how fortunate they are to have a decent Christian master. No tears are shed, but in their eyes is "a look of silent agony" that Marschalk can't bear to witness, and which devastates Ibrahima and Isabella.

On this bitter-sweet note, the steamboat *Neptune* churns upstream on the swollen Mississippi River, with Marschalk waving farewell from the landing, and the children and grand-children struggling not to weep. Ibrahima and Isabella had never imagined that freedom could be so painful.

| 13 |

The advent of cheap, accurate, mass-market DNA testing has confirmed a difficult truth about African Americans. They are overwhelmingly the product of miscegenation, nearly all of which was beyond their ancestors' control. Virtually no African Americans today can claim pure African descent, except for recent African immigrants. The five leading DNA companies have slightly varying figures, but taken together, they indicate that the average African American is about 75 percent sub-Saharan African, 22 percent European, and 1 or 2 percent Native American.

By tracing paternal ancestry through Y-DNA, geneticists have found that a third of African American men today are directly descended from a white male ancestor who fathered a mulatto child in the slavery era, "most probably from rape or coerced sexuality," in the words of Henry Louis Gates Jr., professor of African American studies at Harvard, and presenter of popular television shows on black genealogy. "White and black citizens are bound together in the most fundamental way possible—at the level of the genome," he writes, and yet divided by the racial pseudoscience originally devised to justify slavery and perpetuated in slightly shifting forms ever since.

Miscegenation was everywhere in the antebellum South, but it was also taboo, and often adulterous, so white society, and white women in particular, performed mental gymnastics to pretend that the abomination wasn't happening, and certainly not on the scale that it actually was happening, even though the living, breathing evidence was all around them. In Natchez and New Orleans—laissez-faire river towns with a French and Spanish influence and a historical shortage of white women—the taboo against miscegenation was much weaker, and its inevitability more accepted. In both places, the extralegal system of *plaçage* allowed white men to enter into common-law marriages with black or mulatto women known as *placées*. Crucially for these women and their children, *plaçage* granted them inheritance rights to the man's property and wealth, and the likelihood that they would be freed in his will.

The local customs surrounding miscegenation were particularly fascinating for Mimi Miller, the head of the Historic Natchez Foundation. The wife of Ron Miller, who was told to come back to Nellie's when he wanted some pussy, Mimi is a living encyclopedia of Natchez history, with a phenomenal memory for genealogy. Over decades of burrowing into local records and archives, she has discovered an extraordinary degree of intertwining in the bloodlines of the old white and black families.

"Was it all rape?" I asked.

"That's what I assumed when I got here," she said. "Then I started reading the diaries and letters, which you have to regard with some skepticism, and the wills and court cases, which tell you more than anything. Unfortunately, there's nothing from the enslaved women, and those are the voices you most want to hear."

In the court records, she found cases where the slave owner had freed one of his female slaves, lived with her until he died, freed and educated the children they had together, then left the woman his property in his will. William Barland, a wealthy planter and downtown property owner, was one prominent example. "You can talk about the unequal power relations there and question if the woman really had any choice," said Mimi. "But these were stable, affectionate, long-term relationships that greatly improved the lives of those women and their children."

"How common were these relationships?"

"It was very common for white men, when their wives died of yellow fever, or whatever else, to take up with one of the enslaved women in the household, and a lot of those became lasting relationships. Natchez was highly unusual in that those relationships were out in the open and tolerated here, like they were in New Orleans, and hardly anywhere else."

Having said all that, Mimi didn't want to give me the wrong impression. These were interesting exceptions to the horrifying general rule. "White men were raping enslaved women all over the Natchez District, all over the South, in their homes, in the quarters, and out on the plantations. There was seduction too, if you can call it that. Offer a teenage girl a pretty ribbon or a few coins."

The question of what to do with the "mulatto" children inevitably followed. Some fathers sold their own children in the slave trade, often under pressure from wives who couldn't stand looking at the living evidence of what their husbands had done. Other fathers raised the children in their own households, to which their wives responded in different ways—with cruelty, with surprising kindness, and with incredible feats of self-deception. "Any lady is ready to tell you who is the father of all the mulatto children in everybody's household but her own," wrote the antebellum diarist Mary Boykin Chesnut. "Those, she seems to think, drop from the clouds."

Natchez had an unusually large population of free blacks—1,400 during the 1830s—and most of them were freed by white fathers who had raised and educated them. The majority were poor, "peddlers, prostitutes, laborers, fishermen or woodcutters," according to historian Clayton James in *Antebellum Natchez*. A few inherited wealth from their white fathers, and a few more became successful small businessmen and members of a free black middle class. As Jeremy Houston pointed out on his African American heritage tours, and Mimi Miller confirmed, these men became the leaders of the black community during Reconstruction because they had the education and the ties to white society.

At the Historic Natchez Foundation, Mimi Miller introduced me to an elderly African American brickmason named Duncan Morgan, a master craftsman who had worked on all the antebellum tour homes. He was related to several old white slaveholding families and bore this knowledge with ease, even with a measure of pride. Morgan was also a former president of the Historic Natchez Foundation, a ten-year board member at the Mississippi Department of Archives and History, and a revered authority on local history.

He was well into his eighties now, walking slowly, but still working with bricks and mortar, and very sharp mentally. His skin was light brown and his face was dominated by a large pair of glasses. I had heard that he was one of the few people in Natchez who could move with equal ease through the black and the white communities, and I asked him if that was true.

"I've always been very comfortable in my skin. It's possible that I'm better known among whites, but everybody respects me, I hope, because I'm genuine. And in any given group, I might just be the most intelligent person." He smiled to indicate that humor was intended with that last remark.

He was related to Anne MacNeil and Beth Boggess, the elderly white sisters at Elms Court, who had taken me deep into their family history during Pilgrimage. His great-grandmother was the daughter of a Surget, the Surgets being an extremely prominent family. His grandfather's grandmother was born at Concord, the domain of the Yellow Duchess, as the mixed-race daughter of one of the Minor men.

Morgan gave me some more of his genealogy, then concluded, "I'm Old Natchez."

I asked him what that meant.

"Old Natchez never embraced poor white trash, but if you were mixed, you were acceptable. If you trace it back, it's all intertwined here. When I was growing up, black and white children played together as equals until they were fifteen or sixteen. Then a line of demarcation appeared, and I had to start calling the other children Miss and Mister."

He remembers riding around town with his grandfather, who would point out houses and tell stories about the families who lived there. Being of mixed race himself, young Duncan found the stories about other mixed families particularly interesting. "In so much of the South, it was the white man going down into the plantation quarters, but it wasn't like that here. Those relationships were more direct and out in the open. The fathers usually recognized the children and often freed the mothers so the children would be born free. We had a free black middle class here, which would have been an impossibility in the rest of Mississippi."

"Was it always white men with black women? I asked. Did it ever happen the other way around, or was that too dangerous and taboo?"

"It happens now openly, black men with white women. It happened before the Civil War too, but it was very secretive. I don't think the whites today know about it, but the stories were passed down through the black community. I would hear them from my grandfather and other people. It was mostly white women having revenge affairs on their husbands."

I asked him to elaborate.

"The man would be having an affair with a mulatto woman, and his wife would get mad about it. She'd start having an affair with one of the lighter-skinned men in the household.* When she got pregnant, the baby would get passed off or disappear, or she would take a trip to Europe for several months. That was the usual way of doing it."

The woman would come back from Europe without the baby, or with the baby and some far-fetched story. The child was from her cousin who had tragically died—her cousin in Spain or Sicily, which would explain the "Mediterranean" complexion. People would whisper about it, but whites would maintain the polite fiction and the next generation would learn it as fact. The house slaves, on the other hand, knew exactly what had happened, talked about it openly, and passed down the true stories.

I asked Duncan Morgan if he knew of any specific examples, but he didn't. Mimi Miller had heard something about a hand-

---

* According to the historian Martha Hodes, in her book *White Women, Black Men: Illicit Sex in the Nineteenth-Century South*, it was a rare but persistent phenomenon and the sex was usually coercive and an expression of white power. One technique, employed by plantation wives and their daughters, was to threaten a rape accusation if the man refused their sexual advances.

some butler at Monmouth, but she didn't have any names or corroborating information. The stories that Duncan Morgan had heard from his grandfather were probably the last dying echoes of these highly secretive affairs, although the living descendants were presumably still walking around.

———

From the Historic Natchez Foundation, it was two blocks to the former residence of William Johnson, a barber and businessman who was a pillar of the free black middle class before the Civil War. His mother had been owned by his father, Captain William Johnson, who petitioned the Mississippi state legislature to free their mulatto son at the age of eleven. In the petition, sounding like one of those conflicted slave owners who thought slavery was wrong, Captain Johnson expressed his desire to give "Liberty to a human being which all are entitled to as a birthright, & extend the hand of humanity to a rational Creature, on whom unfortunately Complexion Custom & even Law in This Land of freedom, has conspired to rivet the fetters of Slavery."

Captain Johnson had already freed William's mother, and his sister, who had married a free black barber. This was one of the few professions that free blacks were allowed to practice. They were not actually free at all, but subject to numerous laws and restrictions, and required to carry their papers at all times. They occupied a shaky middle ground between free white society and the unfree world of the enslaved.

William Johnson apprenticed as a barber with his brother-in-law, then gradually built up a small empire of barbershops in Natchez. The men whose faces he shaved, and whose hair he cut, were white and included some prominent citizens with whom he formed close relationships. He would go hunting with them and break a powerful racial taboo by dining with them. He would also help them find work for the mixed-race children that they kept producing.

The William Johnson House is a three-story brick building, and its current status as a National Park Service museum owes everything to a discovery in the attic in 1938. From 1835 until his wretched murder in 1851, Johnson kept a detailed diary about his life and the daily goings-on in Natchez. It ran to 2,000 pages in leatherbound volumes, which his descendants had put in the attic and forgotten about. Some historians describe it as one of the most unusual and significant diaries kept by any American in the nineteenth century.

His original wooden desk stands in the front parlor of the museum-house. He would stay up by candlelight when the rest of the household was asleep and jot down his earnings, loans, and expenditures, items of local news and barbershop gossip, and brief descriptions of his days. Johnson had no talent or ambition as a writer, and the diary reveals no deep, complicated thoughts. He was a conservative businessman who took the world as he found it and tried to get ahead while remaining honest in his dealings, and honorable in his reputation.

He loved to hunt, fish, ride, and gamble. He played dominoes and billiards and drank gin, brandy, Madeira, and champagne. He had a good library of books and kept up with current affairs through various magazine subscriptions. He traveled to New York and Philadelphia and particularly enjoyed his frequent trips to New Orleans, where free blacks lived under less scrutiny. His diary, published at 791 pages by Louisiana State University Press, is a long slog to get through because so much of it concerns small financial transactions, but it's the most revealing record that exists about everyday life in antebellum Natchez, written from the perspective of a free man of color with a thriving business, a happy marriage, eight children, and up to twenty slaves.

The two biggest frustrations of the diary are that Johnson never records an emotion about his father, or an opinion about the morality of slavery. Born a slave himself, then freed, he appears to have had no qualms about enslaving others, and you can't help asking yourself, Why not? Was he identifying white, as Ser Boxley believes? Was he engaged in some sort of self-deception? Among his books was a Bible-based defense of slavery—did that assuage his conscience or justify what he wanted to do anyway? Or was he just the ambitious product of a society that measured a man's worth by the number of human beings that he owned? Johnson inherited seven slaves from his formerly enslaved mother, Amy, and bought the rest at various markets around Natchez.

> Buisness Tolerable fair, I was at auction to day at the Sale of Mr. Philomel Greens, 20 hands. They were sold at the Court House in Lots or Familes. . . . I Bot an old man by the name of Ned for Only fifteen Dollars." —February 27, 1850

Most free blacks did not own slaves, but mainly because they couldn't afford them. Those that prospered usually did buy and enslave people. Like most slave owners who kept diaries, William Johnson recorded many annoyances and exasperations concerning the people he owned. When his slaves were obedient and efficient, he treated them well. He gave them money, praise, gifts, passes to the circus and the theater. He taught them how to read and write. And when they were disobedient, careless, or troublesome, he felt no compunction whatsoever about reaching for his whip.

From a modern perspective, the systematic whipping of helpless enslaved people is one of the most upsetting aspects of the regime, but attitudes towards whipping were very different in the nineteenth century. Husbands routinely whipped their wives and children. Navies flogged their sailors. Teachers flogged their students. All across the American South, whites were whipped in public for minor crimes. Frederick Douglass wrote that everyone in the South seemed to want the privilege of whipping someone else. Perhaps the saddest whippings of all were delivered by slaves to their own children. They knew that if their children were allowed to grow up sassy or disobedient, much worse whippings would be in their future.

William Johnson whipped his slaves with varying degrees of severity depending on the offense. "Good Flogging with Big Whip" and "very Seviere Floging" were at one end of the spectrum, and "tap or two with my wriding whip" was at the other end. When he heard something shaking the loft, went upstairs, and discovered a young male slave having sexual congress with a Muscovy duck he gave him "a Genteel whiping."

One slave named Steven gave William Johnson more trouble and heartache than the rest put together. He stole, he shirked, he ran away to get drunk and would often end up in jail. To make it worse, Johnson liked him. Steven was intelligent and good company when sober, but he was an alcoholic and couldn't stop himself from binge drinking. Johnson had tried giving him a hundred lashes, putting him on the chain gang, turning him over to be brutalized by the town guard, but none of it worked. He had tried kindness and lenience. That didn't work either.

Steven's behavior was a direct threat to William Johnson's

freedom, which could have been revoked for his failure to control a troublesome slave. So he came to the painful decision to sell Steven. The first time he tried, at the Forks of the Road, Johnson couldn't go through with it, and he brought Steven home instead. On New Year's Day 1844, having wept and lost a night's sleep, he took Steven down Under-the-Hill and sold him for $600 to a Mr. Cannon heading downriver. "I gave Steven a pair Suspenders and a pr of socks and 2 Cigars, Shook hands with him and see [him] go On Bourd for the Last Time. I felt hurt but Liquor is the Cause of his troubles; I would not have parted with Him if he had Only have let Liquor alone but he Cannot do it I believe."

Ser Boxley was outraged when the National Park Service decided to renovate the William Johnson House and turn it into a museum. In his view, William Johnson was not a part of black history because he thought white, owned slaves, looked up to whites, and looked down on blacks. Like many of Ser Boxley's assertions, this was an oversimplification, but not without evidence to support it. When Johnson writes that his apprentice barber Bill Nix is a "pure pure Negro at Heart and in action," he is not paying him a compliment. Johnson's best friends were other successful free people of color, but he also had a close association with Adam Bingaman, a Harvard-educated planter-politician, and an ancestor of the two sisters at Elms Court.

Johnson would loan out his slaves to Bingaman when he needed extra hands. In return, Bingaman invited Johnson to graze his nag horses at his Fatherland plantation and breed them to his celebrated studs. The two men were avid horse-racing fans. Bingaman's mixed-race family, by an enslaved woman named Aimee, had a close, affectionate relationship with William Johnson's family. The two men were at the core of a small subcommunity of white men, black mistresses, mixed-race children, and free blacks, held together by mutual empathy and dependence. They looked out for each other's interests, found apprenticeships and marriage partners for free black children and, in the case of Bingaman and Johnson, found genuine pleasure in each other's company.

Adam Bingaman, top of his class at Harvard, fluent in six languages, a former Speaker of the Mississippi House and president of the Senate, ended up abandoning white society in Natchez. He moved to New Orleans with Aimee and their mixed-race children, so they could live together more freely. William Johnson stayed in Natchez and continued to prosper. He bought a farm called Hardscrabble and got into a feud with his free black neighbor Baylor Winn, who had cut some timber on Johnson's land without permission. On June 16, 1851, Johnson rode out to Hardscrabble with his son William, a free black apprentice, and a slave. Gunshots rang out and Johnson was hit in the lungs, back, and arm. As he died, he named Baylor Winn as his murderer.

The white population of Natchez was outraged, but a hitch in antebellum law prevented justice from being served: people with Negro blood were not permitted to give evidence against whites in court trials. Baylor Winn, who was indicted as a mulatto, convinced the court that his blood was white and Native American. That meant the three witnesses to the murder—Johnson's slave, son, and apprentice, all of whom had African blood—couldn't testify against Baylor Winn. So he walked free, even though no one in the court disputed the fact that he had murdered William Johnson in cold blood.

What is the legacy of all that miscegenation in Natchez, apart from its obvious genetic influence on the African American community? How is it remembered and dealt with? Did it continue after Emancipation and the Civil War, and how does it influence race relations in the town today?

According to Duncan Morgan, the old tolerance of relationships between white men and black women continued into the 1930s and 1940s, even as Jim Crow anti-miscegenation laws took hold in Mississippi and the rest of the old Confederacy. He remembers interracial couples living together openly in the 1940s. They would go to the Northern states to get married because it was illegal to marry across the color line in Mississippi. Then they would come home to raise their children in Natchez, which was segregated and white supremacist, but still fairly lenient and broad-minded when it came to miscegenation. "They were very solid, respectable families," said Morgan. "Nobody bothered them until the poor white trash started coming here."

In the late 1940s and 1950s, the first factories opened in Natchez. Poor rural whites from the surrounding counties flocked into town for those jobs and soon stocked the ranks of a resurgent Ku Klux Klan. They were mostly Scotch-Irish dirt farmers and sharecroppers. Their people had reaped none of the economic benefits of slavery. What they had was extraordinary resilience and a fierce, bristling, touchy pride, which was largely based on their alleged superiority to the only people below them in the social hierarchy.

"They had the hatred and meanness towards blacks that one associates with overseers and slave catchers," said Duncan Morgan. "Some of them were probably descended from overseers and slave catchers who were put out of work by Emancipation. They were inflamed by the sight of black-and-white couples openly raising their children together. What had been tolerated here for many generations became much more dangerous, and more taboo. People had to be more discreet or go up North, and it really wasn't talked about, at least not in the white community."

In Natchez today, the walls of silence that built up around the subject are crumbling, and the taboo is falling away. Miscegenation in the past is not an abstract concept, like it is in most of the country, but familial. "The town is full of black and white cousins who are just now getting to know each other," said Mimi Miller. "It's become almost fashionable to claim your black cousins and bring them to the coffee shop or invite them to a family reunion."

Motivated by a sense of generational guilt, moral duty, and a desire to heal racial divisions, the two sisters at Elms Court, Anne MacNeil and Beth Boggess, tracked down some descendants of a slave that their great-grandfather had impregnated and invited them to a family reunion. Twenty years previously, that would have been socially unacceptable in Natchez. Breaking another powerful Southern racial taboo, they invited their African American guests to join the white people in the swimming pool.

The African American mayor of Natchez, Darryl Grennell, is descended from two prominent old white families, who have now claimed him as a cousin. On another branch of his family tree, he's descended from a white tax collector who married his black mistress. "I think of my white ancestors and relatives as part of my extended family," Grennell says, "even though I was raised black and my parents were civil rights activists."

One of my regular lunch companions in Natchez was an African American woman named Beverly Adams. She was the director of student services at historically black Alcorn State University, and the host of a local talk-radio show. She also enjoyed acting. She had appeared in the Greg Iles Tableaux and portrayed Isabella in a PBS documentary about Ibrahima called *Prince Among Slaves*. That experience had permanently altered her sense of identity.

"I had never heard of Ibrahima until they started making that film," she said. "Then I found out from the researchers that I'm a direct descendant of Ibrahima and Isabella."

"How did that feel?"

"There was pride in having African royalty in my family, and sadness because of what happened to him—it's such a sad story, and really a difficult story for me, because I'm also a direct descendant of the family who enslaved him. I already knew about them. In my family, they were always called the Rapist Fosters."

Learning of the connection, one of the Foster descendants, a spry octogenarian called Nan Foster Schuchs, invited Beverly to a Foster family reunion. Over the strenuous objections of her family, and strong criticism in the black community, Beverly accepted the invitation and met the descendants of the people who had raped her ancestors and ruthlessly exploited their labor. Nan welcomed her with such warmth and honesty that an unlikely friendship formed between the two women, and they were now doing presentations together for tourists and curious locals, taking turns to tell the story of Ibrahima, Isabella, and the Foster family.

"It's so hard for black people to let go of bitterness, that Anglo people gained so much wealth on the backs of our people and treated us as badly as they treated us, but it has to be done to move forward," Beverly told me. "We have to talk about these things, no matter how difficult it is, and then I truly believe it can get better. Nan Foster and I have taken a small step in the right direction."

I suggested that there were similarities to South Africa, which had instituted "truth and reconciliation" hearings after the end of apartheid, based on open and honest discussion. Mississippi was also a post-apartheid society, I said, facing many similar issues.

Beverly was quick to correct me. "It's not just Mississippi. The North is segregated too. This is work the whole country needs to do. White people need to understand the bitterness we feel about slavery. There's pride that we survived the whole experience and came through it with dignity, and then success-fully fought for our civil rights, but a lot of white people act like it's no big deal, or we should be grateful for what we have now. They haven't even begun to understand."

| 14 |

April 1828. The steamboat *Neptune* churns its way north against the full force of the Mississippi River in its annual spring flood. A small, basic, noisy craft, with belching steam pipes and a paddle wheel on one side, the *Neptune* is nothing like the magnificent floating palaces that will ply the river in decades to come. Standing on the deck, free at last, but heartsick over their children, Ibrahima and Isabella observe the passing floodscape—clumps of unhappy cattle on tiny islands, marooned farmhouses, drowned forests, sheets of outspreading water where the riverbanks used to be.

They pass Memphis, a small settlement on a bluff, founded nine years previously. They reach the confluence where the clear waters of the Ohio River join the muddy Mississippi, just south of Cairo, Illinois, and they make the northeasterly turn into the Ohio. Twelve days out from Natchez, the *Neptune* docks at Cincinnati and they disembark.

This is the first big American city that Ibrahima has seen, a thriving river port ten times the size of Natchez, with grimy red-brick buildings and warehouses full of flour, pigs, and whiskey, waiting to be shipped downriver to the Lower Mississippi Valley.

It is also the first place he has ever been, in Africa and America, where slavery does not exist and is forbidden by law.

Walking through the busy streets, in his white-turbaned costume with yellow boots and a scimitar fastened at his waist, Ibrahima causes a sensation, and his story proves irresistible to the three Cincinnati newspapers. A bona fide African prince, taken captive in his youth, enslaved for nearly forty years in Natchez, is now on his way home to become a prince again and perhaps assume the throne as king. In Cincinnati, Ohio, it translates into instant celebrity.

Ibrahima welcomes the attention and the publicity because he urgently needs money. The State Department sent just enough to pay for his passage to Washington, but Marschalk spent half of it on his Moorish costume, and no provision was made for Isabella's travel expenses. The State Department doesn't even know of Isabella's existence, let alone that she's on her way to Washington, and intending to join her husband on his voyage back to Africa. Learning of this predicament, the *Daily Gazette* makes a plea to its readers: "It is earnestly hoped that the citizens of Cincinnati will contribute what may be necessary to aid her in that journey."

To garner the contributions, Ibrahima parades through the streets, a "grave looking elderly personage in Moorish dress," as another newspaper describes him. His eye-catching appearance, in combination with the excited, sympathetic newspaper coverage, generates more than enough money to continue the journey, and it plants a seed in his head. Maybe he can do the same thing in other places and raise enough money to buy his children out of slavery.

In late April, Ibrahima and Isabella board another boat and travel up the Ohio River for 370 miles to Wheeling, West

Virginia. Then comes an exhausting, bone-shaking, joint-in-flaming week on the public stagecoach through the ragged roads of Pennsylvania and Maryland. By now, newspapermen all over the Northeast have caught wind of his story and are tracking his progress and spreading his fame. Perhaps inevitably, they are also sensationalizing the facts, publishing inaccuracies, leaping to faulty conclusions, and then arguing about them.

Ibrahima is dubbed "The Unfortunate Moor" and the "Prince of Timbuctoo." The rattling public stagecoach is described as his own luxurious private carriage. Since Ibrahima's father is dead, the notion takes hold that the "King of Timbuctoo" is returning home to claim his rightful place on the throne. A fist-thumping editorial in a Philadelphia newspaper demands it: "He is entitled to the Throne!" But all the publicity is welcome, no matter how inaccurate, because it increases his fundraising opportunities.

When he gets to Baltimore, he meets with William Swaim, the sympathetic assistant editor of an antislavery newspaper called *Genius of Universal Emancipation*. Explaining to Swaim why he needs money urgently, Ibrahima loses control of his emotions. In the next issue, Swaim publishes an account of Ibrahima's story and a plea for contributions: "Though this victim of ruthless misfortune has lately stepped into the enjoyment of his natural rights, he has children remaining at Natchez. While he related to us this painful truth, the tears gushed from his eyes and rolled down his cheeks."

By pure coincidence, Henry Clay, Ibrahima's champion in the State Department, is passing through Baltimore at the same time, so Ibrahima approaches him in a hotel and introduces himself. The secretary of state is a tall Kentuckian famed for his charm, wit, and charisma, and he greets Ibrahima like a friend. Clay promises to help in any way that he can and advises him to proceed directly to Washington and meet with President Adams. Ibrahima tells an acquaintance that he is "highly delighted" with Henry Clay.

Leaving Isabella in Baltimore, Ibrahima catches an uncomfortable stagecoach to the nation's capital. Washington is a smaller city than Cincinnati, and apart from the Capitol building, nothing about it is impressive. The White House is only partially built. Pennsylvania Avenue is a weedy unpaved road with chunks of stone thrown in its mudholes. The city has no sewer system, and no lighting at night. And for Ibrahima, it is a return to legalized slavery.

In addition to its 2,000 resident slaves, Washington is a major regional hub for the slave trade, and enslaved men, women, and children are kept in pens and dungeons all over the city. Visitors from the North and Europe are shocked to see processions of chained and manacled human beings being led through the streets of the young republic's capital.

Ibrahima chooses a quiet, low-key hotel called Williamson's Mansion House on Pennsylvania Avenue, where he has heard, correctly, that he will be treated as a gentleman. On the rainy morning of the fifteenth of May, he walks the two muddy blocks to the uncompleted White House and joins the group of people waiting to ask favors of the president. When Ibrahima's turn comes, he is ushered into an office on the second floor, where John Quincy Adams, a short, bald, stocky man with a cold austere manner, examines his visitor with dark penetrating eyes and greets him in an unexpectedly high-pitched voice. Ibrahima, who was born to be the leader of a nation, does not feel intimidated by President Adams and regards him as an equal, even though Adams has all the power in this encounter, and Ibrahima has a lot of explaining to do.

Also in the room is Samuel Southard, the secretary of the navy, who is charged with arranging Ibrahima's voyage to Morocco. Now Ibrahima has to inform these gentlemen that he is not, in fact, a Moroccan prince and has no wish to go there. He wants to go to Liberia instead, then proceed overland to his homeland of Futa Jalon, not far from Timbuktu. And one more thing: he will also require passage for his wife.

Describing the meeting in his diary, President Adams writes a slightly confused account of a confusing situation: "Abdel Rahman is a Moor, otherwise called Prince or Ibrahim, who has been forty years a slave in this country. He wrote, two or three years since, a letter to the Emperor of Morocco, in Arabic, in consequence of which the Emperor expressed a wish that this man might be emancipated and sent home. His owner, residing in Natchez, Mississippi, offered to emancipate him on condition that he should be sent home by the Government. He came in while Mr. Southard was with me, and we had some consultation how and when he should be dispatched to his home, which he says is Timbuctoo."

The only reason Henry Clay and President Adams took an interest in Ibrahima's case was to improve diplomatic relations with the emperor of Morocco. The president could have easily ejected Ibrahima from his office as an impostor and a time waster, or sent him back to Natchez, but Adams takes the shifting ground in his stride and agrees to the unexpected request from his unusual visitor.

Knowing that he will never have such extraordinary access to power again, Ibrahima then attempts to push his luck even further. As Adams writes in his diary later that day, "He has left at Natchez five sons and eight grandchildren—all in slavery; and he wishes that they might be emancipated, and be sent with or to him."

It is hard to discern what the president really thought of this petitioner in his "native costume," who was not a Moroccan prince after all and did not appear grateful for the government's help in securing his liberty, or its largesse in offering to fund his repatriation, but instead kept introducing one problem after another that he expected the government to solve—a wife, a completely different destination, a total of thirteen children and grandchildren. Of all the favor seekers in the White House on that rainy morning, the elderly Muslim from Natchez, with his claims of royalty, exotic costume, dignified manners, and limited Afro-Mississippian English, must have seemed the most entitled, the most improbable, and perhaps the most pathetic.

President Adams promises a decision about the children and grandchildren at a later date, and that appears to have been the end of the meeting.

| 15 |

Kerry Dicks had a finely tuned appreciation for the Southern Gothic side of Natchez. She could see it with detached irony and describe it with morbid wit, even though she was not observing from a safe comfortable distance. Murder, suicide, eccentricity, madness, and dark transgressive behavior in decaying antebellum mansions were all part of her family inheritance. She would talk about it while drinking wine among the graves in the Natchez cemetery.

Even at the height of summer, the wine was always red. White wine has its virtues, but its color lacks vibrancy and gravitas, and it seemed disrespectful to drink it with the dead. Before opening the bottle, Kerry would walk me through the beautiful old cemetery, with its live oaks and cedar trees, marble monuments and mausoleums, and introduce me to various dead people. On our first visit, she took me to a plain stone marker inscribed LOUISE THE UNFORTUNATE with no further information.

"She came to Natchez to marry her beau, but he died on her," said Kerry in her un-Southern accent. "She started out working a few jobs on the bluff to support herself. Then she made a slow and sad descent Under-the-Hill, starting out as a waitress, I think, and ending up as a lady of the night. Either the doctor who treated her when she got the clap, or a priest, or one of her clients, took up a collection when she died so she could be buried up here, as a kind of return to respectability as a corpse."

At the grave of the Yellow Duchess—Katherine Lintot Minor, 1770–1844—Kerry turned bitter and scornful, as if they'd had a falling-out recently. "That batshit crazy bitch was supposedly buried with a bunch of gold in her coffin to keep the whole color-scheme thing going. Ugh. And look at the inscription. Doesn't it make you want to puke? You know she wrote it herself."

The inscription read IN ALL THE RELATIONS OF LIFE SHE WAS AS NEAR PERFECT, AS MORTALS ARE PERMITTED TO COME.

Kerry knew a lot about coffins, death, and decay. As a teen-ager, she had enjoyed playing Ouija board in the cemetery at night, and she had started coming here as a toddler. "I have pictures of me in diapers, eating sandwiches, and drinking water from the spouts that you use to fill the vases on the graves. It's a family propensity, apparently. My uncle tells a story about this frail old lady called Cousin Agnes, who would wake him and my dad up before dawn, and they would get in the Cadillac, with a big, silent black man behind the wheel, and drive out here to the cemetery. They were little boys, nine and seven, maybe even younger."

She took a sip of wine and smiled at the craziness of it. "Cousin Agnes would unlock the family mausoleum, get the black guy to pry open one of the coffins with a crowbar, and show them a moth-eaten Confederate uniform with a decayed corpse inside it. She would smoke a cigarette and say, 'Boys, that's your great-great-so-and-so.' I'm not sure how much skin he had left then—he's all bones now—but he still had an im-pressive beard. Then they would get back in the Cadillac, and she would drop the boys off back in their beds. This happened numerous times."

Cousin Agnes was Agnes Marshall, whose husband dropped dead during a big party at Stanton Hall. She was mortified that he might spoil the party by dying, so she got people to remove his body and continued drinking and socializing. Then she went on to another party, which turned into a wake for her husband.

In her embrace of morbid, crazy stories, and her ironic pride in being a citizen of Natchez, which she described half jokingly as "an open-air lunatic asylum," Kerry went a little further than most, but the attitude was fairly commonplace. Elodie Pritchartt, who was a generation older, relished the weirdness in her hometown and could talk about it for hours. Among the upper crust, there was a definite pride in Natchez's reputation for eccentricity, and people often became defensive when it was suggested that other places in the South might be equally eccentric. Brett Brinegar, the head of the annual Natchez Literary and Cinema Celebration, had tried living in Savannah, Georgia, another town renowned for eccentrics. "It was way too normal for me," she said. "I couldn't handle it." On a weekday evening at Elodie's house, over cocktails, I met Wayne Bryant, a middle-aged gay man steeped in Natchez lore and garden club history. He enjoys visiting Savannah, but when I asked him if it was as weird as Natchez, he was insulted by the question. "Not in a million years," he huffed.

When the garden club elite gathered at cocktail parties in each other's antebellum homes—the basic unit of social interaction—they would tell one outlandish story after another, and invariably start conjuring up the extravagant characters of the past, such as Katherine Miller, the founder of Pilgrimage. The most extravagant character of all was probably Buzz Harper. He died shortly before I got to Natchez, but he was talked about so often that his presence lingered. He drove a Rolls-Royce and often wore a full-length mink coat, and a huge diamond stickpin. He was six feet four, although people would often exaggerate this to six feet six, or six feet eight, with unusually long limbs and an immaculate silver ponytail. He ate his steak raw, lightly seasoned with salt and pepper, and he was a close friend of Anne Rice, the bestselling author of vampire novels.

My friend Tom Ramsey, who grew up in Vicksburg, sixty miles upriver from Natchez, told me that Buzz Harper was "in the outer stratosphere of gay." Tom, now a chef in New Orleans, used to work in a Vicksburg menswear store where Buzz Harper bought clothes. Entering the store in his long mink coat, with a gold-handled antique cane and a manservant, he would strike an elaborate quartered pose and start discussing the details of his next four-piece suit—a three-piece suit with a matching car coat.

A few years later, Tom and a friend bumped into Buzz Harper on Royal Street in New Orleans. Buzz, in his usual suit and tie, massive cuff links, and giant stickpin, was accompanied by a short German bodybuilder in knee-length spandex shorts, combat boots, a tank top with the German Imperial eagle emblem, and small, round, black sunglasses. The German stood there saying nothing and holding four Airedales on a leash.

"Are you going to introduce us to your friend?" asked Tom.

"Oh," said Buzz. "That toy doesn't speak a word of English." Then Buzz asked to see the bottle of wine that Tom was carrying. "My dear boy, I can't stand to think of you drinking those dregs," said Buzz, and peeled off a $100 bill.

Wayne Bryant was Buzz Harper's personal chef for two years. The job required great flexibility and speed of execution. "He'd have no plans in the morning," said Wayne, stroking Versace the flatulent dog on Elodie's couch. "By the evening we'd have twenty-four for formal dinner with servants, and it might be a Monday night, and everyone would end up playing the tambourine and singing gospel songs."

Buzz was an interior decorator and antiques dealer by trade, completely unscrupulous in his business dealings, but otherwise kind and generous with courteous Southern manners. "He would offer to resize women's rings and replace the jewels with fakes," said Wayne. "He sold a twenty-carat Burmese ruby for $70,000 to my husband's mother. She had it appraised and discovered it was glass. You know, Buzz's wife is still alive and living in Palm Springs."

"Wife?" I said.

"Oh, yes. They always told people they were cousins. I don't know if they were ever legally married, or if it was a ruse so Buzz could look more respectable and gain better social entrée. He came from Newport, Arkansas, and he was the judge there in this tiny little town that might have had a red light."

In Natchez, they lived in three different antebellum homes that Buzz lavishly redecorated. It crushed him that the garden clubs never put one of his homes on tour during Pilgrimage.

"You can't go and vomit chintz and expect to be put on tour," said Wayne. "Buzz used to say, 'Once you go rococo, you never go back.' He had these big blackamoor statues. Choctaw is what Buzz's home would look like if he were alive, blackamoors everywhere and the dining room table set twenty-four/seven. I don't know what it is about Arkansas that breeds these strange fellas who come to Natchez to show off their china."

It was Buzz Harper who persuaded the famously tanned actor George Hamilton to buy property in Natchez and nearby Church Hill in the 1980s, allegedly in a money-laundering scheme for Imelda Marcos, the kleptocratic first lady of the Philippines. Buzz also recruited a string of young gay men from bars and clubs in New Orleans and brought them up to Natchez, where they became known as Buzzettes. He held breakfast parties that were designed to showcase his grand entrance, descending the staircase of an antebellum mansion in a long flowing robe. Wayne Bryant, Kerry Dicks, and several other people described Buzz Harper as the gayest man in Mississippi, and being dead was no impediment to this honor.

Southerners are a storytelling people, and Natchez contained a vast trove of Southern Gothic stories. To check the truthfulness of these stories was usually impossible, and you had to assume that they had been embellished. On the other hand, when it was possible to check the facts, the wildest stories were often true in every last detail—the fiery demise of the beloved whorehouse madam Nellie Jackson, for example. Or the "Goat Castle" murder of Kerry's great-great-aunt Jane Surget Merrill, which kept the whole nation riveted in the 1930s.

Jennie Merrill, as she was known, came from the old planter aristocracy, and she had been a famous beauty in her youth. In 1876, when she was barely a teenager, her father was appointed US ambassador to Belgium, and the family moved in the most elite European circles. After her father's death, she returned to America and based herself in New York City for the next twenty years, working with the photographer Jacob Riis on his crusade for tenement reform. In her mid-thirties she moved back to Natchez for a quieter life and started up a semi-clandestine affair with her second cousin Duncan Minor.

Miss Jennie was known in Natchez for a sharp temper and strange habits. She refused to stop for red lights in her Model T Ford or accept traffic tickets from the local police, who gave up trying. Her fashion sense remained stuck in the 1890s—mutton-sleeve dresses and small, tilted Empress hats. As she got older, she became reclusive, seldom leaving Glenburnie, her antebellum home and estate. She saw almost no one except for the African American servants and workers, who she treated imperiously, and her cousin-lover Duncan Minor, who visited every night.

The neighboring antebellum estate, Glenwood, was occupied by Dick Dana, a once-aspiring concert pianist who had smashed his hand in a window-sash accident (according to most accounts) and had undergone a complete mental collapse (undisputed). He had given up bathing and shaving, and he often wore nothing except a burlap sack with a hole cut out for his head. He had staring eyes, a foot-long beard, and was known as Wild Man by local African Americans. Dana spent most of his time climbing in the big trees that grew on the property. He liked to swing on vines and perch on high branches. People remember him howling at the moon for hours.

At the time of the murder, in 1932, Dick Dana was fifty-three. Glenwood, a two-story Greek Revival mansion that had been his childhood home, was filthy, rotting, and inhabited by a herd of goats. He lived there with another eccentric, Octavia Dockery, an unsuccessful poet, who looked after Dana or at least kept him fed. She was in a long-running feud with her aristocratic neighbor Jennie Merrill, and while class tensions were involved—Jennie thought Octavia was trash, and Octavia resented it—the feud was mainly about goats.

Since both parties refused to build a fence, the Glenwood goats would wander across the property line into Glenburnie and wreak havoc in Miss Jennie's flowerbeds. The police had been called on numerous occasions, but Octavia Dockery refused to restrain her goats, so Jennie Merrill had started shooting them when they came onto her property. In apparent retaliation, Dana and Dockery persuaded an itinerant black man named George Pearls to rob Miss Jennie's house. In a scuffle during the robbery Jennie Merrill was shot and killed.

Her body was found a hundred yards away, dumped in a thicket. Dana's and Dockery's fingerprints were discovered inside Miss Jennie's house, and they were charged with the murder. George Pearls left Natchez that night and was later shot and killed by a deputy sheriff in Arkansas for resisting arrest. He had the gun that killed Miss Jennie in his possession when he was shot, and was convicted posthumously of murdering Jennie Merrill. Then Emily Burns, his temporary girlfriend, who was at the scene of the murder but otherwise innocent, was put on trial as accomplice to murder and swiftly convicted by an all-white jury.

Even though their fingerprints were inside Glenburnie, even though Dick Dana, who almost never washed his clothes, was washing stains out of a shirt when the police arrived, Dana and Dockery were not indicted for any crimes. The press called them

Wild Man and Goat Woman, and Glenwood was nicknamed the Goat Castle. It was an unbelievably squalid ruin, as photographs confirm. The chimneys had fallen down, the roof leaked, the columns were crumbling. Several windows were broken and the front gallery was rotting away.

Inside, the house was ankle-deep in animal droppings, dust, filth, and debris. It was full of cobwebs and infested with rats, mice, fleas, and other vermin. The dust lay so thick on old magazines that their titles couldn't be read. Chickens nested on bookshelves. Cats, ducks, and geese lived in the house. The goats had eaten most of the rare-book collection and stripped off the wallpaper as high as they could reach.

Dana and Dockery subsisted on goat meat, which they cooked on bedsprings in the lovely old marble fireplaces, often using antique furniture for firewood. The Goat Castle Murder, an irresistible tale of aristocratic decay and eccentricity in the Deep South, was a front-page story for weeks all over the country, and it made news in Europe, where a few elderly princes and dukes probably remembered the young American beauty Jennie Merrill.

The first Natchez Pilgrimage had taken place in the spring of that year. Now, in the fall of 1932, thousands more people came down the long unpaved road to Natchez to see the Goat Castle and meet Wild Man and Goat Woman in person. Dana and Dockery started charging a twenty-five-cent admission fee. She cleaned up the house, but not too much, because she knew the squalor was a draw. So, of course, were the goats. They could be seen chewing the cud on the second-story balcony, and peering out through broken windows at the crowds.

Dick Dana began performing for the visitors on a dusty

out-of-tune piano that geese had been roosting in, and there are still a few people in Natchez today who remember his demented musical performances. One of them is Margaret Guido, the current owner of Glenburnie, who reports that the ghosts of Jennie Merrill and Duncan Minor are active in the house, but not causing any trouble: "I'll feel her come behind me when I'm ironing, and I'll just say, 'Oh, Jennie, is that you?'"

After Duncan Minor died in 1939, from natural causes, ownership of Glenburnie passed to Kerry's grandfather, and there was another violent death. "My grandfather had a maid there called Old Flora, who lived in a slave cabin, and I'm afraid this stereotype only gets worse," Kerry told me one afternoon in the cemetery. "She was a witch doctor and would draw magical symbols in the driveway with a broom. I can't remember her husband's name, but he was a drunken wife-beater, and he came for her with a shotgun one day. She ran up into the big house and slammed the front door shut, and he was so drunk that he slipped climbing up the steps and shot himself dead. That's the story that I grew up with."

In the 1970s, Kerry's father had a druggy hippie commune in Glenburnie. His name was Ian Dicks, and Kerry describes him as a "brilliant man who was totally nuts." When she was eight years old, he hung himself in the Homochitto National Forest, outside Natchez. By the time the body was discovered, it had turned black, and people initially thought that an African American had been lynched.

"Then there was my grandmother." Sitting on a stone wall by a grave, Kerry poured another glass of wine. "She threw a party on the same day that her ex-husband married someone else. She invited a whole bunch of people, and then she went into her bedroom and shot herself through the head. Yeah. My great-grandmother committed suicide five years later, on the anniversary of her daughter's suicide. She jumped out of a window—or perhaps fell out—but given the timing, I seriously doubt it."

I gave Kerry my sympathies, not sure what else to do.

"It's okay. It's an interesting legacy. I quite enjoy the Gothic details. But, yeah, that's me, descended from slave drivers and suicides, just a ball of confusion and repressed sexual violence, going to cocktail parties."

There were so many parties, especially during Pilgrimage. A typical Saturday began with mimosas and Bloody Marys at a morning brunch party. Then there would be a choice of lunch parties at tour homes, and cocktail parties in the evenings. Some of these parties were planned and catered with servants and bartenders. Others were impromptu.

One Sunday afternoon, I was invited to a gathering at Elodie Pritchartt's house, but the other guests canceled, so she texted her godmother, Valerie Swinney Bergeron, to see what she was doing. Valerie was a larger-than-life character who loved gin and gossip, carried a bright pink pistol in her purse, and was reputedly a crack shot. She had a heavily sprayed helmet of hair with a Cruella de Vil streak, and she laughed like a short burst of machine-gun fire. Her brother had cut off his own penis during a drug episode, and she referred to him as No-Weenie Swinney. Valerie was in the mood for company, so Elodie and I went over to Pleasant Hill, an antique-filled 1840 Greek Revival where Valerie lives with her husband John. Architectural historians describe it as a "cottage," but it has seven bedrooms and three bars.

Valerie flung open the front door in a pair of voluminous

white palazzo pants, gold sandals, and a blue blouse with an an-
chor motif. Her trademark hairstyle was marvelously immobile.
"I can't stand it another moment!" She spoke fast at high volume.
"I need a divorce from this awful man today! The Saints lost, Ole
Miss lost, I had three martinis at lunch and I'm having a hard
time spitting them out. Come inside, my dears. Behold the awful
man. Let's have a drink."

John Bergeron, a dignified businessman with horn-rimmed
glasses, a neatly trimmed white beard, and a patrician South
Louisiana accent, rose from the antique sofa, utterly unflustered
by his wife's histrionics. He made us all drinks, then sat back
down and scrolled through his gold iPad, making occasional
laconic remarks.

Valerie was dreading the imminent approach of her seventi-
eth birthday. "I'll wake up on the morning of my seventy-first year
and turn into a hag, but I've always wanted to drive a tugboat,
so I'm doing that with Carla Jenkins," she said, referring to Miss
Bettye's daughter. "When I turn seventy-five, I'll go skydiving."

"You already have the helmet for it," said John.

Valerie fake-laughed. "Ha-ha-ha-ha. Actually, Elodie darling,
you know how much I love Big Sexy Hair, which comes in the
big red can at Walmart? They've got an even stronger hairspray
now, and that's what I'll use when I go skydiving. I forget what
they call it. Great Big Fabulous Sexy Hair, or something."

Valerie was mad about a photograph that Elodie had posted
on social media. It showed Valerie wearing a hoopskirt with
a pink Android phone in one hand and a gin and tonic in the
other. "I could be a target for the blacks if they see it," Valerie
said. Elodie laughed. "I'm serious," said Valerie. "A black woman
came up here when I was wearing my hoop and she said, 'Why
do you perpetuate this?' I said, 'What's *this*?' She said, 'You know,

this-this-this.' I said, 'Are you referring to my fashion statement? Do you know who Queen Victoria is?'"

"Was," corrected John from the couch.

"I said, 'She's the woman who invented this fashion to hide her fat white ass. That was in the 1800s when this house was built. We're historical reenactors.' That woman marched down off the porch. They will not let go of the idea that this is about the Civil War, and slavery, and being racist. They cannot appreciate how beautiful these homes are, and what they do for the local economy."

Having said her piece on that subject, Valerie tried a sip of rosé, then switched back to gin and began gossiping furiously about Katherine Miller and various dead relatives. At one point she leapt to her feet, furious at some man buried decades ago. "You son of a bitch," she snapped. "You need to be slapped halfway into next week and shot through the eyes. And I'm the woman to do it, god-dammit. Shrinking-violet time is over and it's not coming back."

She turned to me. "If you don't think Southern women are the best, you need to raise your standards." Then she turned to John, who was placidly swiping through photographs of Angelina Jolie on his iPad. "I can't stand to be married to you for another single minute! This time it's really over. I'll see you in court."

John smiled in an affectionate, long-suffering way. He got up from the couch on his old aching knees and poured us all another round of drinks. "Honey," he said in that beautiful cultured drawl that reminded me of a fine aged wine. "This guy is a writer. He's bound to be taking notes."

He was right of course.

———————

There was a man from Nashville named Scott Smith who dressed like Jiminy Cricket in a top hat, vest, and tailcoat. He worked part of the year as a tour guide in Natchez and found great amusement in what he called "the madness" that went on in the old houses. He was a good friend of Ginger and James Hyland, who had started running paranormal tours of their home, a palatial Italianate mansion on five acres called The Towers. Photography was not allowed, "out of respect for our Ethereal Inhabitants."

Scott was on the front doorstep with a small group of paranormal enthusiasts when I arrived. He gave me a business card that said JIMMY THE CRICKET and told me to brace myself: "This is the most over-the-top home in Natchez." When Ginger and James came out on the doorstep, Scott gave them a silver mirror from Nellie Jackson's whorehouse, with Nellie's name engraved on it—a true Natchez treasure. "After the fire, one of the whores stole it and sold it to Buddy Fly," Scott said.

Ginger's hair was blond, medium length, and carefully styled. It cascaded in little waves and curls and shone like pearl. She was wearing black slacks and a yellow blouse, and the aura of wealth hung around her like perfume. She was the only child of Lawrence Hyland, a brilliant engineer who helped invent radar and developed the Hughes Aircraft Company for Howard Hughes. She handed me her business card, which announced her as THE LIONESS. I guessed her age at seventy.

Her husband James was about three decades younger, with theatrical mannerisms and a slightly twitchy energy. He was wearing frayed-cuff jeans with tasseled black velvet slippers and twirling a golf club. A few years ago, James had gone through a nightmarish court trial after being accused of having sex with a fifteen-year-old boy. The key moment came when James's attorney, Rusty Jenkins (Miss Bettye's son), asked the accuser if James had any scars, tattoos, or notable marks on his body. The accuser stated that he couldn't remember any, whereupon Rusty asked James to drop his pants and lift up his shirt. Visible to the whole courtroom was a dramatic ten-inch-long appendectomy scar running from his navel to his groin. James was found not guilty on six counts of sexual battery, and soon afterwards he married Ginger and changed his last name to Hyland.

Still twirling his golf club, James collected the tickets, opened the front door and led us inside The Towers, whereupon we gasped and wowed. It would take the rest of this book to adequately describe the lavishness of the interiors, or Ginger's collections of antique furniture, jewelry, laces, glassware, Chinese gaming counters from the 1700s, inkwells, opera glasses, watch fobs, jeweled pens, ornamental pen wipes, wreaths of human hair. She had 350 beaded purses on display, and 500 antique eyewash cups. The assault on the senses, and the powers of comprehension, was overwhelming. The deluge of extravagant glittering visual information coming in through the eyeballs had a stupefying effect on the brain.

James stood in the blue parlor, with its blue silk wallpaper, blue-upholstered rococo furniture, blue peacock feathers, and a hundred other blue things, and he started describing the paranormal activity in the house. At first, he was lighthearted and jokey about it, but it soon became apparent that he and Ginger were true believers, and they had gone through some serious shit with the ghosts in their mansion.

"We've had furniture slowly gliding across the floor, flickering lights, and the piano chair will drag itself out into the middle of the room," he said. Activity was strong in the music room, where Ginger had encountered her first true apparition after buying the house. "A solid black silhouette, it turned, it went to the wall, it exploded into vapor," she said.

They attributed most of the paranormal activity to the tragic history of the Fleming family, the original owners of The Towers. "All their children died here," said Ginger. "By gunshot, infected spider bite, horse accident, a cracked skull after slipping on the dining room floor. Kate died of pneumonia, aged seventeen. She laid out four days because her father couldn't stand to bury her. Our bed-and-breakfast guests hear a man moaning, and we attribute that to Mr. Fleming. The music box plays by itself sometimes. Perhaps we can attribute that to Kate."

The antebellum household was run by a slave known as Mammy Caroline, who was born in the governor's mansion in Kentucky. "She was large and in charge," said Ginger. "She had twin baby girls, and after the slaves and servants were liberated on Emancipation Day, she went down to the Devil's Punchbowl, where thousands of freed slaves were congregating in a Union army camp. There were sanitation issues, and her baby girls died. She smuggled their bodies out in pillowcases and buried them here. Mammy Caroline was buried in the family cemetery, which was almost unheard of in segregated Mississippi. She smoked a pipe, and people still smell a sweet smoke here when the humidity is high."

The Towers was a headquarters for the Union army during the Civil War. Ulysses S. Grant reputedly rode his horse up and down the hallway on Christmas Eve 1863, and his ghost was supposed to reappear every Christmas Eve, according to Natchez lore. "We can make light of that because we haven't seen him," said James. "But there is a young soldier who manifests."

Another ghost was named Johnny. "We have a 1,700-square-foot master bedroom upstairs," said Ginger. "I'd been getting disturbing reflections in the mirror, and then at two thirty in the morning, I hear a Weed Eater, and I see a light in the backyard. Then I see a gigantic orb, which resolves into a male figure, and he's holding my Weed Eater, and I remember seeing the auburn stubble of his whiskers. He says, 'I have obtained this equipment so I may acquire your attention.' I asked him not to disturb my bed-and-breakfast guests. I told him we were at peace."

James pointed to a window with his golf club. "Right there was a little girl with a big red ball. And the top-hat person, and those two women." He was looking a little freaked out now.

Ginger had more experience with the spirit world; it had been necessary to perform an exorcism at her house in California. She assured James and the rest of us that the situation at The Towers was now in hand: "The spirits of the house become protective if you do a positive restoration. We had a ceiling medallion shatter recently, and the chandelier underneath it was completely un-damaged. That medallion was in a thousand pieces, and each one was as hard as a rock. There's no way that chandelier could be undamaged, but it was. So you see we're working together now."

"That's right," said James. "It's really okay. We're getting a much more comfortable, protective energy."

"We're sharing the house," said Ginger. "I heard the two women talking to each other in the dining room. One had such a warm, beautiful, motherly voice. She told the other one, 'It's okay. We're all one. We're all connected.' Tears poured out of my eyes. I'm a part of this property now. And the trees. I bless the house every night and turn it over to them, and it's so loving."

When the tour was over, I sat down with James and Ginger, and we drank some wine. James said, "In Natchez, it's smarter to be more afraid of the living than the dead. This is such a gossipy, incestuous little town. We really don't go out anymore, but stay here in our Shangri-la. The paranormal stuff gets intense sometimes, but it's really okay."

As I got up to leave, Ginger told me to come back at Christmas. "We're going to have 167 trees this year, and they'll all be decorated from my costume-jewelry collection. The whole house will be decorated, too. I promise you, you've never seen anything like it. My husband is an absolute genius when it comes to decorating."

As I walked across the grounds to my vehicle, with the antebellum mansion glowing in the dark, and life-size bronze statues of elk and deer and bear looming up in front of me, the world beyond Natchez had never seemed so far away.

I came across a few different theories that attempted to explain the oddities of life down here. One I have already mentioned. Eccentricity is not only tolerated, but celebrated. It makes life more interesting and provides rich material to a storytelling people. So oddballs get free range, and bizarre behavior is not discouraged and even appreciated if it's not too destructive. "We don't put our crazy relatives in the nuthouse, like they do up North," a retired librarian told me. "We put them in the front parlor and give them a cocktail." Another woman phrased it slightly differently: "We don't hide our skeletons in the closet. We set them down on the front porch and tie a bow on them."

Other theories roped together the isolation, the heavy drinking, the obsessive ancestor worshipping, generations of first-cousin marriages, and the psychological pressures of Southern history. Those pressures exert themselves most powerfully on black Southerners, but white Southerners feel them too in a different way. They are required to reconcile their history of enslaving, raping, and lynching with their proudly held beliefs in honor, graciousness, and Christian decency. They have to deal, in some way, with the foolhardiness of secession and crushing defeat in a war they were convinced they would win. They have to square their well-earned reputation for kindness and hospitality with their equally well-earned reputation for violence and bigotry.

The traditional methods for dealing with these pressures have been evasive. White Southerners have denied the facts and created self-serving mythologies. They have blamed outsiders and blamed "the Negro." They have hurled themselves into religion, craving innocence and absolution, and into the whiskey bottle, craving release and oblivion. All of these methods, it seemed to me, have a warping effect on reality and do little to prevent the buildup of pressure, which then expresses itself both in artistic creativity—Mississippi has produced more great writers and musicians per capita than any other state in America—and in blown psychological gaskets and erratic behavior.

The burden of history is made heavier because Southerners can't perform the sleight of mind that comes so easily to Americans in places such as LA and Orlando. They can't forget the past or pretend that history doesn't matter. They don't believe it's possible to make a fresh start with a clean slate. In 1951, William Faulkner famously wrote that the past is never dead. It's not even past. He also said that Southerners don't study their history, they absorb it.

During one of our wine-drinking sessions in the cemetery, Kerry Dicks made a similar observation: "The trouble with Natchez is that the dead won't die properly and let us get on with our lives. They just keep hanging around. They demand a seat at the table. They can't bear to be ignored, so we have to talk about them all the time. The worst thing is that they won't stop judging you. I don't believe in ghosts—at all—but I can feel it physically when my dead ancestors are embarrassed by my behavior."

Natchez, she thought, was being consumed by its past. "We

resurrected our history in order to sell tickets and make money from it, but it's more powerful than we are. It's like we resurrected a monster and now we can't control it. Sometimes it feels like progress is impossible, because the dead are running the show."

16

May 15, 1828. Having said goodbye to President Adams at the White House and made his plea for the liberty of his children and grandchildren—tormented by their enslavement, he finds it difficult to think of anything else—Ibrahima walks down Pennsylvania Avenue to the head office of the American Colonization Society. Located in the downstairs rooms of a brick building, and decorated with West African handicrafts, it is directly across the street from where he is staying.

The Society was founded in 1816 by a Presbyterian minister from New Jersey. Its mission is to encourage and enable the mass emigration of free blacks to the American colony in Liberia on the west coast of Africa. Away from the pernicious influence of American racism, they will be able to reach their full potential as human beings and also spread the gospel of Christianity in the dark continent. The Society's members include Northern abolitionists, guilty Southern slaveholders who want to free their slaves and send them "back home," unrepentant Southern slaveholders who think that free blacks are an outrage and a menace, and sympathetic allies of free blacks including the lawyer Francis Scott Key. He is also a poet, whose best-known work is "The Star-Spangled Banner."

Set to the tune of an eighteenth-century English drinking song, it will later be adopted as the national anthem.

It was Cyrus Griffin, the disabled attorney in Natchez, who first wrote to the Society and suggested that Ibrahima would make an ideal candidate for repatriation. The Society's leaders read his letter with great interest, and they have been following Ibrahima's progress in the newspapers. Meeting the aged Fulani prince in person, they are delighted to find him exactly as they were hoping. John Kennedy, the office manager, finds him "truly dignified in his deportment & manner," and "acute and intelligent on every subject." One of these subjects is African geography. When Kennedy shows Ibrahima a map and points out Cape Mesurado on the Liberian coast, where the colonists have founded the town of Monrovia, Ibrahima points to Timbo and states correctly that it is less than five hundred miles away.

Home is within his reach now, but the prospect of never seeing his children and grandchildren again is agonizing. If he goes back to Africa without them, he tells the Society's board of managers, he fears that he will die from misery, longing, and despair. He has heard nothing back from the White House, or from Henry Clay, who promised to help, so Francis Scott Key and two other men form a committee to find out what the government intends to do.

Henry Clay provides them an answer. The US government will pay for Ibrahima's passage to Africa and meet his expenses during his stay in Washington, but it will not buy his children and grandchildren out of slavery. The administration doesn't give its reasons, but they are obvious. Ibrahima is of no diplomatic value, and he is a political liability in an election year. President Adams is already under fire from the South for his antislavery views. If he were to spend taxpayers' money on the mass emancipation of Ibrahima's progeny, his opponents would seize on it gleefully and blow it up into a scandal. It would be a gift to his challenger Andrew Jackson, and the pro-Jackson newspapers.

Ibrahima absorbs this blow, which is powerful but not unexpected, and turns to his backup plan. He proposes a fundraising tour of Northern cities, to be arranged and publicized by the American Colonization Society. He can use his newfound fame, and the drawing power of his Moorish costume, to appeal for money to liberate his children and grandchildren, while simultaneously generating publicity for the Society and its colony in Liberia. The board approves this plan, and in the rush of enthusiasm and optimism, a number of thorny questions recede into the background. One of them is this: how much money will Thomas Foster require for thirteen people, in the unlikely event that he's willing to sell them?

The first fundraising event takes place at a vast panoramic painting of Niagara Falls, displayed in a rotunda near the White House. It is said to be such an accurate depiction of the natural marvel that viewers get wet, and now they will get to meet a genuine African prince as well. The Society promotes his appearance at "The Falls" with a special announcement:

> We are requested to state that Prince Abdraman [*sic*],
> of Timboo [*sic*], will attend, in Moorish costume, at the
> Panorama of the Falls of Niagara, today, from 10 o'clock
> A.M. 'til 6 P.M.—Where the public will have an opportunity
> of seeing this interesting Personage, who has been the subject
> of singular and extraordinary vicissitudes.

Admission is twenty-five cents, and the management has agreed to give Ibrahima half of the take. The prince who spent forty years as a slave is now a show-business novelty act. Sitting there for eight hours in his billowing white pantaloons, long blue jacket, and yellow boots, with a crescent on his turban, he signs autographs and astonishes many people—who ever heard of a literate African?—by writing out the opening sura of the Koran in elegantly formed Arabic.

He makes similar costumed appearances in private homes in Washington, and on Capitol Hill, where he is given the honor of attending committee meetings. Even the slaveholding Southern politicians are impressed by his courtly, dignified manners, and Congressman Edward Everett of Massachusetts later declares, "If there was ever a native-born gentleman on earth, he was one." Rather than collecting cash on the spot, which might appear grasping and tawdry, Ibrahima has a leatherbound "subscription book," in which donors write down the amount of money they wish to give, to be collected by the Society's agents at a later date. When Ibrahima presents Edward Everett with the subscription book, the congressman puts himself down for $5.

Then Ibrahima goes back to see President Adams with the subscription book in hand. Adams has been unable to supply taxpayers' money to free Ibrahima's children and grandchildren, but perhaps he will reach into his own pocket. It is the final meeting between the two men, and the president describes it briefly in his diary: "Abduhl Rahaman brought me a subscription book to raise a fund for purchasing the freedom of his five sons and his eight grandchildren, to which I declined subscribing." Adams doesn't say why he declined, but his office is besieged by petitioners every day, and he is probably tired of strangers asking him for favors.

Henry Clay is more amenable. Hearing of Ibrahima's fundraising tour of Northern cities, the secretary provides him with a short but valuable letter.

Washington, 5th June, 1828

The bearer hereof, Prince, is a Moor, reduced to captivity near a half century ago. The Executive of the United States, has obtained him from his master, with a view to restoring him to his friends and country.

He and his wife, Isabella, intend visiting some of the Northern Capitals of the United States.

I take pleasure in recommending him to the kind and friendly offices of all in whose company he may fall.

H.Clay

What Henry Clay has forgotten or decided to ignore, along with President Adams, the American Colonization Society, and possibly Ibrahima himself, is the terms of the agreement that the administration struck with Thomas Foster. It stated that Prince "should only enjoy liberty in his native country" and be transported there directly. Until Ibrahima and Isabella reach African soil, according to the agreement, they are still Foster's property.

Adams and Clay have already broken the agreement by allowing Ibrahima to remain in Washington as a free man and a public figure. This is precisely what Thomas Foster was determined to prevent—Prince gallivanting as a free Negro on American soil and stirring up trouble. Now, with his letter of recommendation, Clay has committed an even more flagrant breach of the agreement. When Thomas Foster hears about it, during Andrew Jackson's presidential campaign, he boils with rage and looks around for targets on which to unleash his vengeance.

17

During my rounds in Natchez, I would sometimes stop in to see William Terrell, the genial editor and publisher of the *Bluff City Post*, the local African American newspaper. It was a one-man operation with a ramshackle office on the edge of downtown. There was a front counter where Terrell accepted notices and advertisements, and decades of photographs and memorabilia stuck to the walls. He was a fine conversationalist and would talk to me about local news and politics, opinions in the black community, and African American history. One morning I asked him about the Deacons for Defense. I had been intrigued by the group ever since hearing about them on Jeremy Houston's tour.

The idea of black people arming themselves in clandestine paramilitary groups, and threatening to kill white people, ran so counter to the usual civil rights narrative of nonviolent protest and moral appeals to the American conscience. Yet it had proved extremely effective, not just in Natchez, but in other towns in the Deep South where the power of the Ku Klux Klan was a major obstacle to racial progress.

"The Klan had the bully mentality, and the Deacons understood that," said Terrell. "The best way to deal with a bully is to stand to up him, and if he's armed, you better be armed, too.

Easy to say that now, but it took a whole lot of courage for a black man down here in 1965, when the Klan was killing and torturing and bombing, and law enforcement was full of Klan and Klan sympathizers."

I asked him if it might be possible to interview any of the surviving Deacons.

"Hmm. The ones that are left are getting up in years. They took a vow of silence, to never talk about the Deacons to out-siders, but maybe enough time has passed now. I'll put the word out, but I can't make any promises."

Two days later my phone rang with an unrecognized number. I had met the caller briefly at Holy Family, a predominantly African American Catholic church. "You're interested in talking with one of the Deacons for Defense?" He gave me the name and number of James Stokes, who had been one of the leaders and organizers. I called Mr. Stokes immediately. He had trouble understanding my British accent, so I affected a white Missis-sippi drawl, which he understood perfectly. He said his health wasn't too good, and it was difficult for him to leave the house, so we agreed to meet there the following morning.

His small brick house was right around the corner from where the author Richard Wright had lived as a boy with his grandparents. The neighborhood was still struggling and poor. Harsh sunlight reflected off the broken glass in the weeds. A twelve-year-old circled on a bicycle, curious to see a white man in the neighborhood. I knocked on the front door. No response. I called his phone. No answer. I thumped on the door with a fist, then a flat palm, while shouting "Hello?" and feeling a sudden stab of dread that he might have died in the night.

The front door opened and a frail old man appeared. He was wearing a white shirt and gray slacks, with two or three days of white stubble on his dark skin. He wasn't expecting me. He seemed to have no memory of our telephone conversation the day before. Politeness got me through the door—his more than mine.

He sat down in a wheelchair and gestured for me to sit on the couch. A television was going loudly in another room. There were plastic flowers on the coffee table, porcelain leopards above the fireplace. A strip of flypaper hung down from the ceiling, covered with dead flies. "I thank God for every day I'm still here," he said. "I got both my knees operated on. It's cut down on my speed and standing time."

Once he started talking about the old days, he gained strength and energy. He was born in 1928. His father was a sharecropper on a plantation outside Natchez. Generations of his ancestors had worked the same land as slaves. "My mother raised thirteen head of children. The more children you had, the better your farm was." You had more mouths to feed, but you could farm more productively once the children were old enough to work.

When he was growing up in the 1930s, his family had no idea that the Great Depression was going on. It was just the same hard times and bitter racism as usual. He remembered a group of police officers and sheriff's deputies cutting off a man's penis and dragging him up and down the road for running a social club. "They was all Klan. They hated black folks like you wouldn't even believe. They cut off another man's penis and stuck it in his mouth. They would whip people with barbed wire." At seventeen he joined the US Army and went to Europe towards the end of World War II.

"I could sing pretty good, and I was assigned to the regimental choir. I enjoyed my stay in the army. I went to Rome, Naples, and Salzburg, Austria. I ate the best of foods and slept in the best of motels. It was an honor for me. I give the credit to the old, unlearned people who said, 'Whatever you do, stick close to God.'"

I asked if he saw any combat.

"No, I never did, but the Klan didn't know that and I wasn't about to tell them. They thought all the Deacons were combat veterans and sharpshooters, and that's exactly what we wanted them to think. The truth is that about forty percent of us were from the army. The rest were older men who could care less about living or dying and knew how to shoot from hunting. Most of us had been to jail. I wasn't afraid of anything, probably didn't have the sense."

"Why had so many gone to jail?"

"Ninety-nine percent of the people who were picked up on a Saturday night were black. The police and the judge were unlearned. They didn't know anything about the law. It was to get money out of you. You had to pay a fine. If you had a good-looking girlfriend or wife, the police department had men who would proposition her, so you could get out that way. After we organized the Deacons, a lot of that stuff ceased."

The main reason why they organized the Deacons for Defense and Justice was to protect civil rights workers and protesters and prevent more people from getting killed and maimed by the Klan. Natchez in 1965 was seething with violence and tension. Some senior FBI officials thought it was more likely than anywhere else in the country to explode into a full-blown race war. I asked James Stokes about this.

"We were ready to go to war. We had plenty of guns and ammunition, two-way radios, hand grenades. We spread the message that if any more blacks were killed, we would kill two whites to catch up."

When the Ku Klux Klan reorganized in western Mississippi and eastern Louisiana in the 1950s and 1960s, it succeeded in forming what some historians call a "Klan nation." The rule of law was so corrupted by Klan infiltration and intimidation that the whole region operated as a kind of rogue state outside the US Constitution.

Within this Klan nation, the most diabolical element was a secretive underground cell called the Silver Dollar Group, headquartered in Vidalia, Louisiana, right across the river from Natchez. Most of its members worked in the Natchez factories. They carried a silver dollar minted in the year of their birth and gave up their Klan robes for civilian clothes. They were frustrated with what they saw as a lack of aggression among the other local Klan chapters, even though Klansmen were burning down churches, beating civil rights workers, abducting suspected NAACP members and stripping them naked, whipping them like slaves, and forcing them to drink bottles of castor oil, a strong laxative. That wasn't enough for the Silver Dollar Group, which is credited with dozens of savage beatings and five murders in 1964 alone. They burned one man alive and killed another in a hail of bullets at a highway ambush. Two teenage boys were whipped and drowned in the Mississippi River.

Their territory covered several counties on both sides of the river, and nowhere else in the American South during the 1960s was there such a concentration of Klan atrocities. In August 1965, George Metcalfe, the leader of the NAACP in Natchez, was car-bombed. Investigators are certain that Red Glover, the leader of the Silver Dollar Group and an ex-navy explosives expert, was behind the crime, but he was never convicted. George Metcalfe survived with severe injuries, and the streets of black Natchez erupted in fury at the bombing. Hundreds of angry young men hurled bricks and bottles at police cars and threatened white motorists. Some were armed with pistols and rifles. James Stokes was in the thick of things, trying to stop white motorists from getting hurt, and trying to keep the white police from attacking the rioters.

He was part of a group of armed men who coalesced in the melee as a kind of security force. If the police started shooting, they decided, they would start shooting police officers. Like many working-class blacks in Natchez, they rejected the principle of nonviolence preached by the middle-class civil rights leaders. A new chant was forged in the streets that horrified those leaders: "We're going to kill for our freedom!"

With George Metcalfe in hospital, leadership of the local NAACP was taken over by Charles Evers, the brother of slain civil rights icon Medgar Evers. Charles was living in Chicago at the time of his brother's murder, working as a hustler, bootlegger, numbers runner, and, in his words, a "cathouse proprietor." He came back home to Mississippi and led the struggle in Natchez in his brother's honor. Coming from the streets, he instantly recognized the power of violent threat and used it as a bargaining chip while paying lip service to the nonviolent principles of the civil rights movement.

The day after the car bombing, a mass meeting was held in the black community and a list of demands was drawn up. It called for the immediate desegregation of all public facilities and institutions, more black police officers, a black representative on the school board, equal protection for blacks under the law, jobs for blacks at white-owned businesses, and a public denunciation of the Ku Klux Klan. They also demanded that city employees address them with the proper Southern courtesy titles, *Mr.*, *Mrs.*, and *Miss.*, instead of *uncle*, *auntie*, *hoss*, and *boy*. City officials rejected all the demands and called in the National Guard. Evers ramped up the boycott of white-owned stores. The Klan held a series of marches and rallies, burned crosses in city parks, and intimidated civil rights protesters.

Against this background, on September 10, 1965, James Stokes and a group of like-minded men gathered in the back of James Jackson's barbershop for the first meeting of the Natchez Deacons for Defense and Justice. They borrowed the concept and the name from the Deacons chapters in Louisiana, founded in the previous year, but they insisted on being independent because they didn't want to pay the $100 joining fee. James Jackson, the barber, led the meeting, which was filmed by a documentary filmmaker named Ed Pincus, who was in Natchez documenting the civil rights struggle. The resulting film, *Black Natchez*, is still widely available.

"I'm not doing this because I dislike white people," said Jackson in his barbershop. "I love white people . . . but when people is killing me off . . . the Ku Klux Klan—that's who I'm against completely. . . . It's time for us to do something."

"You may have to come into hand-to-hand combat with some of them white cats," said another man. "You may have to shoot somebody. It's as simple as that, man. . . .You know about the Klans. No one have to tell you about them. So you got to know the risk that you're taking."

They swore each other to secrecy, but apparently felt comfortable with Pincus filming it. They vowed to never tell their families that they were Deacons or to reveal anything under police interrogation. The most feared and despised police officer in the area was a Klansman named Frank DeLaughter, known by African Americans as Big Frank DeLaw. He stood six feet four and weighed 285 pounds. He handcuffed his black suspects to a chair, peppered them with racial obscenities, then went to work with a cattle prod, a fire hose, a leather strap, a torture device for snapping thumbs, and a derringer. These were the horrors that flew to mind when the Deacons talked about police interrogations.

"So if he puts his gun beside my head and say, 'I'm going to blow your damn brains out,' well, shit . . . just let him blow it out," said James Jackson.

They discussed the necessity for beating up "Uncle Toms" who were breaking the boycott of white-owned stores. "Flat out beat him with your bare hands. Okay? It's not but thirty-five dollars for fighting and disturbing the peace. You give him a good whupping, then we pay the thirty-five dollars." Another says, "And when I get him on the ground, I'll stomp him. And while he's down there, I'll tell him what it's for."

One recruit was put off by this talk: "I don't know if I can whup anybody as bad as you say. Stomping them and all that." That was okay. Delivering beatings to Uncle Toms wasn't mandatory.

Half a century later, in James Stokes's living room, I asked how many members there had been. He refused to tell me. He had broken his vow of silence, but he wouldn't break his vow to never reveal the number of members. I thought back to James Jackson, the militant barber, at that initial meeting: "Like, we know all the Klans, just about, right? The point is that they don't know who is a Deacon. That's the advantage, man. Like they may know two or three Deacons, but they don't know who else over there is a Deacon."

The Deacons were always armed, and they brandished their weapons openly. I asked Stokes how they got away with this. He smiled. "We organized a hunting club with badges and insignia and registered it with the city. That was our cover. There was a clause in our charter that we were authorized to carry guns. We were hunting alright, and once the Klan found out we were hunting them, they weren't visible like they used to be."

The Deacons would send men to spy on Klan meetings out in the country, Stokes said. They patrolled the black neighborhoods of Natchez, questioning white interlopers. They escorted and protected civil rights workers and enforced the boycott against white stores by stopping Uncle Toms who shopped there, throwing away their groceries, and sometimes "whupping on them a little." During marches and demonstrations, they wore their weapons openly and occasionally drew them and surrounded white troublemakers.

In September 1965, the city fathers got a court order passed, outlawing marches and picketing without a permit. Over the first weekend of October, nearly six hundred African Americans gathered in churches, intending to defy the order and march. Among them were James Stokes's wife and daughter. When they came out of the churches, they were all arrested, and three busloads were sent to Parchman, Mississippi's notorious state penitentiary. Most of them were in their late teens and early twenties. The youngest was a thirteen-year-old girl.

They were taken to the maximum security unit. The men were forced to strip naked. Women and girls were stripped of their coats and sweaters, but allowed to keep on their dresses and undergarments. As a kind of sniggering, sadistic joke, all the prisoners were forced to drink a large dose of laxatives and crammed into cells with only one toilet and hardly any toilet paper. The mattresses had been removed from the metal bunk beds, and there were no blankets. The cells were so cold that the prisoners were forced to lie on top of each other and huddle together to keep warm, but the laxatives and the lack of toilet paper—you can imagine their shame and misery, with the white guards pointing at them and cracking jokes: "Look at the monkeys in this cage."

They were kept for three to six days. Fire hoses were turned on them. None of them were charged with any crime, but James Stokes's wife, and many others, never recovered from the trauma of the experience. "She died from the affliction of some of that treatment," he said. Then he stared at the wall for a while.

In November 1965, Stokes was invited to go on a fundraising tour of California by Clifton Boxley, who was not yet Ser Seshsh Ab Heter-CM Boxley. "Going from Mississippi to California was like coming out of a dark room into the light," said Stokes. Speaking at churches and colleges, he requested contributions for radio equipment, uniforms, and cars, and kept quiet about the guns. He brought thousands of dollars home, which the Deacons spent mostly on pistols, .303 semiautomatics, and ammunition. "We'd get them in pawnshops," he said. "Those .303s would stop a car in a minute."

The nonviolent moderate black leadership was eclipsed in Natchez by Charles Evers and the Deacons. "To us, nonviolence was a sign of weakness and submission to the white man," said Stokes. "Nonviolence was letting the Klan whip on us, and police officers have our wives and girlfriends. It was our guns that changed everything. They were our protectors, and we kept them clean and oiled."

Nearly every other civil rights campaign in Mississippi ended in failure, requiring the federal government to step in, but on December 3, 1965, the city government and the white elite in

Natchez, feeling economic pain from the boycott, agreed to nearly all of the demands. The schools and hospitals and all city facilities would be integrated. More blacks would be hired by the city, and by white merchants. Improvements would be made to black neighborhoods. The white establishment did not agree to the courtesy titles, but promised to fire whites who used racially demeaning language.

Having won a historic victory in Natchez, Charles Evers and the Deacons took the campaign into the rest of southwest Mississippi. "The rest of the civil rights folks didn't like him, but Charles Evers was a great leader," said Stokes. "We'd be the security when he spoke in Fayette, in Woodville. If white people would spit on us, we'd get them out of the crowd and give them a good whupping. It was just beautiful. For the black folks out in the country, to see a black man give a white man a good whupping was a revelation. It helped them get over their fear."

Stokes said that the Deacons were fortunate that they never had to kill anyone. "The Klan got scared was the main reason. We would keep them guessing, keep them worrying. They never tried to confront us." Then he remembered that someone did get killed, another black man, Aaron Liberty, a part-time police officer in Woodville. "He was a Tom who would take news back to the whites, and he was harassing James Williams, a loyal man. One of my loyal Deacons killed him." Court records show that Leon Chambers was sentenced to life in Parchman for the murder, but Stokes said that a Deacon named Gable McDonald did the killing. After the case went to the US Supreme Court, charges were dropped against Leon Chambers, and McDonald, who confessed to the murder and later recanted his confession, was never prosecuted.

———

After 1965 there was no more violence from the mainstream Klan chapters, which were dissolving in acrimony and thoroughly penetrated by FBI informants. Only the Silver Dollar Group continued terrorist activities. Its leader, Red Glover, was furious that George Metcalfe had survived the car bombing, and he was stunned by the courage, determination, and victory of the civil rights activists, which did not fit his racial stereotypes at all. The first revenge target was a young activist and Deacon for Defense named David Whatley, who was attempting to become the first black student in the white high school in Ferriday, Louisiana. In January 1966, an explosion at his home in Ferriday failed to detonate a bundle of dynamite, and Whatley escaped with his life.

Glover admitted two new members into the Silver Dollar Group after they murdered Ben Chester White, a gentle, timid sixty-seven-year-old farmhand who was not involved in civil rights and always deferential to whites. His last words before he was riddled with bullets were "Oh, Lord, what did I do to deserve this?" Martin Luther King was marching to Jackson, Mississippi, at the time, and Claude Fuller, one of the gunmen, hoped that such a brutal murder of a completely innocent man would shock King into coming to Natchez, where the Klan could assassinate him. But King stayed away.

The following year, a massive explosion killed Wharlest Jackson, the former treasurer of the NAACP, who had just received a promotion at the Armstrong tire company, into a job traditionally held by white men. He was driving home from work in his truck. Pieces of his body flew for hundreds of yards. Red Glover was the FBI's prime suspect, but they lacked eyewitnesses and a convincing trail of evidence, so he wasn't prosecuted. The Silver Dollar Group became compromised by informants and ceased its activities in 1967. The fifty-two members included a core of fifteen murder suspects. Only one of them was ever convicted, decades later towards the end of his life. The rest walked free.

James Stokes, who ran a service station during the civil rights struggle, then a car dealership, became an associate minister at the Zion Hill #1 Baptist Church. I had read that the Deacons for Defense disbanded in 1967, but he said that wasn't true: "We never disbanded. We had a meeting on Thursday last week."

Memories of the civil rights era were vivid and powerful in the black community, and sometimes traumatic. James Stokes, and the other surviving Deacons, were often approached in public and thanked for their courage and achievements. In the white community, it was the complete opposite. The struggles, marches, and violence of the civil rights era were poorly understood and largely forgotten. I asked Regina Charboneau if she had heard anything about Klan violence or civil rights protesters getting hauled off to Parchman when she was growing up. "Absolutely not," she said. "My mother was pro–civil rights, but she kept us completely sheltered from the whole thing."

Then Regina told me about a dinner party she had attended in New York City in the 1980s. The conversation turned to civil rights and Mississippi. Regina announced to the table that it had been entirely peaceful in Natchez with no drama or conflict whatsoever, which is what she'd always heard from her family and the white community. After dinner, a former FBI agent and family friend took her aside and had a talk with her. Only then did Regina learn for the first time about the Klan murders and atrocities, the Klan infiltration of local law enforcement agencies, the protest marches, the boycott, and the Deacons for Defense.

In early 2015, as Natchez planned its tricentennial celebrations, Darrell White, the director of the African American museum, was invited to a meeting and asked how the black community would like to participate. "Black folks aren't interested," he said. "There's too much pain in those three hundred years, too many open wounds." They asked for an example and he cited the Parchman episode, when James Stokes's wife and daughter and at least 150 other would-be marchers were hauled off in buses and abused in the state penitentiary.

The committee members thought he was making the whole thing up. One prominent white citizen said, "No one in this town was ever sent to the penitentiary for walking down the sidewalk." Darrell White came back with a two-inch stack of the city arrest records, and three people who had gone through the ordeal. When they told the white mayor and the tricentennial commission what had happened, it came as a genuine shock, because white Natchez, with a few quiet exceptions, had erased the entire episode from its collective memory banks, just as it had erased the memory of the Forks of the Road slave market until Ser Boxley started his campaign. For a small, gossipy town obsessed with its past, Natchez could perform extraordinary feats of amnesia.

Hyde Carby, a young white lawyer, and a grandson of Miss Bettye Jenkins, took on the task of writing an apology from the city of Natchez to the victims of the Parchman Ordeal, as it became known. For inspiration, he read Martin Luther King's "Letter from Birmingham Jail" and listened to the Drive-By Truckers singing about the duality of pride and shame they felt as white Southerners. "I knew we had one chance to do this right, and it had to be as direct and unequivocal as possible," Carby said to me when I met him.

He wrote an extremely moving, eloquent apology that made no excuses. When the white mayor, Butch Brown, read it out in City Hall to the survivors of the ordeal, tears came rolling down their faces. "They never believed it would happen," said Darrell White. "Why would they? An apology like that has almost never happened in Mississippi before, and rarely in the rest of the country."

Now the city, led by the new mayor, Darryl Grennell, was erecting a monument to honor the survivors of the Parchman Ordeal, and others who were arrested for attempting to march. The "Proud to Take a Stand" monument, a black granite wall with the names of all the 439 people who were wrongfully arrested, will stand in the grounds of the city auditorium. "It's the first monument in Natchez that addresses a very traumatic, difficult, but ultimately victorious era in our history," said Mayor Grennell. "No tour of civil rights history in the Deep South will be complete without a visit to this site."

18

The hand that wielded a sword against the Bambara, a wretched hoe in Thomas Foster's fields, and in all probability a long rawhide whip as Foster's driver, now carries a leatherbound subscription book through the streets of Baltimore. This is the first stage of Ibrahima's fundraising tour with the American Colonization Society, and despite the best efforts of the local representatives, it is not going well. His costume is attracting less attention than usual, and money accumulates with disheartening slowness.

Baltimore is so profitably invested in the slave trade that the idea of donating money to buy people out of slavery seems wrongheaded, perhaps. Or maybe the plight of an old semi-freed slave in a Moorish costume is simply of no interest for most people in this business-minded city. After a week of soliciting, Ibrahima has only $420, and that includes everything he raised in Washington from the nation's ruling elite. It is less than half the purchase price for one of his sons, and he has thirteen children and grandchildren in bondage to Thomas Foster.

Ibrahima gives up on Baltimore and goes to Philadelphia, where the Society has many well-connected supporters. One of them assures him that raising $1,000 will be easy. Ibrahima is soon invited to the mayor's office, where he signs autographs for an audience and impresses a newspaperman with his fluent right-to-left Arabic script. On the Fourth of July, he delivers a speech at the Sixth Presbyterian Church on Spruce Street, and the minister gives him the proceeds of the collection plate.

Working the streets and coffeehouses with his subscription book, he finds himself in competition with other supplicants, including a man with a written claim that Indians cut out his tongue. Philadelphia is a pleasant city, clean and orderly, but its inhabitants are far less generous than he was promised. Six weeks in the City of Brotherly Love produces only $350.

Reaching Boston in August, he secures meetings with the editors of six different newspapers. He wants to win them over to his cause and also clear away any suspicions about his identity. The story of a captured prince returning home to Africa and soliciting donations has spawned a few imitators and impostors. A brazen college student assumed the name Abdullah Moham-med and traveled the Northeast claiming that he was kidnapped by pirates in Syria. He fooled a state governor and a professor of Eastern literature and enjoyed many free meals and places to stay before his ruse was unmasked. The self-styled "Almourad Ali" managed to collect $1,500 in the Northeastern states for his passage home to Turkey. Then it was discovered that his one and only home was in Albany, New York, where he was in trouble with the police.

Ibrahima has no trouble convincing the Boston editors that he is the genuine article, and they are impressed by his princely bearing and intelligence. They give him plenty of sympathetic newspaper coverage, with appeals to the generosity of their readers, but Ibrahima is struck down with fever on the day of his first appearance and unable to get out of bed. When he recovers, he makes an alteration to his costume. He discards the scimitar as unnecessary, replaces the white turban with a green fez, and ties a broad red sash around his waist. Walking up and down State Street with a long blue cape over his arm, he attracts considerable attention, including the raucous mockery of children.

Boston's Negro leaders, despite their opposition to the Society's mission of sending black Americans to Liberia, are delighted to meet an African prince. They throw him a parade and a banquet with hundreds of guests. Speaker after speaker praises Ibrahima, bemoans the cruelty of his fate, implores God's help in purchasing the freedom of his offspring, and vows that Southern slavery must be destroyed, with violence if necessary. Ibrahima applauds these fiery abolitionist speeches along with everyone else.

He has no idea that detailed descriptions of the banquet, the antislavery speeches, and his applause will reach Natchez. Nor does he know that Thomas Foster has been opening and reading all the letters Ibrahima has written, with the Society's help, to his children and grandchildren. Or that Cyrus Griffin, the disabled attorney, published an article that included a withering quote from Ibrahima about Natchez planters: "You no pray often enough—you greedy after money."

Thomas Foster is already furious with President Adams and Henry Clay for not sending Prince directly to Africa as promised. He's furious with Prince for gallivanting around the Northeast like a free man and promising liberty to his children and grandchildren. Then comes news of this radical Negro abolitionist banquet, and another letter from Prince, telling his children that the fundraising tour will now be extended to Providence, Hartford, New York, and points beyond, with no mention of a departure date for Africa. Prince also mentions a possible visit to Natchez, in which case Foster vows to re-enslave him.

A large portion of Foster's ire is directed at "Colonel" Andrew Marschalk, the rotund, many-chinned, blowhard newspaper editor who initiated the campaign for Ibrahima's freedom and promised Foster that his agreement would be honored. To preserve his own reputation and deflect Foster's wrath, Marschalk now reverses his support of Ibrahima.

He writes a 5,000-word handbill painting Ibrahima as a radical abolitionist who wants slaves to rise up and murder their masters, and he accuses the Adams-Clay administration of enabling and supporting this bloody agenda. And so Abd al-Rahman Ibrahima, who has been a prince, a slave, a show-business novelty act, and a costumed beggar, now becomes a tool in the 1828 presidential election campaign, in which proslavery Andrew Jackson is challenging antislavery John Quincy Adams.

Marschalk publishes 1,500 copies of his incendiary handbill, and it is widely copied and distributed by Jackson supporters in Mississippi and Louisiana. It begins by describing "a shameless violation of a written contract of Messrs. Adams and Clay with Mr. Thomas Foster of this state" and goes on to characterize Ibrahima as the "travelling emancipator" of the "emancipating Administration." Repeating some of the overheated rhetoric from the Boston banquet, Marschalk warns that it "will excite the Negroes in the southern states to rise and massacre [*sic*] their masters."

Marschalk is denounced as a shameless liar and troublemaker by the planter elite in Natchez, but downriver his handbill is taken seriously. In Louisiana, a newspaper editor describes Ibrahima as "a cruel and vindictive African tyrant, crafty, deceitful, proud, and ambitious" and repeats the claim that he is a "travelling emancipator" who has been plotting with John Quincy Adams to destroy slavery. The editor uses block capitals to emphasize the monstrousness of the conspiracy: COADJUTORS OF THE HOUSE OF TIMBO . . . TIMBO AND QUINCY! QUINCY AND TIMBO!

In the November election, Andrew Jackson carries Mississippi and Louisiana easily, helped a little by Marschalk's handbill, and beats Adams to become president-elect. Ibrahima continues his fundraising tour into 1829, but wisely decides to depart for Liberia before Jackson is inaugurated in March. In early February, he and Isabella make their way to Norfolk, Virginia, where the Society has chartered a ship to Liberia.

Despite raising $3,500 on his fundraising tour, neither Ibrahima nor the Society's agents are able to free any of his children or grandchildren because angry old Thomas Foster is now refusing to sell them at any price. Ibrahima's sons strike back at Foster, or so it appears, by sabotaging his cotton crop. Most of it is rejected by the buyer because the white fibers are so entangled with sticks, leaves, husks, and other debris.

| 19 |

Racial divisiveness, inherited from slavery and Jim Crow, was the ongoing curse of Natchez. The schools were divided, and the town was divided over the schools. The vast majority of white children went to fairly successful private schools, even if it bankrupted their parents to send them there. The vast majority of black children went to the public schools, which were rated F by the Mississippi Department of Education. Most African Americans resented the obvious racism of this separate and unequal school system, which put their children at an unfair disadvantage. They blamed whites for abandoning the public schools in the wake of court-ordered integration, and for not caring about the education of black children. Most whites, on the other hand, blamed black administrators and black social problems for ruining the once-thriving public schools.

The business community was divided. There was a white Chamber of Commerce and a black equivalent. The head of the white chamber, Debbie Hudson, had tried repeatedly to persuade her African American counterparts to amalgamate, but they weren't interested. There was too much history in the way. The African American mayor, Darryl Grennell, had campaigned on a platform of overcoming racial divisiveness to promote economic development. "We need to stop thinking about black and white and focus on the color green," he said in his speeches. His landslide victory indicated that most people in Natchez agreed with him and were willing to work together, but changing old habits and mindsets was proving difficult, especially in the political arena.

Grennell's attempts to bridge the racial divide were being torpedoed by Phillip West, the head of the school board, and Joyce Arceneaux-Mathis, a powerful alderwoman. Both were African Americans who had grown up in the 1960s and built their political careers on fighting for the black community against white racism and discrimination. They did not take kindly to Darryl Grennell's victory, and Arceneaux-Mathis went after him on his first day in office.

One of the incoming mayor's prerogatives has always been to pick the city attorney. Grennell chose a white man for the job, and Arceneaux-Mathis led the majority-black board of aldermen in voting down the mayor's pick for the first time in history. She nominated an African American attorney instead and told the local newspaper there could be no better choice. Unless skin color was the only consideration, this was obviously untrue. Her nominee had been city attorney when Natchez lost a judgment for failing to respond to a $1.8 million lawsuit by a court-ordered deadline—a clear case of ineptitude that had cost the city a lot of money. After a public outcry against her nominee, Grennell got his pick, casting the tiebreaker following a 3–3 vote.

Natchez has an unusually weak mayoral role in its city government, and this was also hampering Grennell's efforts. The mayor has no vote unless it's to break a tie on the board of aldermen (the term *alderpersons* has not caught on down here). Grennell had four African Americans on his board, and two whites, and most of the voting ran 4–2, relegating him to the sidelines. People had started talking about "Mayor Arceneaux" because Joyce was calling the shots, and she seemed to have it in for Darryl.

I would stop in periodically at City Hall to interview Grennell, an even-tempered former microbiology professor with a penchant for quoting the poet Robert Frost. Handsome, bald, and light skinned, he worked out at the gym every morning with impressive results. He wore tight-fitting shirts and suits, and when he rolled up his sleeves, you could see brightly colored tattoos of orb-weaving spiders and tropical flowers. His body language was confident and masculine, and when he rested his jaw on his fist, or leaned forward in his chair to make a point with an outstretched hand, or hooked one leg across the opposing knee, it looked slightly exaggerated and actorly. You got the feeling that his muscles yearned to flex and bulge.

"The gym is a stress release," he said, when I asked him about his political frustrations. "So is baking. I love to bake, and I give everything I bake to other people. I also enjoy frogging [hunting frogs], and going fishing. And believe it or not, I crochet, which is a great stress release."

He wanted to end the racial divisiveness because he thought it was the only logical solution to the city's problems, and the right thing to do, but he was also influenced by his family tree. Among his forbears were two prominent white men who had recognized their mixed-race children, and a white tax collector who married his black mistress. "I think of my white ancestors and relatives as part of my extended family because those were loving relationships. But I don't think of myself as biracial or mixed, because I was raised all the way black."

His father was a prominent civil rights activist who formed an organization called the Black Dot Club. "They had small black dots tattooed on their chests, and their job was to transport civil rights workers in and out of dangerous situations, including John Lewis, who is now a US congressman. My mom was pregnant with me when she was put on a bus, hauled off to Parchman, and abused by the prison guards."

That was one reason why he had led the campaign for a monument to honor the survivors of the Parchman Ordeal. Darryl was proudly African American and he revered the civil rights movement, but unlike Ser Boxley, Phillip West, and Joyce Arceneaux-Mathis, to name three locally prominent examples, he didn't resent white people for all the terrible things they had done in the past, and for the continuing racism in large swaths of the white community. Instead he took heart that race relations had come so far, without denying there was still a long way to go.

Darryl was the first gay black mayor in Mississippi, and one of the first in the nation, but he never presented himself that way or claimed that he had made history. He didn't want to be defined by his race or his sexuality, believing that character and accomplishments were far more important. He openly acknowledged that he was gay, and planned to marry his partner, but he didn't make a big deal about it. Most people in laissez-faire Natchez didn't think it was a big deal either, although he had caught some criticism from conservative African American church ministers and their followers.

On the wall of his office, near the portrait of Ibrahima, was a framed first edition of *Horton Hears a Who!* by Dr. Seuss. Darryl found the book's message of everyone coming together to save a community to be inspiring and politically relevant. I asked him why he thought Joyce Arceneaux-Mathis was so antagonistic towards him. Was it personal? A story was going around town that she had called him a "yellow motherfucker" to his face during a black caucus meeting at her house, referring to his light skin tone after she'd drunk a few glasses of gin. He had no comment on that alleged incident. "I really don't know what she's got against me."

He thought it was possible that she didn't like him because he was light skinned and gay, and equally possible that she disagreed with his efforts to move Natchez beyond race-based politics. "The problem with divisiveness is that it doesn't lead to prosperity. It holds us back. We use up all our energy fighting over a pie that is getting smaller and smaller as our population and tax base declines. Trent Lott [former US senator from Mississippi] used to say that Natchez is the best-kept secret in America. I want to make it a treasure for the whole country to enjoy. To do that, we've got to tear down these walls of division, and I'm optimistic that we can do it."

He was pleased to see whites and African Americans working together on a $25 million plan to develop downtown and attract more tourists, even though other African Americans thought it was yet another boost for the rich white part of the town. Darryl was also encouraged by the conversations about racial healing that were taking place in Natchez, his electoral victory, and his religious faith. "I've asked God for guidance. Things will happen when He wants it."

———————

One of Darryl Grennell's biggest supporters during his election campaign was Greg Iles, the bestselling thriller writer and the most famous person in Natchez. He had just published the final installment of an epic 2,300-page trilogy about race, corruption, and murder in Natchez and Louisiana; all three books reached number one on the *New York Times* bestseller list and were being published in thirty-five countries. When he returned from his book tour, Iles invited me to his secluded country house to talk about politics and race relations in his hometown, and what he described as the "broken school system" that was imperiling its future.

Driving through the woods outside Natchez, I reviewed what I knew about Greg Iles. He was almost entirely nocturnal and had lost a leg in a recent car accident. He played guitar in a charity rock band with Stephen King and other bestselling authors. Some people in Natchez criticized him for being arrogant, but most people seemed to like and respect him, even if they disagreed with his outspoken liberal politics. It was obvious from reading the *Natchez Burning* trilogy that he was a true master of the page-turning thriller, and that he had thought deeply about the stubborn complexities of race in the South, where slavery had bound two peoples together in mutual antagonism and dependence, and the contradictions in that original relationship had never been resolved.

Reaching the entrance gates, I punched in a security code. The gates swung open and a smooth, winding road led me through forty acres of grounds to a large impressive house, just shy of a mansion and built long after the Civil War. Greg Iles, tall, in his late fifties, with reddish hair, opened the front door in jeans and a T-shirt. He had a neatly trimmed beard, black-framed glasses, and an engaging grin. "Come on in, man. I'll tell you what I can. Natchez is a complicated little place with a lot of problems."

I followed him into the kitchen. He was limping only slightly on his prosthetic leg and seemed full of energy and good cheer. He introduced me to his second wife, Caroline, who was considerably younger than him and pregnant with their first child. She gave a strong impression of being kind, intelligent, and down-to-earth. We all chatted for a while and ate from a cheese platter, then Greg led me down into his basement recording studio and writing room. It was a bunker, a masculine command center where day and night were banished, and he would write in a kind of manic fugue state for twenty hours or more at a stretch, sometimes thirty-six hours straight without sleep. There was a rack of expensive guitars and a fridge full of Tab sodas and Heinekens. I asked him about growing up in Natchez—when did he first become aware of race and racism?

"I don't know how aware I was of the racism, but when I was five years old, there was a massive Klan rally a mile from my family's house." This was in October 1965 at Liberty Park in Natchez. Klansmen came from all over the South, and the press estimated that 3,700 people were present. "My dad walked me down there because he believed in witnessing historic events. There were thousands of people and it was chaos, and here's what I remember. Not only the Klan robes on the men, women, and children. What is seared indelibly on my mind is the horses wearing robes. You talk about something scary. You see the horses in these ghost robes, and the men hollering, and the guns, and holy shit, man, I was five years old!"

His parents grew up dirt-poor in rural Louisiana, but they didn't have the deep, implacable racism that is so common among impoverished whites in the Deep South, and so necessary to their pride and self-respect. They met at a small Louisiana college, where they both excelled academically. Then his father became an army doctor and they were stationed in Germany, where Greg was born.

"That was a blessing. These two Southern people who had

grown up in a very insular way got exposed to Europeans, Yankees, people from all over America who were in the army. They traveled as much they could—Italy, Paris. But what impressed them the most was the aftermath of the Second World War, and the awareness of the Holocaust. When they came back to the South and moved to Natchez, and the civil rights movement started to happen, my father looked at it in exactly the same way as he looked at the situation of the Jews in Germany. He was in complete sympathy. So was my mother."

Greg's father treated more black patients than any other white doctor in Natchez, often without payment. He also treated a lot of Klansmen and kept his views to himself. He was the first white doctor in Natchez to hire an African American nurse and desegregate his waiting room, but it always weighed on him that he didn't do more. "He was afraid of his family being ostracized or run out of town," Greg said. "It was a legitimate concern in those days."

Growing up in Mississippi in the aftermath of Jim Crow was similar to growing up in post-apartheid South Africa. The legal architecture of segregation and white supremacy was gone after a long, bitter struggle, and the children of both races were now feeling their way into an uncertain new reality that they were also shaping. One of Greg's most powerful childhood memories, right behind the Klan rally, comes from his elementary school after desegregation, when the first three or four black students were admitted and the white students ostracized them. "I will never forget seeing those kids, standing alone, out on the playground, completely isolated. That is a kind of violence to a kid, and you could see so clearly what they were going through. It was a brave thing of their parents to put them in there, and black parents and kids had everything to gain, but, man, those kids have stuck with me my whole life."

In the following years, more and more black children started entering the Natchez public schools, and more black teachers started teaching, until a racial tipping point was reached that caused whites to flee into the private schools. "It happened all over the South," Greg said. "You had people who did it for the knee-jerk reason that they just didn't want their kids going to school with black kids. Then you had people like my dad, who really wanted it to work, but saw the educational standards slipping. If you fill up a school with kids who've had an inferior education to date, you have to teach at the pace of the slowest kids. And some of those black teachers really weren't qualified for the job."

When he was in fourth grade, Greg Iles came home one afternoon and told his parents that his black teacher had misspelled something on the board and he had corrected her. He thought it was a funny story, but when his parents heard it, they yanked him out and put him in a private Episcopal school. "It's a sad story, and I don't like relating it. But it's that anecdotal stuff that affects people's decisions."

I had assumed that the white flight from the public schools happened all at once, but he said there was an intermediate phase in the 1970s and 1980s that many Natchezians, black and white, remembered with pride and nostalgia. In that era, one public high school, North Natchez, was entirely black, and the other, South Natchez, was racially mixed and majority white with better facilities. According to Iles, "Both schools were powerhouse athletic schools statewide, and they both gave a pretty damn good education, by Mississippi standards I should stress."

In 1989, Phillip West, now the head of the school board, led a lawsuit to shut down North Natchez and make South Natchez the single high school for everybody. Greg Iles thought Phillip West was an embittered, self-serving demagogue with the same disregard for factual truth as Donald Trump. But he had to admit that West and the other plaintiffs, "from a moral, philosophical, and ethical perspective," had been entirely justified with that lawsuit.

The problem, as Greg saw it, was the result of that lawsuit. "As soon as they won it, many, many more whites left for private schools. South Natchez became predominantly black. I think it's ninety-five percent now. The football team fell apart, and academically it became one of the worst schools in America. It doesn't get any worse than an F rating in Mississippi. If you're looking at this from the outside as a moral experiment, the lawsuit was obviously the right thing to do. But if you live here, and you want to put your kids in that system, you go, 'Well, what was the point of that? You destroyed public education in Natchez.'"

Faced with the choice of paying private fees or sending their children to a failing school, many parents, black and white, were choosing instead to leave Natchez and move somewhere with decent public schools. It was one of the major reasons why the population was shrinking—Adams County had lost 17 percent of its people since 1980—and it also made it difficult to attract new businesses to the area. Greg Iles, who sent his children to a private school, had tried to lead a movement of whites back into the public schools, but it had gotten nowhere, even with his most ardently liberal friends. Again, it was the anecdotal stuff. "I can show you a video on my phone of a brawl at that school, right out in the open. It's mostly girls hitting each other and ripping hair, no adults within sight for at least two minutes, just an out-and-out brawl. My friend is just not going to put his daughter into that situation."

In the last few weeks, the simmering racial tension over the schools had boiled over into open conflict. Led by Phillip West, the Natchez–Adams County school board had tried to convince the voters to pass a $35 million bond for a new Natchez high school because the old building was in disrepair. The bond issue had been defeated, with the vote split on racial lines. Now there were demonstrators in the streets, lawsuits flying, threats of a boycott from the black community, explosive accusations on both sides.

The racial divide was swiftly turning into a chasm, and Greg Iles was concerned that racial violence could break out for the first time since the 1960s. Needless to say, most people in Natchez owned guns, including Iles, who has a large collection. It's one of Mississippi's defining characteristics: even the liberals are armed to the teeth.

For most people in the African American community, it was glaringly obvious why whites hadn't voted in favor of the $35 million school bond. Their children were in private schools. They didn't want to pay more taxes to improve a school that was over 90 percent black because they didn't care about black children. Darrell White, the director of the African American museum, spoke about white voters with a look of deep disgust on his face.

"One hundred dollars a year was the average property tax increase," he said, smoking a cigarette outside the museum. "You pay money so your children don't go to school with ours, and you won't pay a hundred dollars a year so our children can have a better school? You're not going to invest because we still have a segregated school system that benefits and rewards whites. And then you get mad when some of us point out that this is racist. You start screaming and hollering, 'How dare you call me a racist?'" He shook his head and ground out his cigarette butt with his heel.

For most people in the white community, it was glaringly obvious that a new building wasn't going to fix the public education system, which was spending almost twice as much money per student as the private schools, and achieving far worse results. I interviewed a white teacher named Mary Ann Blough, who had taught in the public schools. She said that socioeconomic problems in the black community posed a major challenge for educators; Phillip West and other school board members often made the same point.

She singled out drug-addicted babies, fetal alcohol syndrome, malnourishment, and the many children who couch-surfed between various relatives. These were heartbreaking challenges, but she claimed that school administrators made no real effort to tackle them. "The people in charge blame the whites, blame the parents, blame the teachers, blame the students, and now they're blaming the buildings. The facilities are run-down because they haven't maintained them properly. They say there's no money for maintenance, but they spend a fortune on hiring consultant after consultant. Oh my God, so many consultants when we didn't have any textbooks or paper."

After the $35 million bond issue was voted down, the Natchez–Adams County school board, which had already spent $360,000 on architect fees for the new high school, basically ignored the result of the vote. In a special meeting announced only three and a half hours before it started, the board members voted to borrow $9 million to fund school construction and renovation and use their power to raise taxes in order to pay for it. They also approved another $25 million to be raised in the future.

Kevin Wilson, a white business owner with several properties in town, estimated that his taxes would increase by $20,000 a year. At the next school board meeting, he presented a petition with 3,338 signatures, calling for the $9 million loan to be put on a public ballot, so the voters could decide if they wanted it or not. The petition did not meet the legal requirement to overturn the board's vote, so the board ignored it.

Phillip West then read out a statement saying that the opponents of the school board "do not care about the education of the children who attend public schools" because they had the same shameful mindset as whites fifty years ago, whereupon the meeting degenerated into an angry shouting match, with West hurling accusations of racism, and white people yelling back at him. Someone shouted that West didn't care about taxpayers' bills. He shouted back, "You weren't concerned about the bills when I wasn't allowed to go into the schools, when I was paying taxes. Don't give me that BS."

After West shouted down a middle-aged white woman, her son walked up to him and said, "I'll drag your ass outside." West kept ranting and pointing his finger as other board members tried to calm him down. Having called the white people racists, he then delivered a lower parting blow: "I'm a Christian, and evidently most of them are not." The police were called, a fuming West was led out of the room by other board members, and the meeting was adjourned.

Following this debacle, Kevin Wilson sued the school board. Phillip West filed assault charges over the "drag your ass outside" threat, denounced Wilson's lawsuit as racist, and went on another angry televised rant about white people at an NAACP meeting. At the next school board meeting, white protesters picketed the building and held up signs: OUR SCHOOL BOARD IS SNEAKY, WEST IS THE WRONG DIRECTION, and MR. WEST, I'M NOT RACIST. They received some encouraging honks and thumbs-ups from white drivers, and some rude hand gestures and race-based obscenities from black motorists.

One of Kevin Wilson's businesses was vandalized. Someone beat on the door of his stepson's house at three in the morning, and then drove away. A white couple, John and Marcia McCullough, started a campaign to get the state education department to declare a state of emergency, take over the failing school district, and fire all the school board members. Concerned about violent reprisals, the McCulloughs kept loaded weapons close to hand.

State takeovers of predominantly African American school districts happened with depressing regularity in Mississippi and nearly always followed the same pattern. After the whites left for private schools, or other school districts, educational standards declined as the influence of multigenerational poverty asserted itself, and payrolls became bloated from extravagant and often nepotistic hiring practices. The superintendent of one school district in the Mississippi Delta was found to have thirty-six relatives on the payroll, many of whom were collecting their paychecks without setting foot on school property. In poor African American communities with hardly any economic opportunities, the school system was primarily seen as a source of employment, and the more jobs it could furnish the better.

Judging from payroll documents obtained through a Freedom of Information request, the Natchez–Adams County school district was functioning more like a patronage system than a normal American educational system. The district had over 700 staff, including teachers, for approximately 3,400 students—or one employee for every 4.9 students. There were 70 administrators, not including principals and assistant principals, for those 3,400 students. A typical American school district has about 50 administrators for 20,000 students.

F-rated Natchez High, with 700 students, had four principals and four assistant principals, all making between $50,000 and $82,000 a year plus benefits. By contrast, the A-rated public high school in Tupelo, Mississippi, with 2,100 students, had just one principal, working with one assistant principal. My repeated requests to interview Phillip West and the other school board members were denied, so I don't know how they would justify these hiring practices. In one public meeting, West said they needed more personnel, not less, because the district had so many impoverished couch-surfing children.

The argument that whites didn't care about the public schools in Natchez because their children were in private schools obviously had some validity, but it was strongly disputed by some of the white people I talked to. Greg Iles, a liberal Democrat, and John McCullough, a conservative Republican, saw the issue in exactly the same way. In McCullough's summary, "Any white person who doesn't care about the public schools is a fool. The whole future of this town depends on fixing the public schools, so we can stop our population decline and attract new families and businesses. If we can't fix the schools, I'm afraid we're going to lose the town."

———

Mayor Grennell hated to see the town so angrily divided over the schools. It was the opposite of what his election was supposed to achieve. "It's frustrating, but there's nothing I can do about it. I don't have any power over the school board, and there's no changing their minds, so I don't let it stress me. I focus on the positive and put my trust in God."

There were some positive developments. A biracial group of prominent citizens, including Phillip West, was meeting once a week in private to talk about the schools and the divisions in the community. At the meeting I attended, West kept ranting and raving, but a timetable for progress was nonetheless hashed out with his agreement. A new organization, Natchez United, had formed with the goal of fostering racial unity and helping the public schools. Its leader, Dr. Marvin Jeter, was a white educator with an impressive track record of turning around failing schools in poor communities, both in Mississippi and Oklahoma. He had swept-back blond hair and was wearing an open-necked pink shirt with a gold chain when I met him for lunch at Cotton Alley Café on Main Street.

"People are stuck looking at this as a black and white issue, when they should be asking, 'How can our kids succeed in school?'" he said. "And it's really very simple. It's not part of the human condition to want to fail. If children know for an absolute fact that you have faith in them, that you genuinely care about them, and you're not going to quit on them, they will succeed in school. And if they doubt any of that, they will look for a way to succeed on the streets instead."

Dr. Jeter had a PhD in education administration, and a ten-page résumé of high-ranking education jobs. He had learned that having faith in the students was the secret to turning a school around, but he believed another kind of faith was even more important. "The first thing we need to do is bring God back into the community," he said, as if Natchez, a town of 15,000 people with 111 churches, was a wasteland of atheists and backsliders. "Only He can heal the deep wounds here. Unless the faith-based community comes together, anything we do will be a Band-Aid and the wounds will continue to bleed out. We're working with Bishop Stanley Searcy, an African American minister that I know from Oral Roberts University. I'm praying Phillip West will join us, too."

Another faith-based group working on racial reconciliation was Mission Mississippi, a statewide organization founded by an African American minister in 1993. It provided a forum for black and white Christians to meet regularly, talk about race as openly and honestly as possible, and form biracial friendships while simultaneously strengthening their religious devotion. Beverly Adams, Ibrahima and Isabella's descendant, was a member, but lately she had been struggling to retain her hope.

"I believe in what we do at Mission Mississippi, but it's hard work and slow going, and I'm concerned that we're not having much impact on the community. Even on a personal level, it's difficult." Through the organization, she had formed a solid friendship with Helen Smith, a powerful figure in the Natchez Garden Club who lived in an antebellum home called Texada. Beverly had received there in a hoopskirt a few times, which had raised more than a few eyebrows among her African American friends, colleagues, and family members.

"The other day Helen invited me to a party, and we're encouraged to socialize in each other's communities, so I went. I didn't feel uncomfortable at the time, although I was aware that I was the only black person at the party, except for the men parking the cars, and the women working in the kitchen and serving the food. It was afterwards that it really hit me, and I started to feel really uncomfortable. Have you seen the movie *Get Out*? It was like that, just a whole lot of white people trying to be cool with the black person in the room, and it was just . . . I don't know. I wished I hadn't gone."

Mission Mississippi also encouraged its members to attend each other's churches, but it was proving difficult to do. This was the main topic on the agenda at the first Mission Mississippi meeting I attended. "There's a difference in church culture," Beverly said to a group of thirty people. "We clap and shout and say, 'Mm-hmm,' and it gets loud when the preacher and the musicians are going all out. We can see white people trying to get with it, but they're uncomfortable, and we're uncomfortable in white church because it's so quiet, and we're thinking, 'What's wrong? Where's the spirit?'" She suggested a new initiative: they should go as a group into each other's churches one Sunday a month and arrange for pulpit swaps with black preachers in white churches, and vice versa. The idea was well received and plans were laid.

It seemed to me as an outsider, raised in secular, multicultural London, that these earnest faith-based initiatives fostered healthy discussions and could only do good in a place where religiosity was so strong. But they also revealed how deeply divded the town really was, and how difficult it was to see things from the other group's point of view. In the fight over the schools, for example, two sides were immovable in their clashing opinions. Almost no whites believed that a new school building would fix the public education system. Nearly all blacks thought their children deserved a school building that wasn't falling apart, and that it was racist to think otherwise.

Another example was Mammy's Cupboard. Mission Mississippi had held a discussion about the towering Aunt Jemima–themed restaurant and pie shop on Highway 61. I didn't attend that meeting, but heard about it from Kathleen Bond, a superintendent in the National Park Service and Mission Mississippi member. "Most whites at the meeting did find Mammy offensive, or at least problematic, but one woman saw it as a complimentary representation of African American cooking talents and hospitality, and another found it quaint," Kathleen told me.

Two African American women bluntly explained to the group what Mammy's Cupboard represented to them: enslaved servitude was the proper role for a black woman, and everybody had easy access to what was under her skirt. One of these women would always try to distract her children when she had to drive past Mammy's, in the hope of averting angry scenes in the car. That was something the white people hadn't considered. No structure in town was capable of enraging their children in the same way.

Beverly Adams accepted that change was hard for people, but she felt discouraged by the younger generations, who didn't seem interested in making the effort. "These younger whites think racism has nothing to do with them. They say, 'I never owned slaves. I don't hate black people. Y'all need to get over this stuff.' They don't get it at all, what it's like on our side. And the younger blacks don't believe it will ever change. They think this is the way it will always be."

20

Ibrahima and Isabella are the last passengers to board the *Harriet*, a handsome 275-ton ship anchored near Norfolk, Virginia, and chartered by the American Colonization Society for passage to Liberia. Already aboard and eager to depart are 150 free black colonists, described by a visiting journalist as "very orderly and decent people. . . . Many of them, except for the color of their skins, would have been valued members of society in the United States." Over half of them are literate, most are skilled in various trades, and all are Christians. Part of their mission in Africa is to civilize the natives by spreading the gospel. Several ministers with the Society have made strenuous efforts to convert Ibrahima to Christianity, and while he has listened politely, his faith in Islam has never wavered. It is something that he will bring back to Africa intact.

On February 7, 1829, the *Harriet* casts off from her moorings and rides the cold wind into the open ocean. Ibrahima and Isabella are free from the land of their enslavement, yet slipping even further away from their children and grandchildren. They still hope to see them again, reasoning that Thomas Foster is old and his heirs will sell if the price is right. Ibrahima has left the $3,500 from his fundraising tour with the Society for this purpose, and he yearns for the day when his American family will be reunited in the kingdom of his forefathers.

The smell of the Atlantic Ocean, the pitching and rolling, the flapping sails and creaking timbers, evoke memories of the cramped horror voyage on the *Africa* forty years ago. But this time he is a guest of the US government with a handwritten passport from Henry Clay, and he and Isabella are berthed in a comfortable stateroom. While he was in New York, Ibrahima sent a letter in Arabic to his brother in Futa Jalon, saying that the good people of America have liberated him from slavery, and that he will be returning home shortly. What an astonishment this letter will cause in Timbo, from someone long since given up for dead.

Ibrahima has no plans to claim the throne, resume military command, or take any part in governing his country. Instead he intends to establish himself as a trader between Futa Jalon and the colony in Liberia. For thousands of years, bound captives have marched in misery along the trade routes of West Africa, but Ibrahima's experiences have convinced him to disavow the trafficking of human beings. One of the most challenging tasks he has set himself, upon his return to Futa Jalon, is to convince his relatives and countrymen to give up this lucrative trade, which is a key source of guns and gunpowder.

After thirty-seven days at sea, with favorable winds and all passengers in good health, land is sighted. Cape Mesurado, on the Liberian coast, comes into focus as a narrow strip of beach and a broad band of lush green vegetation. For Ibrahima, this is a homecoming. But the great majority of the colonists were born in the United States, and many of them are shocked by the naked Kru boatmen who paddle out to meet the *Harriet*. The African

American colonists will also be surprised to learn that the Kru refer to them as "white people." *

Disembarking at the port of Monrovia, the capital of Liberia, their eyes are comforted by more familiar sights. The town has a hundred houses built in the Anglo-American style, a church, a library, and a jail, which contains a miscreant Englishman who tried to escape his debts. Hundreds of colonists come down to the docks to greet them, with the women in formal dresses and men wearing frock coats and top hats. The Society's agent in charge is a white American named Dr. Richard Randall, a former army surgeon who Ibrahima met in New York and entrusted with the letter to his brother.

Dr. Randall, who is suffering the after-effects of a fever and finding it difficult to walk, tells Ibrahima that he sent the letter with a Mandinka messenger to Timbo, and is still waiting for a reply. Ibrahima immediately writes a second letter and sends it via Freetown, Sierra Leone, which has good connections with Futa Jalon, and Dr. Randall sends news of his arrival up the rivers.

The Society provided Ibrahima and Isabella with a house frame, but when it's unloaded from the *Harriet*, another colonist insists that he paid for it and refuses to let it go. A promised keg of nails also fails to arrive. This leaves the elderly couple facing the torrential downpours and chilly nights of the rainy season in a flimsy bamboo shelter, with no prospect of building a house. A far more serious oversight concerns a letter that fails to arrive in

---

* In pockets of the colony, some of the African Americans establish large plantations and build Greek Revival mansions, which they fill with African servants. Some whiten their faces with powders, to further emulate Southern slaveholders, and impose forced labor and indentured servitude on the indigenous Africans. Even in the 1940s, their descendants wear hoopskirts and top hats to formal occasions.

the *Harriet's* mailbag. Written by the Society's board, the letter said that Ibrahima and the other new arrivals should be immediately moved to Millsburg, an inland town with a much healthier climate than fever-ridden Monrovia.

Within a week of landing, one of the *Harriet's* passengers is dead. All the crew members fall sick, and one dies. Within a month, seven more colonists are dead. Then the fever claims Dr. Randall. Within a few months, thirty of the new arrivals are dead. Ibrahima falls sick too, but recovers. He gets a letter written to New York warning that Monrovia is a death trap, and he makes plans to depart for Timbo as soon as the rainy season is over. Dr. Randall's replacement has agreed to spend $500 on supplies for the journey. All the arrangements are in place.

As soon as he reached African soil, Ibrahima began praying to Mecca five times a day, and following all the prescriptions and commands of the Koran. Now he starts reading and writing in Arabic again, and manuscripts pile up in the bamboo shelter during this grim season of rain and funerals. He also plans out his business enterprise. Most of the trade with Futa Jalon goes through Freetown in Sierra Leone, but with his royal connections in Timbo, and goods from his merchant friends in New York, Ibrahima feels confident that he can steer a good portion of the trade further south through Liberia. He can make a handsome profit by supplying his people with guns, powder, tobacco, linen, sugar, combs, knives, and other goods. In return, he can get ivory and gold from Futa Jalon and export it to America with palm oil and rice produced in Liberia.

Sometime in late June, with the rain lashing the bamboo walls, torrents rushing through the streets, and more people dying of fever, Ibrahima contracts diarrhea. He thinks nothing of it, but it takes hold and weakens his entire system. By the time he calls the doctor, it is too late, and Ibrahima knows it. One of his final requests is for his manuscripts to be sent to Timbo.

It is tragic that he comes so close to returning home, and as the life drains out of him, he must wonder what on earth will become of Isabella, marooned in a sickly outpost on an unfamiliar continent, without her husband, children, and grandchildren. On July 6, 1829, at the age of sixty-seven, Prince Abd al-Rahman Ibrahima dies in Monrovia with Isabella at his bedside.

21

Even in the garden clubs, which most African Americans regarded as bastions of white supremacy, some people were trying to bridge the racial divide and work towards reconciliation. Regina Charboneau was determined to racially integrate the Pilgrimage Garden Club, even though she could think of nothing more horrifying to its founders. It would be a historic moment for the city, a landmark of racial progress, and a personal coup. She thought the PGC board was ready for black members, and if some women in the rank and file couldn't handle it and defected to the other club, then that was where they belonged.

Regina was convinced that the Natchez Garden Club was more racist and more attached to Confederate trappings than the PGC. "But they're not all racists," she clarified. Chesney Doyle, the Tableaux director, was one obvious exception. Another was Helen Smith, Beverly Adams's friend from Mission Mississippi. Regina was now hearing rumors that Helen was attempting to integrate the Natchez Garden Club, and while Regina didn't think that was possible, it added a step of urgency to her own efforts.

I went to see Helen Smith to see if the rumors were true. A tall woman with an open, direct manner, she had lived in Iran, Scotland, and Dallas with her oil-business husband, before coming home to Natchez and moving into Texada, which her parents had restored in the 1960s. The house was built circa 1798 and had once been used as the capitol of Mississippi. Duncan Morgan had removed the worn exterior bricks from their crumbling mortar, turned them all around, and reset them in new mortar that precisely matched the faded original.

Helen sat me down with a cup of coffee in the front room. "The racism I saw growing up here, and the alcoholism, were the two main reasons why I left for so long. When I came back, I knew there had been progress. There was a doctor on one of the committees I joined, and he was black, and no one talked about 'that nice black doctor.' I thought to myself, 'I can live in this place now. No one is talking about what a nice black man he is.'" That doctor was Rod Givens, one of Greg Iles's best friends. A few years before, the Pilgrimage Garden Club had invited Dr. Givens's wife to become a member, but she had declined, and that ended the first attempt at racial integration among the Natchez garden clubs.

Helen wanted to reach a point in Natchez, then in Mississippi and the nation at large, where people no longer use race as the primary identifier. "That's the end goal of my work in Mission Mississippi, my actions and my prayers. Why should it matter so much?" When I asked her how much progress she had made, she said, "I've reached the point now where I can have lunch with black housekeepers and host mixed dinner parties."

If you live somewhere urban, liberal, and cosmopolitan,

that might sound like a pretty feeble marker of progress, but in the Deep South, eating together at the same table in someone's home has proved one of the most difficult taboos to overcome. It has often been observed that black and white Southerners find it easier to have sex with each other than to eat supper together. "When we bought this house ten years ago, I had to warn my neighbors that some of my house guests would be African American," said Helen. "I told them, 'Don't be surprised, don't be alarmed, and do not call the cops.' They've got used to it now, which is a small sign of progress in itself."

Helen was "offended" that her garden club had no African American members, and the rumors were true. She intended to do something about it. As a kind of icebreaker in her campaign to integrate the club, she had taken Beverly Adams and two of her friends to a garden club function, and it had gone fairly well. "I don't know if we're ready for black members quite yet, but people are willing to talk about it now. It might be because nobody wants to ruffle my feathers. I'm in charge of repainting Magnolia Hall, and it's costing a fortune."

Magnolia Hall is the Natchez Garden Club headquarters and flagship building, and while it might stand out as an impressive mansion in any other Southern town or city, it looked rather ordinary next to Stanton Hall, as the ladies of the PGC were glad to point out. When the painting and restoration work was completed, or perhaps sooner if she sensed a shift in the winds, Helen Smith intended to make a proposal to her board: "Ladies, when you're ready, we need to target seven to ten black families. We'll serve them candlelit dinners at Magnolia Hall, and everybody has to serve them. We have to invite them *en masse*, not put a couple of people on the spot."

Regina Charboneau, meanwhile, was trying to go through Beverly Adams's sorority, an African American women's club that held dressy social functions and did volunteer work for youth groups and other causes in the black community. Regina approached Beverly about doing a joint event with the sorority and the Pilgrimage Garden Club, maybe a fundraising dinner or a picnic benefit, with a view to future joint events, followed by invitations to join the garden club. Beverly wasn't interested.

"I like Regina, and some of the other garden club women I've met, but only some," Beverly told me. "With the others, there's no mistaking their racism. It is written all over them, and that doesn't mean that they're evil, or lacking in other qualities, but as a black person, it just makes you want to stay away from that world. And from our perspective, there's nothing pretty about the history that the garden club is preserving, and making money from."

Beverly was astonished when I told her that Regina and Helen belonged to separate garden clubs. Her eyes widened when I talked about the rivalries and backbiting, the lawsuits and padlocks, and the feeding of laxatives to the hounds during Tableaux, so the other club's court would have to step out through dog shit in their crowns and gowns. "That's crazy," Beverly said. "I thought there was one garden club. Two clubs? And they don't get along? Why?"

———————

I gained a deeper understanding of that question in the living room of Chesney Doyle's mother's house. Kathie Blankenstein was a second-generation stalwart of the Natchez Garden Club; she had been Queen during the Korean War. For my benefit,

she had invited over another NGC member, Nancy Hungerford, the mother of Greg Iles's pregnant wife, and laid out an
amazing collection of scrapbooks from the early years of Pilgrimage.

Working through the scrapbooks, I found no critical coverage. Correspondents from New York, California, and London,
England, wrote about the Natchez Pilgrimage in the same way
as Mississippi journalists. They were charmed by the mammy
costumes, the liveried butlers, the "pickaninnies" eating watermelon, and all the rest of it. It was a delightful glimpse of the
Old South.

When I reached 1936, the headlines were about the "War
of the Hoopskirts." This was when the garden club ladies split
into two opposing factions and began feuding and scorning
each other, as they have been doing on and off ever since.
"We in the Natchez Garden Club refer to the Pilgrimage Garden Club members as Pills," said Blankenstein. Her tone was
playful, but not entirely. They also used the term as an adjec-
tive. Talking about one antebellum home, Kathie asked Nancy,
"Is it Pill?" When they referred to Katherine Miller, the main
instigator of the Hoopskirt War, they called her "I, Katherine," because of her exaggerated self-regard, and because that's
what the Natchez Garden Club had been calling her since the
1930s.

The War of the Hoopskirts was about money, although loyalty was also a factor. In the first four years of Pilgrimage, the
garden club made $33,000 after expenses. Roughly $14,000
went to the owners of the antebellum homes, leaving the club
with $19,000. Most of the non-homeowners wanted to use
that money to buy and restore more historic buildings. The
homeowners, led by Katherine Miller, wanted the lion's share

of the money because it was their houses that the pilgrims came to see. "We've got the merchandise on the shelf," she would say, and explain how expensive it was to maintain an antebellum home. In June 1936, Katherine Miller led her faction out of the Natchez Garden Club and formed the Pilgrimage Garden Club, taking seventeen of the twenty-six tour homes with her.

"Essentially they were mad about money, and they had a big fight and put on separate Pilgrimages," said Blankenstein. "I, Katherine, begged my mother to come over to the new club, but she was loyal and disapproved of what they were doing. As far as she was concerned, I, Katherine, had betrayed the Natchez Garden Club and fallen from grace. Oh, it was terrible. It broke up bridge clubs. It broke up lifelong friendships. My mother and her childhood friends ended up being bitter enemies until they died. And it was maddening. Those women had no loyalty at all! It was just a business to them, and they were social mavens. That's why they went with I, Katherine."

"We're the original garden club," said Nancy Hungerford. "Sometimes we can't help feeling mad that they took so many of our homes away from us. And the Pills act so snooty sometimes, like *they're* the real garden club, just because they've got more homes and money."

Blankenstein said, "We did a bad thing, too. We had an injunction brought against them. We nailed notices to their homes saying they had to be closed. They sued us. It went to court. Tempers were flaring on all sides."

A lot of the energy that went into the Hoopskirt War, and the Pilgrimage itself, stemmed from the fact that well-to-do white women didn't work in those days, and they had black servants to do all the household chores. "You had a lot of very smart, energetic women who didn't have enough to do until Pilgrimage and the Pageant came along," said Hungerford. "They poured themselves into it. The Pageant was amazing in those days because all the girls were in ballet school. When they danced the Soirée, you could have put it in an MGM movie."

I asked what the husbands were doing while all this was going on. Kathie Blankenstein smiled. "The husbands were sitting there miserably, enduring it, and writing checks. That was their role and it still is to a certain extent."

———

With Beverly Adams and her sorority sisters out of the running, Regina was now pinning her integration hopes on Debbie Cosey, who she counted as a friend. Debbie and her husband Gregory had restored and remodeled the old slave quarters at Concord, the former domain of the Yellow Duchess, into a bed-and-breakfast. Regina's board had now voted to include Concord Quarters as a Pilgrimage tour home, to be advertised in all the leaflets and marketing, and to receive a share of ticket sales. In the small, self-contained world of Natchez, this was big news—the first African American tour home.

"It's a way for us to acknowledge slavery and allow an African American business owner to tell that side of our history," said Regina. "And Debbie is wonderful. You'll love her. You must go there and stay the night. And maybe you can see if she might be open to joining the garden club. I really think she might be ready."

Debbie Cosey was wearing a loose-flowing dress with an African print, and her gray hair was natural. As Regina predicted, I did feel a strong rush of affection for Debbie as soon as I met her. She has a warm, earth-motherly charisma and a big personality that seems strong, extroverted, vulnerable, and sensitive at the same time. She was standing outside the old slave quarters with her husband Gregory, who smiled broadly, pumped my hand, and let his wife do the talking. It was their first morning on tour, in the Fall Pilgrimage, after nearly five years of renovating the building and gambling with their finances. "Oh Lord, I'm nervous, you'll have to excuse me," said Debbie. "I've never done this before. I've been in the hospitality industry all my life, but people always handed me a script. Okay, here goes."

She took a deep breath, settled her nerves, consulted her notes through glasses, then started reciting the history of the building. The Concord Quarters was constructed in the 1820s, during the reign of the Yellow Duchess. For a slave quarters, it was surprisingly large and impressive, with an upstairs balcony and five stout white columns rising up to support the roof. "They built it like this to match the big house. Outside, it was a status display: 'Look at me, I'm so rich even my slaves live in a big fine house.' Inside it was nothing. There were dirt floors downstairs."

The great mansion at Concord burned down in 1901, leaving only its magnificent curving, double-flight marble staircase climbing up into the air. In time, the staircase collapsed, weeds grew over the marble chunks, and all that remained of Concord was the old slave quarters, boarded up and forgotten as an African American neighborhood formed around it. "It was in really bad shape when we bought it, and covered in green," said Debbie. "It was a big green monster, but we love architecture, and we could see its potential. We had to buy it, even though the bank wouldn't lend us any money. We didn't even know it was a slave quarters until my friend Mimi Miller told me."

"How did that feel?"

"Oh, my. I knew I had to save it then. I got really busy. I got very emotional. I wanted to know who they were that lived here. A lot of black people were mad at me. They said, 'You should just let it die,' and 'I didn't know slaves had houses,' and 'Let it fall in.' It was hurtful."

Debbie led me inside. The rooms were small but beautifully decorated with antique furniture, cut flowers, Afrocentric art on the walls. The descendants of the family that had owned Concord, and its slaves, offered Debbie the original china from the big house, but she turned it down. "I don't want Concord china in here," she said to me. "I mean, come on, this is the quarters. I have my mother's china in here."

There was a strong sense that the house had been reclaimed and redeemed, and Debbie had performed ceremonies to help this process along. "I decided this was the Queen Mother's room," she said, standing in the largest bedroom and referring to the matriarch of the enslaved household. "I came in here, and I got out my Bible and I introduced myself. I said, 'I want to save your house. My name is Debbie. I'm so sorry for what happened to you.'"

She showed me an ancient-looking shoe that they had found half buried in the dirt floor. She was certain it had been worn by an enslaved child. "My baby grandson put his arms out to be picked up by a ghost, right where we found the shoe," she said matter-of-factly. After the Yellow Duchess died, an inventory of her property was compiled, and Debbie had obtained a copy of the original handwritten paperwork. The inventory included a list of all the furnishings in the famous Yellow Room, and 120 Negroes worth $43,325.

"The name of this house is Concord, meaning 'harmony,' and that's how we want to live. We have chosen to live with the past. We hope to open a dialogue between white and black. We want to glorify the enslaved people of these quarters. Now, if you'll follow me outside, I'm going to sing. I do that because I do that."

We stood outside in the autumn sunshine, and the hairs stood up on my arms as Debbie Cosey sang the old gospel song "Oh, Freedom" in a stunningly beautiful contralto voice: "And before I'd be a slave / I'd be buried in my grave . . ." I knew the Roberta Flack version, "Freedom Song," and Debbie's rendition was every bit as powerful and impressive. By the time she finished, there were tears in my eyes. "I'm going to sing that for tourists," she said afterwards. "And we're going to do weddings, because we have got to bless a bride here."

I spent most of the day at Concord Quarters and stayed the night and had some long conversations with Debbie Cosey. She yearned to know more about the slaves who had lived here, but all she had was a list of 120 names, with their ages and market values, and it didn't specify which ones were the house slaves. She was also frustrated, and saddened, by her lack of knowledge about her own ancestors. She could only trace back her lineage to her grandfather, who was born into slavery in nearby Franklin County.

"I asked him who his father was, and he said, 'Old Massa Jones. Now get on away from here.' My grandfather had white silky hair, blue eyes, and big ears. He looked like a leprechaun, and all he knew was to work you, and work you, on his farm. It's something to see at our family reunions. We've got green eyes and pointy noses. We have people that are black as a panther with blue eyes. My mother had nappy red hair and yellow skin. When I asked her about it, she would say, 'Hon, Mama don't know.'"

Debbie's mother was a cook and a maid who worked for more than thirty years at Hawthorne, the antebellum home of Bettye Jenkins. "When I was young, I wanted a house just like that with canopy beds and a huge gallery," Debbie said. "I loved Pilgrimage because I got paid cash money to make flowers. You know, in thirty years the Jenkins family never once gave my mother a ride home and never once came in our house. Just didn't. But they did pay for my tuition at Alcorn [State University] and that meant a lot."

When Regina proposed putting Concord Quarters on tour, a delegation of senior PGC ladies came to see the house and decide if it was worthy. One of them was Bettye Jenkins. "She latched on to me, we were both tearing up, and she said, 'Debbie, I'm so proud of you!' Jeanette Feltus was here, Ruth Ellen Calhoun, more than twelve of those old fogies! I don't think any of them, bless their hearts, had ever been in a black woman's house before. I couldn't get over their enthusiasm. I thought they'd never leave! Anyway, here I am, on tour in the Natchez Pilgrimage. I've had a lot of criticism from black people, which I understand, but this is what we want to do, and we're doing it, and it's exciting."

It seemed like an opportune moment to ask Debbie if she would consider joining the Pilgrimage Garden Club.

"Regina and I are friends," she said. "We used to fool with

people by telling them we were sisters. But no, I really don't think so. I'd feel like a token."

Regina was still confident that she could bring Debbie Cosey into the fold, but that would have to wait now because a major crisis had broken out between the two garden clubs. "Tableaux is falling apart," said Regina, venting her frustrations in her kitchen. "I'm so sick of dealing with them. It's like the evil, jealous younger sister who just cannot get past her hatred of her older, more sophisticated sister. It's like a bad marriage. I keep thinking that if I do this thing, or that thing, that it will get better, but the truth is they hate us. They have such contempt for us. They call us Pills, for Chrissakes!"

The falling apart of Tableaux, like most historical events, resulted from long-term forces and unexpected catalysts. For years, it had been getting harder and harder to recruit children. Even in the golden age, it had been a struggle to get boys to dress up in frilly little velvet suits and prance around a maypole. It had usually required an indomitable maternal will because most boys hated it. Mothers these days were more likely to accept an adamant refusal from their sons and let them put their energies into sports or other activities. And the girls weren't interested like they used to be, back when they were all in ballet school. "Now they want to play soccer and go on social media and study hard so they can get into college," said Regina. Times had changed, even in Natchez where time is so resistant to change, and the Tableaux, despite the efforts to adapt and modernize it, was still an extraordinary anachronism.

Nonetheless, Regina was happy with Chesney's script and pleased with this year's production, although she and the PGC board saw plenty of room for improvement. "We took out the Virginia Reel because it sucked, and the other club got mad," she said, identifying one of the unexpected catalysts. "In addition to two garden clubs, we have two dance studios in Natchez. One is theirs, the other is ours. Their studio produced the Virginia Reel, so when we took it out, they accused us of attacking their club."

Regina and Chesney agreed that the main priority was to hire an artistic director, and two other theatrical professionals, to improve the amateurish quality of the production. The new hires had been approved by the PGC board, but now Regina and Chesney had received a snubbing letter from the president of the NGC. Not only had the NGC board voted against hiring the theatrical professionals—"We do not find the proposal a sound business venture at this time." The letter also said that the Tableaux chairwomen, not Chesney Doyle, would now decide "all adjustments" to her script and "take full control of the production from this point on." In other words, Chesney had been shitcanned by her own club, and she would now be replaced by Cheryl Rhinehart, who had directed the Tableaux in the old days before Greg Iles got involved.

This was the last straw for Regina. She announced that the Pilgrimage Garden Club was withdrawing from the Tableaux and would instead present its King, Queen, and Court at "A Royal Evening at Longwood." She wasn't yet sure what the Royal Evening would entail, beyond champagne and a spectacular setting. Longwood, a six-story octagonal mansion owned by the PGC, was arguably the most dramatic building in Natchez.

"I've got to put on something for the mothers," Regina said. "They've been volunteering all year, and dreaming of their sons and daughters in the Court. The Queen has dreamed all her life about coming out in her dress, and I get that. We can make it clear that this is the last time if we have to."

The PGC's withdrawal left the Tableaux under the complete control of the Natchez Garden Club, but they had no script. Chesney Doyle, who compared the experience of directing her first Tableaux to "diving headfirst into a blender," had written a letter saying that neither club had permission to use any part of her written script, or audiovisual program. Ann Gaude, who ran the dance studio affiliated with the Pilgrimage Garden Club, was so upset by the schism that she pulled out of the production. "I had her weeping on my sofa," said Regina. "Even people who love the Tableaux are saying it's over. Ann produced Ol' Man River, Maypole, the Can-Can, and the Soirée. That's a lot to lose from the production, but it's not my problem anymore. I'm so glad to be out of it, even though I'll go down in the history books as the one who ended it after eighty-one years of collaboration."

People were comparing the split over Tableaux to the great sundering of the clubs in 1936, and the rumor mill was in overdrive. Regina was hearing that the NGC was going to take Tableaux all the way back to the old days, meaning no more African American performers, no mention of slavery, the return of the Confederate flag, and the return of "Dixie," the anthem of the Confederacy, at the show's climax. Helen Smith told me none of this was true, but Regina's sources said that the NGC Pageant committee members were being careful not to mention their true plans in front of Helen.

Greg Iles was hearing the same rumors as Regina, and he was worried that Natchez was in for a major embarrassment: "If the national media get wind of it and come down here, they'll have a field day. It'll be Natchez, Mississippi, last bastion of the old Confederacy, and Phillip West and Joyce Arceneaux will be glad to tell them that we're all a bunch of racists and nothing has changed in Mississippi."

| 22 |

Soon after he took office and hung Ibrahima's picture on the wall, Mayor Darryl Grennell received a visitor from Liberia, Dr. Artemus Gaye. He was a refugee from the Liberian civil war in the 1990s — a conflict between the Americo-Liberians, descended from the black American colonists, and the indigenous peoples they had oppressed and exploited since the early days of the colony. During the war, Artemus Gaye found out he was descended from slaves in Mississippi.

He fled the violence and enrolled at Northwestern University, just north of Chicago, where he started researching his family history and discovered that he was also descended from African royalty: Ibrahima and Isabella were his seventh-great-grandparents. Dr. Gaye was now making regular trips to Natchez to find out more about his family tree and get to know his Mississippi cousins. It was a reminder that Ibrahima's story did not end with his death. It rippled down through the generations on two continents and continues to affect people's lives today.

From Liberia, a poignant detail has surfaced. When Ibrahima's letter reached Timbo, announcing that the good people of America had liberated him from slavery and he was coming home, a caravan was sent to welcome him. It was laden with thirty pounds of gold, which Ibrahima would have undoubtedly used to buy the freedom of his children and grandchildren in Natchez. In one of his last letters, Ibrahima wrote, "Their emancipation would be paramount to every other consideration." When the caravan reached the town of Bopolu in western Liberia, 150 miles from Monrovia, its leaders learned that the prince had died and turned their horses around.

Thomas Foster, who was the same age as Ibrahima, died of heart disease later that year (1829). His thirteen children inherited extensive cotton plantations and more than a hundred slaves. After the estate was divided, the American Colonization Society purchased Ibrahima's son Simon, his wife Hannah and five children, and his brother Levi. The price was $3,100, which came out of the $3,500 that Ibrahima had raised on his costumed tour. The Society arranged their passage to Monrovia, where they reunited with Isabella after a separation of more than two years. Artemus Gaye is the direct descendant of Simon and Hannah.

If that caravan had continued to Monrovia and given the royal gold to the prince's mourning widow, she could have easily purchased the freedom of her other children and multiplying grandchildren in Natchez. As it was, they remained in slavery until Emancipation in 1863, and Isabella died in Liberia without ever seeing them again. Beverly Adams is descended from the children who remained enslaved in Mississippi, and many more descendants are living in the Natchez area and Southern states. As Artemus Gaye discovered at his first family reunion in Natchez, the name Prince is still widely used in these families. If it was originally bestowed with sarcasm by young Thomas Foster, it has long since been reclaimed as a name that conveys pride in royal African ancestors. In fact, it was Ibrahima himself who first accomplished this by naming his second son Prince.

————————

By the end of the Civil War, Foster Fields was a ruin. The house was deserted, or burned down, or a warren of freed slaves, depending on which sources you believed. Most of Thomas's relatives had gone to Louisiana, Texas, or elsewhere in Mississippi, and most of the gravestones from the family cemetery went with them. But one afternoon in the thick, sweltering heat of August, following vague directions from someone who had seen it years ago, Kerry Dicks and I found what appeared to be the grave of Thomas Foster.

We were trespassing on the grounds of a private house, pulling away weeds, trying to read the blackened inscription on the gravestone, when a pickup truck drove up to us. A sticker on the window read HELL WITH THE DOG. BEWARE OF THE OWNER. The white man behind the wheel was wearing a gray T-shirt and smoking a cigarette. He looked tough, and probably armed, but not particularly concerned. In my British accent, I said, "Hi there. We heard that Thomas Foster, who owned Prince Ibrahima, was buried here somewhere, and we're wondering if that's the grave."

"That's what I figured," he said. "And that's him alright."

We gave our names, and he introduced himself as Chris Gibson. "The Gibsons intermarried with the Fosters. A Gibson was the preacher at the Presbyterian church."

"My family used to live at Foster's Mound," said Kerry, referring to the place where Thomas Foster's brother had lived. "The Junkins, on my mother's side. My great-grandmother was born there." This is a common form of exchange when Mississippians meet for the first time. They want to know about each other's ancestors, and which families they married into. If kinship ties can be established, so much the better. If there was a feud in the past, it could get awkward.

"Come on up to the house and I'll tell you what I know." Gibson drove the few hundred yards, and we followed on foot.

Sweat seeped into my clothes. Sweat dripped off my earlobes. If that was Thomas Foster's grave, I thought, this had to be part of Foster Fields. Ibrahima must have trodden this ground, heard these summer sounds of birds and cicadas, and worked in this punishing heat and humidity. Not for the first time since I moved to Mississippi, I tried to imagine picking cotton in a shadeless field from dawn to dusk, moving down the rows with the babies and toddlers on a nine-foot cotton sack, then trying to cool off at night in a sweaty, airless shack full of fleas and mosquitoes. Solomon Northup's bed was a single wooden plank. More commonly, a slave's bed was a few old rags on a dirt floor. Food was served in a communal trough, as if enslaved people were cattle or pigs.

Chris Gibson lived in an 1870 farmhouse next to a huge pecan tree with lightning scars. "Mother's parents bought this property in 1957 with no idea of the connection to the Fosters. There was a couple named Creasy and George living in the old slave quarters, and they were part of the deal. You had to inherit them with the house. She'd iron clothes and work as a maid. They stayed on for a while until they built a house down the road."

He pointed across his driveway. "The old slave quarters was right over there. It was a four-room house. They hauled it off to Frogmore Plantation in Louisiana and re-erected it as a historical exhibit. I don't know if it was the prince's house or not. It's possible."

"Where was Thomas Foster's house?" I asked.

"The original log-cabin structure is under the grass of my driveway. The big house sat out past it a little ways. Slaves lived in it during the Civil War. When the Fosters came back, they threw a tantrum and refused to live where blacks had lived. That's the story I heard. Foster's fields extended in all directions from here. It's mostly gone to woods now."

He showed us an old cistern from Thomas Foster's day, and a grist wheel that the slaves used to grind corn and flour. Then we walked back down to the grave, and he apologized for its overgrown condition. Gibson owned six businesses in addition to his job as a battalion chief with the Natchez Fire Department, and he was trying to keep up the old house as well.

He showed us two graves in a tangled clump of weeds, brambles, and goldenrod. One had a slim gray stone leaning back and tilting slightly to the side. Its inscription commemorated Thomas Foster's daughter Cassandra Speed, the LATE CONSORT OF JOHN SPEED. She died at forty-four, and IS NOW GONE TO ENJOY IN HEAVEN AN ETERNITY OF INCREASING BLESSINGS AND GLORY.

Thomas Foster's gravestone lay flat on the ground, and it took some work to make out the inscription. Kerry, an aficionado of cemeteries and tombstones, was sure that he had composed the words himself. HE LIVED IN THE DISCHARGE OF ALL THE DUTIES OF SOCIAL ORDER, it began, a clear reference to his slaveholding, AND EXEMPLIFIED THROUGH LIFE THE CHARACTER OF THE DOER OF GOOD AND WAS REMOVED FROM THE BOSOM OF HIS FAMILY TO THAT OF HIS GOD ON THE LAST DAY OF SEPTEMBER 1829. That was less than three months after Ibrahima died in Monrovia.

I thought of all the suffering and pain and misery this doer of good had imposed on his human chattels, and I wondered about the influence of his strongly held Calvinist religious beliefs. The more people he enslaved, the richer he became, and presumably the more certain he felt that he would enter the Kingdom of Heaven, because in Calvinism wealth was the surest proof that you were one of God's elect.

I thought of the black and white children that had played together here, and all over the antebellum South, until the age of twelve when the black children were sent out into the fields. They were old enough to work now and feel the whip. A favorite game among the younger children was to sell each other on make-believe auction blocks, with one child playing auctioneer, and the others boasting about how much they were worth. Plantation children also delivered whippings to each other with flimsy switches, because children use games to neutralize what terrifies them. Standing there at Foster's grave in the rich golden light of August, these visions conjured from history books were like hallucinations.

Downtown Natchez was lit up beautifully for Christmas and hung with garlands, and the town displayed its eccentricity with two unique yuletide traditions. The first was Ginger's Jeweled Christmas. As promised, Ginger and James Hyland had spent five weeks decorating 167 Christmas trees with her costume-jewelry collection. Paying guests were invited to tour the mad glittering spectacle with Scott Smith in his Jiminy Cricket outfit and then drink champagne. The second unique Natchez tradition was the Santa Claus Parade, which Regina Charboneau described as the only police-escorted drunk-driving event in America.

"You've seen how women dominate so much of what goes on here," she said. "Well, the Santa Parade is men only. They start drinking early in the morning, and they drive around town and make stops at houses where women have laid out a big spread of food and booze. They descend like a horde of locusts—it all gets decimated in twenty minutes—and then they drive on to the next one. It goes on all day, then there's a cocktail party for Mr. and Mrs. Claus, and another party after that. It's usually on Christmas Eve, so generations of Natchez children have woken up on Christmas morning to find their father passed out on the couch with half-assembled toys all over the floor."

"How do I get into the Santa Parade?" I asked.

"It won't be difficult. But this is one of those rare occasions in Natchez where a woman can't make it happen. You need a man to invite you." She was talking about a straight white man. They were always around, but on the peripheries of the real action, and it was easy to forget that they existed. Twice I had asked Kerry Dicks if such-and-such garden club lady had a husband, and she'd looked confused, as if I was bringing up some obscure, irrelevant detail, and then answered, "I think he might be dead.".

As Regina predicted, it wasn't hard to get on the Santa Parade. I was invited by Miss Bettye's grandson Hyde Carby, the lawyer who wrote the apology from the city of Natchez to the victims of the Parchman Ordeal. I asked him about the dress code. Did I need a Santa hat?

"No. Just a coat and tie, and a good strong liver."

We met before dawn at Greenlea, the antebellum home of Philip and Stella Carby, Hyde's parents. A large painting of Hyde in a Confederate officer's uniform hung on the wall, from his year as King of the Pilgrimage Garden Club. The painting had come under family debate a few years ago because some African American lawyers were coming over to the house. Hyde would have gladly put it in the attic, but the painting memorialized a proud moment for his mother, and she wanted it to stay on the wall. Then Philip spotted a small Confederate flag in the painting that none of them had noticed before. That raised the stakes of the debate because the flag was a more charged symbol than the uniform. A family compromise was reached. The painting stayed on the wall, and an expert was hired at considerable expense to paint away the Confederate flag.

We drank a quick cup of coffee and climbed into Philip Carby's big white SUV. The weather was cool and overcast. As he drove through the quiet streets, Philip said, "This Santa Parade has been going on for as long as anyone can remember. Hyde's grandfather did it for seventy-five years, until he was ninety-four."

Hyde said, "It's a drinking party for men, escorted by cops, and it's a party with a purpose. We throw out candy for kids, and we raise money for needy families. We'll give out Christmas gifts for three hundred kids this year. Seventy-five families will get vouchers for a ham or turkey."

About fifty vehicles were parked outside the Hotel Vue on the edge of the bluff. Inside, a hundred men were knocking back Bloody Marys, screwdrivers, mimosas, and other breakfast drinks. Hyde explained that a new Santa is elected every year by the Santa Committee, and the men I was seeing in red blazers were previous Santas. They had the privilege of addressing each other as "Santa Claus," and putting stickers on their vehicles, announcing the year of their Santahood. This year's Santa, identifiable by his red coat and Santa hat, was in his eighties, and there were concerns about his stamina. "At least the weather is okay," said Hyde. "Santa rides in a convertible, whether it's ten below or raining."

Tommy Ferrell, a former sheriff with a face like a bulldog, told me in grave tones that a scandal had occurred. "Ladies are allowed at the stops, but we had one try to join the parade this year. Fortunately her family got ahold of her and shut her down. If that ever happens, that a lady gets on the parade, and the wives find out, they'll make so much trouble that'll be the end of it."

Tommy knew law enforcement people all over the country,

from his time as president of the National Sheriffs' Association. I asked him if he'd heard of anything similar to the Natchez Santa Parade. "There's nothing else like this," he assured me. "The mayor of LA was here one year. He said we were all crazy."

Hyde walked out of the hotel with a salty dog (vodka and grapefruit juice) in a clear plastic cup, nodded to the police officers and sheriff's deputies outside, and thanked them for the great job they were doing. I followed, holding a Bloody Mary. Dozens more men walked past the cops with breakfast cocktails and climbed into vehicles. Philip Carby doesn't drink anymore, and he had agreed to do all our driving. I wondered about the other drivers. "It's hoped that they refrain, but it's not enforced," Philip said. "If anyone has hit anyone, they've kept it quiet. I don't remember any accidents."

We were joined by Tony Heidelberg, a lawyer, municipal judge pro tem, and one of the few African Americans in the Santa Parade. "I love it," he said. "We're doing a lot of good, and having a lot of fun doing it." Now we heard the wail of police sirens, announcing that the ninetieth annual Natchez Santa Claus Parade was underway. We joined a long procession of vehicles led by the chief of police and the county sheriff. Patrol cars were positioned at various intersections, blocking off traffic, so we could drive through all the red lights in our path. We entered a low-income, mostly white subdivision, where the streets were lined with people. We honked our horns, rang a bell, hurled candy out of the windows, and shouted, "Merry Christmas!" Tony would add variations: "Alright now!" "Yes indeed!"

Exiting the subdivision, we drove down Highway 61 past Mammy's Cupboard—Philip remembered when it was called Black Mammy—and turned into the wealthy Beau Pre subdivision. We all parked outside the 19th Hole and Golf Shop at the country club and swarmed on a spread of sausage rolls, sandwiches, and cocktails. I talked with Tony Byrne, who had been the mayor of Natchez for many years, and a good friend of Nellie Jackson's. He had a kind Irish face full of character, and the red blazer of a former Santa. "Last year we gave away seventeen thousand dollars' worth of toys and vouchers for hams and turkeys," he said. "For a lot of those kids, it's the only Christmas they're going to have. And we get the warm glow of giving away other people's money. So it works out."

After thirty minutes, a bullhorn siren announced that the stop was over, and we scrambled to grab another drink and get back in our vehicles. Police officers at the gates of the subdivision waved to us and smiled as we drove past them. In the passenger seat, I lifted my Bloody Mary in appreciation and smiled back.

The next stop was at a private house downtown. A brunch party was in progress and would continue after we left. Kerry Dicks was there, and it turned out that she was the scandalous woman who had tried to ride in the parade. "My family started it," she said. "And I just don't see why possession of a penis entitles a person to ride, while possession of a vagina is a disqualification. Last year, a guy sneaked me into his vehicle. This year, I thought I'd try to make it official." Tony Byrne and others on the Santa Committee were open to the idea of women riding, but a powerful cadre of older men, including Kerry's uncle, thought it was an abomination. "He vowed to go to his grave before letting a woman ride," she said.

The parade continued through downtown, with candy flying out of the vehicles towards children behind barricades, and came to a halt outside the Braden school building, where the payroll-bloated Natchez-Adams School District was headquartered. Our Santa already looked shaky and tired as he climbed out of the convertible and made his way into the building. "I hope I have the strength to get through this," he said.

We entered an auditorium full of needy families, most of them African American. On the stage, Kerry and her cousin were waiting with bags of toys to give away to the children. Santa made his way to a chair onstage, and Kerry's cousin began reading out the names of children, doing a pretty good job at pronouncing the creative ones—Ahmarrion, Pre'Shaunti, Kelvauntae, Ke'Aashia, Rundraneeka. Kerry led the children across the stage to meet Santa, then handed each child a brown paper sack full of toys.

I stood against the back wall, with the other tipsy white men in coats and ties, uncomfortably aware of how this would look to a critical eye. For us, it was a day of indulgence and privilege, of quaffing free cocktails in expensive vehicles, being temporarily above the law and feeling virtuous about helping the needy. For the families sitting below us in the auditorium, it was a day of accepting our paternalistic charity. On the other hand, it was hard to argue against the excitement on the children's faces, or the value of a turkey to a poor family on Christmas Day.

In the early afternoon, we rolled through an impoverished black neighborhood, and some of the five-cent candy we threw ended up in the gutter, where children scrambled to retrieve it. The next stop was at Natchez Children's Services, a group home and advocacy service dedicated to the prevention and treatment of child abuse. I handed the director, Cherish McCallum, a check for $2,500 from the Santa Committee. She was incredibly grateful, and I experienced that warm glow of giving away other people's money, while the children clambered on Santa's lap for photographs.

Then it was time for our fifth drinking opportunity of the day, at the old downtown railroad depot. A man named Dee had just shot a pigeon and was grinding its corpse under his heel. Fatigue was setting in, and Hyde said it was time to switch from breakfast cocktails to bourbon, or "brown whiskey," as he called it (white whiskey is moonshine). A group of men at the bar were bragging on the safety record of the Santa Parade. "There've been a few dings and fender benders over the years, but we've never hit a kid," one of them said proudly.

"And they will run out in front of you sometimes," said another.

"Ninety years, not a single kid," said a third.

The afternoon followed the same pattern as the morning, cruising through neighborhoods throwing candy, regular stops for more food and drink. I carefully tended and nurtured a bourbon buzz, trying to ride it for energy, but by 5:00 p.m. I couldn't face another drink, and I badly wanted to go somewhere and lie down. Tony Heidelberg had already left, and Philip and Hyde Carby were ready to go home too. As I said my farewells, some people tried to shame me for quitting before the evening parties began. The real stalwarts, they said, kept going all the way to midnight mass.

———

On Christmas Day, Regina Charboneau invited my family for dinner at Twin Oaks. My wife Mariah and our two-year-old daughter Isobel had already been to Natchez several times. Among the first hundred words that Isobel learned to say were Natchez, Miss Regina, and Mississippi River. Ruth Ellen Calhoun had her dressed up in a hoopskirt before her second birthday and thought it would be a marvelous idea for Isobel to start receiving when she was a little older: "It builds such confidence in the little ones. They learn that they can talk to anybody."

Mariah and I had talked about moving to Natchez. There were lovely old houses for sale on some of the prettiest streets in America, at very reasonable prices. I couldn't imagine ever tiring of the view from the bluff, the magnificent trees, the flower-scented streets, the frog orchestras on summer nights, the generosity and hospitality, the stories that people told and the importance they placed on storytelling. Moving to Natchez would be a way to gently withdraw and live at a more human pace. Ultimately we decided against it, mainly because of the schools, but also the shrinking population, the remoteness and isolation, and the relentless gossiping.

To give an example, I cooked an Italian meal one evening for Glenn and Bridget Green at The Burn, their antebellum home. Regina and Doug Charboneau were the only other guests. Now I was hearing from Kerry, who heard it from a trusted source, that I had thrown a big dinner party for all the married gay men in Natchez, cooked them Indian food, then run away with Bridget Green for a dirty adulterous weekend on the Mississippi coast. I couldn't help being impressed by the creativity at work here, but the idea of being perennial fodder for the Natchez rumor mill was not appealing.

On Christmas morning, while Isobel opened her presents, Mariah asked me what she should wear for a late-afternoon Christmas dinner at an antebellum home in Natchez. I had no idea and was too stupid to ask Regina. Mariah put on a pair of perfectly fitting red pants with an ivory sweater and arrived at Twin Oaks to find Regina and nearly all of the Natchez women dressed in chic stylish black. In the rest of Mississippi, women almost never wear black in the daytime except at funerals, and absolutely not on Christmas Day.

A few of the ladies asked Mariah where she was from. When

she told them she was from Tucson, Arizona, and living in Jackson, they immediately lost interest in talking to her. It was Mariah's first exposure to how snooty Natchez can be, and she was amazed by it. "It's a small town in Mississippi," she whispered to me. "They act like it's the center of the world. If you're not from here, or writing about here, or talking about here, you don't count."

One of the guests was Peggy Pierrepont, from the old-money Pierrepont family in New York. She had relocated to Natchez some years ago. "I absolutely adore it here," she said. "Most people are so incredibly kind." She was also keenly aware of the phenomenon that Mariah had just observed. "Yes! There are people here who absolutely believe, who will give you detailed geographical and historical explanations that prove beyond doubt that Natchez, Mississippi, is the center of the world. I find it quite charming."

Following my usual habits, I went into the kitchen, where Regina was assembling the feast. She was delighted to inform me that Debbie Cosey had decided to join the Pilgrimage Garden Club after all, and the board had voted her in unanimously. Now that Debbie had led the way, Regina was hoping that other African American women would join too. Having a properly integrated garden club running Pilgrimage tourism and preserving historic buildings would alter the racial atmosphere of the whole town.

The shrimp and corn chowder was made. So were the biscuits with orange marmalade butter. The grapefruit, apple, and almond salad was in the fridge, along with a chocolate crème brulée trifle to be served with bananas Foster for dessert. Roasting in the ovens were richly seasoned prime ribs, quails stuffed with mushroom dressing, and cauliflowers that she would serve with capers and lemon. Now Regina was frying oysters and duck-fat french fries, while catching me up to speed on the latest Tableaux developments.

She had overturned eighty years of tradition by withdrawing her club, and people were now comparing her to Katherine Miller leading the renegade homeowners out of the Natchez Garden Club in 1936. It was the second great split of the clubs, and to add to the drama, Chesney Doyle was defecting from the NGC and joining the PGC, in the full knowledge that her grandmother Lillie Vidal would be horrified and appalled.

The efforts by Regina, Chesney, and Greg Iles to bring black history into the Tableaux had failed. Contrary to rumor, the NGC was not going to bring back "Dixie" in their production, and while the Confederate flag would be paraded, it was going to bow down at the end to the US flag. But apart from these two details, it would be the old Tableaux all over again, romanticizing the white antebellum aristocracy, with no depictions of slavery and black history. Nor could Regina find a way to incorporate African American history into her Royal Evening at Longwood event, where the new King, Queen, and Court would be presented after the traditional dances, with the young men wearing the traditional Confederate uniforms.

"When I bought Twin Oaks, I tried to hire an interior decorator," Regina said. "He told me, 'You don't need me. If something doesn't belong here, the house will spit it out.' That's what it's like with the Tableaux. You try to put slavery and black history in there, and it just spits it out. There's no way to combine the two things in a way that isn't jarring. This will be the last year for the Confederate uniforms though. When we do the Royal Evening next year, we'll have them in military cadets' uniforms."

I said, "Why not just scrap the whole thing?"

"I'd love to, but it's not that simple. The purpose of the garden club is to preserve these amazing old buildings, and that takes a lot of time and money. To organize all the different fundraising events—Spring and Fall Pilgrimage, Antiques Forum, Save-the-Hall Ball, and so on—you need volunteers, and they need an incentive. Getting their child into the Court has always been the incentive. Take that away, and the whole thing starts to fall apart."

It was time to eat. The food was laid out on platters and serving dishes on the big antique table in the dining room, with candles glowing, the massive Audubon prints on the green walls, the punkah overhead, and the lingering spectral presence of the original owners and their slaves. There were too many people to seat at the big table, so we fixed our plates, as Southerners say, and took them over to three smaller tables set up in the front parlors. It was the best meal I have ever eaten on Christmas Day, by a considerable margin.

We were seated at the cosmopolitan table with some visiting Italians and Australians. They were perfectly nice people, but I didn't want to hear about Italy or Australia, or how their vacations in America were going. I was eavesdropping on the table where the Natchez people had congregated. They were telling stories involving swords and pistols, a raccoon living in an antique tester bed, a man with six sons all named after Confederate generals, a woman named Mary Postlethwaite who was so hooked on genealogy that she slept in the basement of the courthouse among the records.

Now they were talking about an intriguing event at Longwood in 1866. Julia Nutt, the widow of Haller Nutt, one of the wealthiest slaveholders, invited thousands of emancipated slaves to the grounds of her half-built mansion for a picnic, and

I wanted to know why, and what food she had served, and how the townsfolk had reacted. Natchez had hooked me and reeled me in. Like the ladies who gently shunned Mariah, I had lost interest in other places. They seemed dull and predictable. They all belonged to the same elsewhere, where time moved in an orderly progression towards the future, and the dead lay quietly in their graves.

After Christmas dinner, I climbed the creaking stairs and cleared out the last of my belongings from the upstairs rooms. Then we said our goodbyes. Driving back to Jackson through the winter woods and fields, with my wife and daughter asleep, I remembered something that Kerry Dicks had said in the cemetery with the sun sinking down into Louisiana. She didn't know if Natchez had taken a small box and created an entire world inside it, or looked at a small box and mistaken it for the world.

ACKNOWLEDGMENTS

I found Natchez to be an extraordinarily generous and welcoming place. I feel a deep debt of gratitude to everyone who helped me, most notably the Charboneau family, Ron and Mimi Miller, Kathleen Bond, Jim Wiggins, Greg Iles, Kerry Dicks, Ser Boxley, Darrell White, Elodie Pritchartt, the Bergerons, the McCulloughs, Tommy Ferrell, Jeremy Houston, Darryl Grennell, the Jenkins and Carby families, Beverly Adams, David Garner and Lee Glover, Ginger and James Hyland, Jimmy the Cricket, Pulley Bones who was there when I needed him.

The best book ever written about Natchez, in my opinion, is *Prince Among Slaves* by Terry Alford, the story of Ibrahima. It was a constant companion during my time in Natchez, and I relied heavily on its superb research and storytelling.